SPRING FLOWER
BOOK 1: 1931 – 1951

A TALE OF TWO RIVERS

春花
裴敬思醫生的養女：兩條江邊的故事

Yangtze River

Hudson River

Jean Tren-Hwa Perkins, MD

Compiled and Edited by
Richard Perkins Hsung, PhD

Spring Flower: A Tale of Two Rivers
Jean Tren-Hwa Perkins, MD

ISBN-13: 978-988-8769-22-3

© 2021 Richard Perkins Hsung

This book has been reset in 10pt Book Antiqua. Spellings and punctuations are left as in the original edition.

BIOGRAPHY / AUTOBIOGRAPHY

EB138

All rights reserved. No part of this book may be reproduced in material form, by any means, whether graphic, electronic, mechanical or other, including photocopying or information storage, in whole or in part. May not be used to prepare other publications without written permission from the publisher except in the case of brief quotations embodied in critical articles or reviews. For information contact info@earnshawbooks.com

Published by Earnshaw Books Ltd. (Hong Kong)

To my beloved parents,
Dr. and Mrs. Edward Carter Perkins

Contents

Introduction	1
Part I The Great Flood: My Birth	7
Part II The Hudson River: My Home	115
Part III Anguish of Separation: My Awakening	191
Appendices	
1. A Tribute to My Beloved Parents	297
2. A Brief History of Modern China, Including a Tribute to Missionaries	311
3 & 4. Letters with My Parents: Dec. 1950 – March 1951	327
Glossary of Names	367
Acknowledgments	370
About the Editor	375

*The stories told are of actual events,
although some of the names, dates, and locations
have been changed.*

Introduction

Where shall I begin a story that spans more than half a century? I've told my story to many people over the years, and quite a few have encouraged me to write it all down and publish it. Some say it's a fairy tale and can be told to children. I'm not sure about that, but I did have a charmed childhood.

A very long time ago, when I was a junior high student in Yonkers, New York, I fell in love with English literature and fancied becoming an author. But life had other plans for me. I've had plenty of time to contemplate where and how to begin the only book I'll write, and still, it's challenging. Everyone's life is book-worthy, but not everyone sits down to write their story. What makes mine different from others? What warrants the agony of dredging up the past? What would make my story even slightly of interest to the modern reader?

Perhaps this is a common experience among first-time authors. I sat and sat and could barely get beyond lifting a pen or holding a pad. While my heart was racing with all I wanted to tell, my mind was in disarray. And that was on a productive day. On unproductive days, I felt so overwhelmed by the enormity of it all I would lie on the floor among stacks of boxes of documents, photos, and letters and feel paralyzed. At other times, I would hyperventilate until I would practically pass out from the pungent odor of fifty-year-old carbon paper. There were days I'd stare at old photographs for hours with tears streaming down my cheeks, overcome with grief, suffocating as though someone was squeezing my throat, preventing the air from flowing in.

SPRING FLOWER: A TALE OF TWO RIVERS

As the days and months went by, I began to fear I'd never write a single word. My fingers were beginning to feel the onset of arthritis, and I realized I might not be able to handwrite the first draft. Not that long before, I'd had the steadiest hands, but now they were beginning to tremble. So I splurged and bought a typewriter, only to learn that it wouldn't type by itself like a player piano; I still had to do the work. I sat in front of my new typewriter for hours upon hours, staring at the wall in my dimly-lit studio. So I rented a studio with a window, only to find myself staring at a beautiful young Japanese maple a few feet outside the little window, and suddenly I'd be flooded with memories. I began to gain weight from a year of binge eating, so I changed my strategy. I began to jog along a river path to come up with ideas, which I planned to jot down afterward. But I'd fall asleep at the typewriter the moment I got back, exhausted from the run.

During one run, though, on a nondescript, cloudy Sunday afternoon, an epiphany rose up: *The book needed to be about me.* It sounds obvious now, but I hadn't actually realized that till then. Miraculously, I typed five words: "My Life, by Jean Perkins." That became the working title. A few Sunday runs later, I woke up disoriented, lying among archival boxes. As I wiped the moisture from my cheeks, I stared at the boxes, most of which were there because my mother had saved them. And then my cousin Evelyn and her daughters held onto them until I returned to America. Randomly thumbing through one of the boxes, I saw a folder with a chronology of my father's life. *Eureka!* To begin talking about myself, I had to talk about others, especially those to whom I owed my life. The book of my life is really about these most beautiful human beings who gave me life, and those I have had the good fortune to encounter.

I had two sets of parents. The first gave me birth; the second gave me life. My adoptive parents were Dr. and Mrs. Edward

JEAN TREN-HWA PERKINS

C. Perkins. In 1918, my American parents opened the first clinic for men, Water of Life Hospital (WLH: 九江生命活水醫院), in Kiukiang, Kiangsi Province (九江, 江西: Jiujiang and Jiangxi in the pinyin romanization system used today), a rural town on the southern banks of the Yangtze River in Central China. They devoted their time and energy to the well-being of Chinese people—medically and spiritually—for nearly half a century. My father had a Chinese name, 裴敬思, "Pei Jinsi" in pinyin, while my mother's was 裴家紀 (Pei Jiaji).[1]

Without their love and tender care, I wouldn't be alive to this day. And thanks to them, I was given a small role to play in this world. But I'm getting ahead of myself. Let's start at the beginning.

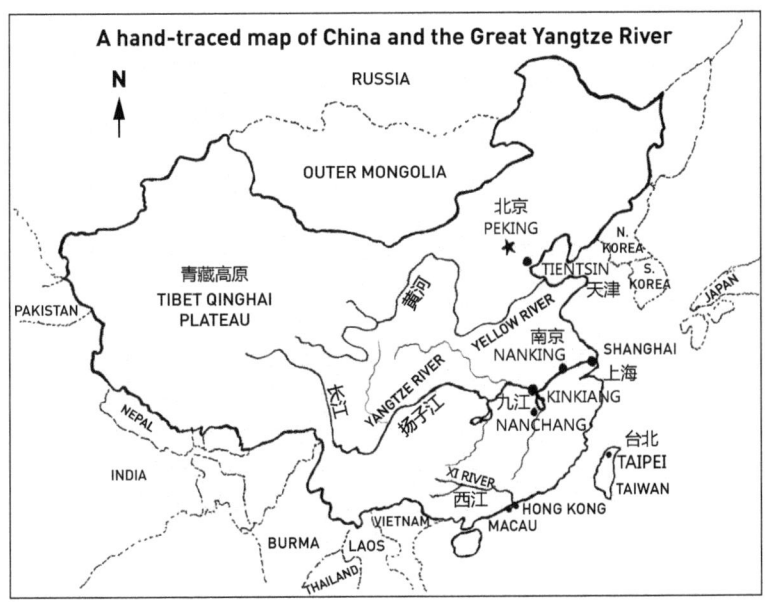

---

1 For a full account of my adoptive parents' background, along with a brief summary of modern Chinese history and Christian missions in China, see appendix 1.

SPRING FLOWER: A TALE OF TWO RIVERS

China has a famous river called the Yangtze River in English and the Long River – Chang Jiang (長江) – in Chinese. Carrying melted glacier water from the Tibet-Qinghai Plateau, whose altitude is 16,000 feet (5,000 meters), the river winds eastward some 4,000 miles (6,400 kilometers) into the East China Sea near Shanghai. Since ancient times, the Great Yangtze River has provided "water of life" for the dense populations of the Southwest, Central, and Eastern regions of China. Wars came and went, and dynasties (朝代) changed hands and names every few centuries, but the great river has always been there. The history of China and that of the Yangtze River have intertwined seamlessly over thousands of years.

The history of the river has not always been one of beauty, ingenuity, and courage. It also includes the Great Yangtze River Flood (長江洪水泛濫) of 1931, one of the deadliest natural disasters of the twentieth century. For millennia, the Chinese struggled against floods, but this one killed nearly four million people from drowning, post-flood starvation, and the spread of infectious diseases. Most of the victims were poor, desolate farmers who received little help from the war-ravaged Republic Nationalist Government that was in power then.

My adoptive mother, Georgina M. P. Perkins, wrote:

> In the year 1931, there was another great opportunity to help the Chinese people, where there was a great flood of the Yangtze River. Ordinarily, at Kiukiang, the river was about 1½ miles wide, but at flood time that year, it was over 30 miles wide! It got even wider downstream, nearly 120 miles wide near Nanking! The flood covered a wide area of the north bank of the river. Kiukiang, on the south bank, was well-flooded,

but not to the same extent. The farmers on the north side lost their tools and equipment. Their animals and homes were completely underwater. So, they came to Kiukiang, where flood relief was carried out. At the WLH, many temporary little homes popped up for flood refugees, and a clinic was held every day for them. We were happy to have milk to give to the babies. We got to know a number of the babies, and one of them was named Spring Flower (春花).

With that, I'll begin my story.

Part I

The Great Flood:
My Birth

1

I was born on a spring night in the Province of Hubei (湖北), in a small town called Hwang-Mei (黄梅镇) located on the northern banks of the Yangtze River straight across from the town of Kiukiang in Kiangsi Province. The year was 1931. In those days, Hwang-Mei was a farming village, mostly poor peasants living in makeshift mud huts with thatched roofs. There were hundreds, perhaps thousands, of nearly identical tiny huts scattered along the riverbank. In one of them lived a poor peasant family with the last name Hu (胡), and on this particular morning, there was a stir of excitement percolating from the hut.

The mother of the Hu family was in labor. She was told that her child would be born between midnight and 2 a.m. A local midwife with no medical training, Eastern or Western, was there to assist with a pair of rusty scissors. Her primary duty was to cut the umbilical cord, and for reasons unclear to me, rusty scissors were the instrument of choice. According to this particular midwife, rusty scissors could bring good luck to the newborn.

In those days, China knew little about sterilization, especially in rural areas. There were no clean towels or disinfected instruments to welcome the newborn. Midwives used patched-up, mud-stained clothes to receive the infant, and they had dirty rags on hand for diapers. Babies born in that environment died like flies from fatal infections like tetanus, not to mention starvation. To survive, these babies had to be tough. At this late hour, these were the last concerns of the Hu family or the midwife.

SPRING FLOWER: A TALE OF TWO RIVERS

Mr. Hu stood at the door, anxiously awaiting the announcement of his child's gender. He paced back and forth, hoping it would be a boy. His wife hoped so, too. Beads of sweat rolled down her face, and yet she made no sound because it would have been improper to yell. This newborn was by no means their first. Mrs. Hu was having her seventh, eighth, or perhaps tenth child, including unborn and stillborn babies. She could no longer recall the number.

Finally, the ordeal was over. With a lusty cry, I made it known that I had come into the world to stay!

"Mm-Ma" is the Chinese equivalent of Mama or Mommy, still the most commonly used name for mother. With birth pangs still reverberating, all Mm-Ma wanted to know was whether it was a girl or a boy. The midwife shook me loose of bloody clothes and handed me to Mm-Ma. Then she picked up the basin filled with red water and headed for the door to tell Mr. Hu he could stop pacing and come in.

Realizing I was a girl, Mm-Ma let out a scream, "No!" Her contractions came back in full force accompanied with mental anguish and the bitter pain of disappointment. She shouted at the midwife, "Come back. Check again. It has to be a boy (你看錯了吧！你再看一眼，這次一定是個男孩)!" Without a word, the midwife walked back to the bed, held me up high and spread my legs wide for Mm-Ma to see clearly for herself.

Mm-Ma screamed again, "My god, not a girl again (天呀—又是個女孩)!" Then she slumped back into her pillow, exhausted and disheartened.

Hearing of my gender, Mr. Hu didn't even bother to enter the hut to take a glance. He hurried to the fields to vent his frustration by whipping the one and only precious water buffalo they had. Oh my, the pathetic water buffalo who faithfully plowed the fields for the family every morning had done nothing to deserve this.

JEAN TREN-HWA PERKINS

Mr. Hu, a man of few words, understood the value of sons to a farmer. For him, it was even more crucial because he was no longer a young man. Asthma and tuberculosis had begun to plague him, leaving him gasping for air. There were three older boys in the Hu family. The youngest, aged twelve and known as Number Six according to the order of birth, was dying from TB during the days leading to my birth. No wonder Mr. Hu was deeply troubled. To make matters worse, Number Six died shortly after my first cry. Mr. Hu believed that I contributed to Number Six's death, because Mm-Ma could not care for Number Six during the pregnancy. Mr. Hu never came home that night.

Mm-Ma had other practical concerns about my being a girl. First, she was already forty and her ability to bear more offspring was diminishing. Although she'd already given birth to three sons, a Chinese family could never have too many. Girls, in contrast, were only trouble. Mm-Ma already had two or three daughters who were not stillborn. While my older sisters were still infants, Mm-Ma had to go door-to-door to find a future mother-in-law for them, never a small task. She had to beg and plead with families who had some level of means to accept her baby girls as future daughters-in-law. Once assured, Mm-Ma left her daughters with them.

Unlike many Chinese families, who would end up leaving their newborn girls on strangers' doorsteps, Mm-Ma was reluctant to do that. She wanted to make sure they had a home where she knew the location, no matter how far away it might be. Doing so, she could close her eyes and sleep with minimal peace in her heart, even while knowing the fate of a daughter was to become a teenage slave if she survived to that age. That was what she had gone through herself.

I was unwanted and unloved because I was a girl. But the chilly reception I received from my biological family on my first day in this world was the norm in old China. Luckily for me, as an infant, I was oblivious to all those machinations, except that I was always hungry.

With a deep sigh, Mm-Ma looked at me and said, "Where on earth will I find yet another mother-in-law?" The thought of bringing me up herself never crossed her mind. I started to cry as if I suddenly understood her agony and that I wasn't wanted. Mm-Ma gently patted my chest to calm me, and she continued to muse, "Girls don't belong to the family. They cannot even carry on the family name, so who cares where they end up." This thought scared her, but also eased her conscience. She tried to smile at me, but I was mad. I closed my eyes tightly and didn't respond. With the thought of an extra mouth to feed, Mm-Ma's smile faded.

"Sons are much more valuable," Mm-Ma unconsciously muttered. "They carry on the family name, produce grandchildren, and take care of their parents when we become old. Woe to son-less parents; they will end up in misery if they live to old age!" She shivered at the thought. "Most important," she concluded, "sons give their parents a decent burial. One has a great face if there is a funeral procession with many sons in mourning."

Mm-Ma was a good woman. She was faithful to her family and did what she thought was best for them. Her thoughts were typical for women of her time, who never had a chance for an education. She was also oblivious to anything going on beyond the bounds of her impoverished village.

At daybreak, Mm-Ma reluctantly and painfully pulled herself out of bed. As a peasant woman, she had no time to idle in bed even the morning after giving birth. She was exhausted, but she had a family to feed. Her husband and two sons would surely be hungry when they finished work in the fields. It was early spring, and a new rice-planting season was upon them.

In those days, wives would wait on their husbands like slaves. This terrible tradition had been in practice for thousands of years and applied to all families — poor and rich alike. Most women accepted this as their fate, bearing it all in silence. A rare few would revolt or run away, only to be brought back and punished severely, often with a brutal beating. Mr. Hu had no intention to change the tradition, but luckily for Mm-Ma, Mr. Hu was mild-mannered compared to many other Chinese men. He only beat her occasionally. But years later, I learned how Mm-Ma became blind in one eye.

Girls could be excellent helpers, but Mm-Ma would never know. Had she kept her eldest daughter, Mm-Ma might have had help that morning, but she hadn't. There was no one else in this dark mud hut except me, and I was of no value to anyone.

Mr. Hu finally returned from the rice fields. He went from beating the water buffalo to pushing it to plow the fields. On seeing his tired and muddy face, Mm-Ma said, "Oh, here you are. Well, she [meaning me] has to have a name, even though she's a girl." Still fuming, Mr. Hu agreed.

Girls were named after flowers that bloom in the season of their birth. For sons, it was another story. Parents would seek out traditional scholars to find a name that would be favorable according to the year, month, day, and time of birth. Also, to protect their sons from evil spirits, a boy's name was used only on special occasions or when he went to school. At home, he would be referred to as a dog, or a tiger or some other animal to trick the evil spirits into believing there were no boys around, keeping their sons safe from harm.

It didn't take long to name me. Practically in unison without much thought, my parents said, "Call her 'Tren-Hwa (春花),'"

which means "Spring Flower." They didn't bother to specify which flower. Since there were so many flowers at that time of year, it was simplest to include them all. Also, they didn't know the exact date on which I was born.

My birth could have been as early as days after the Chinese New Year in 1931. There is a reason why the Chinese New Year is also referred to as "Spring Festival (春节)" (春節). It is less of a lunisolar calendar equivalent of Gregorian's January first but more of an annual celebration to signal the beginning of the spring. For farming purposes, ancient Chinese had devised twenty-four terms to describe seasons and climate shifts throughout the year, and one of them is called *Li Chun* — "the beginning of spring" (立春), which takes place shortly after the Spring Festival, and before the Gregorian calendar's Spring Equinox.

Incidentally, *Li Chun* is also the time when plum trees blossom (梅花) in Southern China, including along the Yangtze River valley. And of course, plum blossom (梅花) historically is a symbol of China, much as cherry blossoms are a symbol for Japan.

I must also note that my name 春花 (Spring Flower) should be romanized as "Chun-Hwa" and not "Tren-Hwa." Perhaps when my Americans parents heard my birth mother say "Chun," it sounded to them like "tren." In any case, the misspelled, or mispronounced, name "tren" would become a saving grace for me many years later.

So Spring Flower I became, whether I was born in February or May. Giving me a name, though, did not mean my parents had decided to keep me. Mm-Ma remained determined to find a future mother-in-law for me and send me away as soon as she could.

For months, Mm-Ma searched in vain, without a glimmer of hope. She didn't enjoy carrying me on her back while trudging along the dirt roads on her tiny bound feet. To win the hearts of a family that might take me in as a possible future daughter-in-law,

JEAN TREN-HWA PERKINS

they had to see me in person, like an interview. With bound feet that were only five inches long and me on her back, she found it challenging to stay upright even on level ground. I don't know how she did it with her bound feet, but during busy seasons, my poor Mm-Ma also had to work in the rice fields. In any event, in my defense, none of this was my fault. I was not her firstborn, and I never asked to be married off at the age of three months.

I should add that Mm-Ma hated having her feet bound. However, for her generation and those before, it was the fashion—and compelled by force. Men would not marry a woman with standard-size feet. The smaller, the daintier a woman's feet were, the increased likelihood she could be betrothed. So Mm-Ma could only walk as fast as her special-made heels would allow her. I wouldn't even call them feet, they were so deformed. All that was left were her toes, ankles, and arches. These fragmented parts had been crushed to pieces and recalcified to make her feet as small as possible. They were a mangled mess.

There was a cruel joke that women had their feet bound so they couldn't run away from their men. Mm-Ma used to think it was funny, but now that she needed to cover as much ground as she could in her search for a future mother-in-law, Mm-Ma wished she had the biggest feet in the world. She also found breastfeeding upsetting. Why should she have to feed a worthless baby girl?

As the months passed, the issue took a turn, and Mm-Ma became afraid she might get attached to me. Taking care of me for an extended period, she might lose the will to give me up. Breastfeeding was a natural form of birth control and would at least delay her next pregnancy. But when mothers breastfed their babies until they were two or even three, it could lead to infantile malnutrition diseases such as vitamin A deficiency and partial or complete blindness.

But I digress. Mm-Ma wanted to be fertile to have another baby boy. She knew she was running out of time. She did have two more births after me; both of them were girls.

As if the frustration I'd brought wasn't enough, the weather was also terrible. What had begun as typical spring showers turned into a steady downpour, day after day with no break in sight. While farmers needed ample water for rice planting, too much could rot the roots and drown the entire plant. Every day, Mr. Hu looked to the sky, hoping for the sun to shine.

While trotting home one day from another unsuccessful hunt for a mother-in-law, Mm-Ma noticed the water levels rising along the northern riverbanks. She also noticed the river was wider. She'd grown up along these riverbanks, and she knew something was wrong. With the rain coming down in torrents, she started to run, and I didn't make things easier for her with my cries of hunger.

As soon as she got home, Mr. Hu walked in from the fields. Mm-Ma, completely drenched, asked anxiously, "Lao Hu, do you suppose there's going to be a flood? The river is rising rapidly." *Lao Hu* (老胡) was a common phrase referring to one's husband. Hu was the family name, and *Lao* means "old."

"It's possible," Mr. Hu answered with a deep tone, as he glanced out the door.

Mm-Ma too looked out and saw the pond near their hut overflowing onto the rice fields, which Mr. Hu had tried all morning to drain.

"If the rain doesn't stop, we are in deep trouble," Mr. Hu rumbled to no one in particular. "There will be no harvest this fall, and we will all starve. The rain is drowning our crops—and us."

Mm-Ma scanned the interior of the hut with our meager belongings. Crude as they were, they were too precious to lose. This hut had been her home for a long time. I never found out exactly when Mm-Ma's mother gave her away as a future daughter-in-law. My parents had been married for at least twenty-five years when I was born. It was not only the custom to marry *young*, but marrying away girls when they were infants was common.

Mm-Ma's wedding bed was the only thing in the house that had a touch of grandeur. It wasn't as grand as the rich had, with fancy carvings on the bedposts, but hers did have a wooden top with strips of traditional blue flower cloth hanging down like curtains that could be drawn at night to keep mosquitos out as well as for privacy. There were painted wooden panels that had seen their better days covering both edges of the bed, so one could use the bed as a table, a desk, or a wooden seat also.

On the other side of the hut were two boards, each the width and length of a door, supported by homemade benches. These were my elder brothers' beds. A not-too-sturdy table stood in the middle of the hut where the family could eat, but more often than not, each person would take a bowl of rice with homemade pickled vegetables and have their meals in the courtyard by the rice fields. Except for Chinese New Year, there was rarely enough food to fill the table.

While Mm-Ma looked around thinking about what to take in the event of a flood, her five-inch bound feet were busy rocking me in a wooden crib, the same crib all the siblings, now dead or alive, had slept in. All mothers in China had wooden cradles. The only way they could get anything done with screaming infants was to rock them with one foot while working with their hands. A Chinese woman's hands were never idle. Mm-Ma was either sewing new clothes from cloth she'd woven on her precious loom or making cloth shoes for the family.

As Mr. Hu fell asleep, Mm-Ma's eyes finally rested on her spinning wooden wheels. At last, she was calm, and she knew she had to work late into the night after wasting a whole day looking for a mother-in-law. Without these late-night hours spinning cloth, the family would not have clothing. It was pitch dark, and Mm-Ma could hear the rain still pouring down. From time to time, she stood up to stretch her legs by the window. As she glanced back at the wooden cradle, she could hear the river rising. She began to think there might be a flood like the ones she'd heard about as a child, and she wondered aloud, "What will happen to us? What will we do with Spring Flower?"

One of the most massive floods in nearly a century was about to hit....

2

THERE WAS no electricity in small towns like the one where I was born. Most farmers used vegetable oil lamps because it was affordable. They grew and made their corn oil. Few people could afford kerosene, let alone electricity. While some families made candles, my family used vegetable oil. Mm-Ma would pour the precious oil sparingly and skillfully into a small dish, and she would then use a dry plant called *Tung Sing Cao* (听信草) as a wick, because it's soft, absorbent, and flexible. The brightness was the equivalent of about two candles. Mm-Ma was proud of the secret recipe her mother had passed on to her.

On this particular dark and rainy evening, to save oil, the family went to bed early. I slept with Mm-Ma, as most babies do in China. It was more convenient for the mother to breastfeed at night without having to fumble to light an oil lamp. And it would be a terrible waste to leave the lamp on all night. Another reason babies slept with their parents was to ward off rats that might otherwise nibble on their little noses. Mm-Ma wasn't taking any chances of my having no nose. What family would accept a future daughter-in-law without a nose?

That spring, an unusual amount of melted snow was pouring into the rivers from the Himalayas and Tibet-Qinghai Plateau, and the levels were rising more quickly than they had in centuries. Overnight, the entire Hwang-Mei County, including Hwang-Mei village along the northern banks of the Yangtze River, was underwater. Rice fields and vegetable gardens vanished. The peak of the flood had arrived. Despite all the warning signs, people had been reluctant to leave their homes, clinging to the glimmer of hope that the rain would stop and the water would recede. The flooding devoured their hopes and dreams.

Mm-Ma, alert to unusual sounds, nudged her sound-asleep husband, "Lao Hu — wake up!"

Getting no response, she shook him and said, "Something's wrong — something is going on. I hear the strangest noises."

Lazily, Mr. Hu opened one eye, and when he heard her words, he opened both eyes wide and scrambled out of bed. "Oh no — come quickly," he said, "Let's go out and see."

As they reached the door, they could hear the water swishing by, each wave advancing closer to the hut. The mud hut had suddenly become riverfront property. The violent splashing had reached their house and was pounding on the wall.

In his youth, Mr. Hu had heard older folks talk about this majestic river flooding, but this was his first experience of it. Looking around, he felt pleased that he'd selected this spot decades ago to build a home for his future bride. Instead of choosing a lower terrace closer to the rice fields, he decided to locate his hut atop a hill. The land belonged to the landlord, but as long as a farmer could pay the amount of grain required at the end of harvest season, the farmer and his family could keep the hut and continue farming the land.

That brief euphoria didn't last. As the light of dawn pierced through the clouds, Mm-Ma and Mr. Hu could see objects floating in the water. They heard cries of distress as a crowd stampeded toward the remaining dikes. With daylight, Mm-Ma could see that despite our hut being on higher ground, the flood was lurching toward us rapidly. It would be dangerous to stay inside since the mud could crumble and bury us alive. The walls were already soaked.

Refugee camps on the southern banks of the Yangtze River during the flood

Mr. Hu and Mm-Ma packed a few essentials and joined the crowd running to the dikes. Though higher than anywhere else, the dikes were quite narrow. We barely got there on time. A few hours later, there was no space left on the dike. With the wind blowing furiously, some who got too close to the edge were tragically blown into the river. Rumors were flying that there was looting going on. Mr. Hu went back to stay near our hut, which by then was knee-deep in water.

For the next few days, the flood wasn't getting any worse, but the water level wasn't receding either. The river, typically a mile or two wide, now extended twenty miles or more, submerging vast areas. In certain regions, the river swelled to 130 miles wide, or more. Many of those who escaped drowning would later die of disease or starvation. A great tragedy had begun to unfold.

In the midst of this devastating tragedy, foreigners, missionaries, and others, even mercenaries, were working with the local Chinese to help. They set up temporary camps with straw or mud huts along the southern banks of the Yangtze, which were less flooded, distributing clothing, food, and medical supplies. Charles and Anne Lindbergh even flew to China to assist, using their plane to transport supplies and medical workers.

In the meantime, Mr. Hu, who was watching over our meager possessions in the flooded hut, set up a straw "teepee" and every few days would bring us a modest supply of food until there was no more. Mm-Ma took as little as possible so that her sons could have more to eat, forgetting that when she didn't eat, I would have little or no milk. I was by then four or five months old.

We were stranded on the dikes for more than a month. Feeling desperate, many farmers from Hwang-Mei village crossed the river to the southern banks in search of help and hope. They became known as the "Yangtze River flood refugees." Days later, some came back saying that they met blue-eyed aliens with high nose bridges who had been kind to them. These foreign devils (洋鬼子) were giving out clothing and food, and giving babies free milk.

Mm-Ma had heard about these foreign devils, but had never seen one. She wondered how she might approach them or if they even spoke her language. So, she talked herself out of crossing the rising river.

"What if none of this is true?" she murmured.

Weeks later, despite seeing more food and clothing brought back by Hwang-Mei villagers, she still doubted it could be real.

When Mr. Hu came to the dike, she asked, "Lao Hu, what do

you think? Should we take a look?"

Mr. Hu did not reply, as he was focusing on stuffing his long pipe with leaves.

Mm-Ma continued, "Maybe we should have a look. Would you take us across the river?"

Mr. Hu nodded as though he agreed with her. He walked to the wobbly wooden dock, saw a few open wooden rafts tied to the wooden pier, and waved Mm-Ma over. He untied one of the boats, and just like that, the three of us rowed across the treacherous water. Mm-Ma held me tightly to shield the wind from my head.

What was usually a thirty-minute ride to the southern bank of the river took more than two hours. The river was a sea with rooftops floating like islands. When we finally arrived, we saw that the city of Kiukiang was also flooded. People were either traveling in boats or wading knee-deep in water. Mr. Hu stayed

Flooded streets near the railroad station

Downtown Kiukiang

Refugee camp near the Kiukiang River Lock Pagoda (锁江楼塔)

SPRING FLOWER: A TALE OF TWO RIVERS

Refugee camp in Kiukiang during the flood where my mother and I stayed

behind by the wooden raft while Mm-Ma carried me, and we waded through the water toward the city. When she saw a passerby, she asked for the place where foreigners were feeding babies. The man kindly pointed and said, "Sen Ming Wha Shrey Eee Yuan (生命活水医院: The Water of Life Hospital), up there on the hill."

By the time we arrived, the morning distribution of milk for babies was over. A young Chinese nurse told Mm-Ma that she should stay at the camp the hospital had set up for flood refugees because there would be another round of milk distribution the next morning. So, Mm-Ma and I were given a hut at the camp, and she got an earful of information from the other refugees. Someone told her that the American missionary doctor had built the Water of Life Hospital, and the new building had just opened. She learned that the locals knew the doctor as Pei Eee-Sen, which is Chinese for Dr. Perkins, with Eee-Sen (医生) meaning doctor, and Pei (裴) for Perkins. Pei is an official Chinese surname listed in the old book called *Bai Jia Shing* (百家姓: "100 Family Surnames").

The doctor's full Chinese name was Pei Ging Tsee (裴敬思), the family name coming first. These three Chinese characters were a transliteration of the word Perkins. Ging-Tsee (敬思) also has a deeper meaning. Ging (敬) means to be respectful, and Tsee (思) implies deep reflection. All foreigners who worked in China during that time were given Chinese names, making it easier for non-English-speaking Chinese people around them.

Mm-Ma's new neighbors at the camp continued to provide information about what they knew or thought they knew. One woman said, "Pei Eee-Sen is a great man and a highly skilled doctor who must be in his eighties." Another chimed in, "He has snow-white hair." A third woman walked over to join the conversation. "He is married to Pei Tse-Mo (裴师母 meaning Mrs. Pei), who is much younger. She is delightful and can even speak Chinese. Pei Tse-Mo also helps with handing out food and milk, but most of that is done by two young nurses, twin sisters known as Poo-Da (浦大) and Poo-Er (浦二), also missionaries from America. When you take your baby for milk, you will see them all."

Mm-Ma thought, "Oh, maybe that was who I saw this morning."

These conversations put Mm-Ma at ease about meeting the foreigners. When the next morning came, she joined a crowd of mothers walking toward the tent where milk would be passed out. Sure enough, the foreigners were already inside the tent standing by a table full of milk jugs and food. She noticed how young they looked. Each had a white cap perched atop her head. They seemed kind and caring toward the waiting mothers and their babies.

With me strapped on her back in an old cloth saddle, Mm-Ma rushed to the forming line. She pressed close to the woman ahead of her. She didn't want to be missed, and so she squeezed a little harder. This motion attracted the attention of two American nurses, Poo-Da and Poo-Er.

SPRING FLOWER: A TALE OF TWO RIVERS

*Refugees in the new Kiukiang Water of Life Hospital compound
(WLH: 九江生命活水医院), 1931–1932*

I should note that these two American nurses were not twins. Their family name was Ploeg, and they were second-generation Dutch immigrants from Grand Rapids, Michigan. Chinese people had been fondly calling them the Ploeg sisters (浦乐姐妹: pronounced "Poo-Le Jie-Mei"). Jie-Mei (姐妹) means sisters; Poo-Le (浦乐) was a transliteration of "Ploeg." The older of the two sisters, Deanetta, became Poo-Da (浦大) with Da meaning big, so she was Big Ploeg. And the younger one, Bessie, was referred to as Poo-Er (浦二) with Er being the number two.

The Ploeg sisters noticed the woman with a baby on her back. She looked unfamiliar to them. Then their eyes descended on me,

JEAN TREN-HWA PERKINS

My biological mother and I (far left) at WLH, ca. 1931

and I wasn't frightened by their gaze or their strange features. Instead, I gave them a big baby smile. That must have touched their hearts, and they gave me a nickname, the Cute Baby.

For the next few days, whenever Mm-Ma appeared with me, the sisters gave me more than my share of milk. Mm-Ma was amazed that such good people even existed on earth. They told her she could come every day for food and milk for her baby. So we stayed at the camp for a month.

Mm-Ma was glad I could be fed once a day, but she herself did not have enough to eat. Her milk was drying up. Being a fast-growing baby, I needed more than what Mm-Ma and the refugee camp could give me. So, Mm-Ma began to walk the streets to beg for food. As time went by, the American sisters noticed that Cute Baby had stopped smiling. I was hungry.

As the floodwaters in Kiukiang finally began to recede, the flood refugees started returning home, or at least returning to where their houses used to be. Feeling she had already been away from home for too long, Mm-Ma waded through what water was still left and wearily crossed the river with other refugees on a boat. As she approached the hill where our hut had been, she saw only a pile of mud.

A mud hut can last for years under ordinary circumstances, as the mud is packed tightly, much like bricks. But, if it's soaked in water for an extended period, eventually it will collapse. With hard work from Mr. Hu and my elder brothers, our few belongings were still all there, though drenched. But since most of our belongings were made of wood, they would dry up once the sun returned. Most important was to rebuild the hut before winter. It was already late summer.

With a deep sigh, Mm-Ma asked, "Lao Hu, what shall we do? Where can we get the materials and with what money? And who will help build it?"

"In normal times," Mr. Hu said, as though thinking out loud, "relatives and friends and neighbors help out. But we'd have to feed them while they help, and there's no harvest now. Where will the food come from?"

"Indeed," Mm-Ma echoed, staring blankly ahead. Then she looked at me, her Spring Flower, thin and weak. During these challenging months, she had grown attached to me, more than she was willing to admit. Of course, her sons were her priority. The oldest, Kuo-Hsiang (阔祥: meaning affluent and blessed), was already fourteen or fifteen.

"If the water doesn't recede, the land will freeze and spell trouble in the spring," said Mr. Hu. "Maybe the boys can go to the foreigner's hospital and offer their labor?" He sounded smart for a change.

"What about Tren-Hwa?" Mm-Ma replied, after another deep sigh. She knew that sooner or later she would have to send me to a future mother-in-law's home. That was the rule.

Mr. Hu said nothing.

"What do we do now, Lao Hu? Spring Flower seems to be

Missionaries caring for children in need at WLH

wilting fast. I'm not sure she is going to make it." Then Mm-Ma began to sob.

Still not a sound from Mr. Hu.

Suddenly she remembered something the flood refugees had said, about foreigners liking to help Chinese girls. Mm-Ma stood, with her eyes lit up. "Lao Hu, please take me back to Kiukiang. Kuo-Hsiang can accompany me this time."

"But you just came back," Mr. Hu said. He appeared confused.

"People told me these foreigners would pick up discarded baby girls and place them in orphanages. Some even take them into their care." By now, Mm-Ma was shouting in excitement.

"And?" Mr. Hu responded dully. Then he understood. "You are right. But will a foreigner want Tren-Hwa?" Mm-Ma sat down, a little deflated.

Moments later, she perked up again. "Maybe. They seemed to like her when we went to get milk and food. The foreigners always gave Tren-Hwa extra helpings. Giving her to foreigners might be the best idea, easier than finding a mother-in-law in these times of flood and struggles." Mm-Ma could contain herself no longer. "Lao Hu!" Mm-Ma shouted, "We shall offer Tren-Hwa to the foreigners. Let's give it a try!"

"It's a thought," he answered, still unmoved, "But will the child take to the foreigners?"

"She showed no fear when facing them," Mm-Ma told him. "And they seem to like her."

After what was probably the most extended conversation in their lives, Mm-Ma and Mr. Hu seemed in no hurry to pursue the idea. Neither wanted to admit to the other that I had found a place in their hearts.

As weeks went by, Mm-Ma sighed while looking at my thin little body. What a bundle of trouble I had been since the night I was born. She knew she had to act quickly or I might die in her arms at any time. So she decided to take me to see the foreigners the next morning, and that Kuo-Hsiang would row us across the river.

As luck would have it, after crossing the river the next day, Mm-Ma stumbled right into Mrs. Perkins at the hospital gate. Without much ado, Mm-Ma screwed up all the courage she had and said, almost in one breath, "Pei Tse-Mo, please take my child, let her be your daughter!" Tse-Mo (师母) means a teacher's wife, a highly respectful appellation.

Mrs. Perkins was speechless. Her thoughts raced back to 1916, fifteen years earlier, when she married Dr. Perkins at the age of thirty-three. He was eight years her senior. They sailed to China for their honeymoon, with the intention of settling down as missionaries for the rest of their lives. Since she was an only child, it was difficult for her to leave her aging parents, although they had given their unconditional support. With their blessing, she and Edward were undeterred in giving their hearts and minds to the Lord and the Chinese people.

Although they'd never talked about it, her only regret was

that they remained childless. Perhaps that is why Mrs. Perkins helped promote the welfare of girls in this rural region. After seeing so many baby girls abandoned at the hospital gate, on strangers' doorsteps, or along the roadside bleeding away, their umbilical cords still attached, she was determined to help as many Chinese girls as she could. She was particularly bent on them getting an education.

She became known for having a number of Chinese "daughters," most in their late teens or older. Some were in college on scholarships Mrs. Perkins had raised through friends in America. Only one of the girls Mrs. Perkins helped was younger. She was enrolled in elementary school and living in the school dorm. To adopt an infant would be an ordeal. Mrs. Perkins was already forty-eight, old enough to be a grandmother. After she recovered from the shock of Mm-Ma's question, she asked, "What's your name?"

Mm-Ma looked confused, perhaps by Mrs. Perkins's accent. The woman standing next to Mrs. Perkins translated for Mm-Ma.

"Oh, Hu—my name is Hu, Pei Tse-Mo." Mm-Ma chuckled and added, "You can speak Chinese?"

Mrs. Perkins nodded. "Mrs. Hu, I am very sorry, this is not a simple matter. I cannot just take your baby. At least I do not have an answer for you now."

Sensing the disappointment, Mrs. Perkins immediately followed up with "Who is this boy? Is this your son, Mrs. Hu? He seems like a brilliant young man. I believe I can help him find work and maybe even go to school."

Mm-Ma's mind was in disarray and had forgotten that Kuo-Hsiang was standing behind us. She quickly bowed and said, "Yes, Pei Tse-Mo, please! Kuo-Hsiang is a perfect boy—thank you. If you could help this boy, you would be our great savior." Mm-Ma pushed Kuo-Hsiang forward and began to press his shoulders downward, gesturing that he should kneel and kowtow in front of Mrs. Perkins.

Mrs. Pekins promptly stopped that.

"No, please no need, Mrs. Hu, please don't do that."

Mm-Ma then made another attempt to hand me over to Mrs. Perkins. "But what about this baby girl, we cannot... please..."

"No, Mrs. Hu, she's your child, she's a child who already has a mother, I cannot just take her away (这是你的孩子, 是个有母亲的孩子, 我不能乱拿)."

Mrs. Perkins sounded firm as she pushed me back into my mother's chest. Crestfallen, Mm-Ma left the hospital with me on her back, puzzled and confused. She thought all foreigners were wealthy and there would be no problem. They seemed to like her baby the last time. She roamed the streets, feeling profoundly sad.

Mrs. Perkins had taken in Kuo-Hsiang, who would be working as an orderly at the hospital and an aide at the refugee camp. She even promised to discuss with Dr. Perkins whether they could help Kuo-Hsiang get an education. As remarkable as all that was, Mm-Ma was still disappointed. Her goal was to give me away.

The Kiukiang streets were mostly cleared of water now. Mm-Ma thought perhaps if she stayed in Kiukiang long enough, she might run into a future mother-in-law. But after begging for a few days, she knew no one would want an extra mouth to feed after a flood like this one.

Reluctantly, Mm-Ma headed home. When she approached the dock looking for a boat, she heard a woman yelling.

"Mrs. Hu, wait—wait a moment, Mrs. Hu!"

Mm-Ma turned around, and it was the woman who had been standing next to Mr. Perkins and helped with translation.

The woman was out of breath. "Mrs. Hu, I've been looking

JEAN TREN-HWA PERKINS

for you for days. Mrs. Perkins asks if you can come back to the hospital to have another chat about your baby girl."

Mm-Ma's eyes lit up.

My thin and pathetic baby face had moved Mrs. Perkins. She had gone home and discussed the situation with Dr. Perkins, but neither could make a decision or find a solution. As was their custom, they prayed for guidance.

Upon arriving at the home of Mrs. Perkins, Mm-Ma fell to the ground and began to sob. She was exhausted and emotionally drained after begging on the streets for days.

Mrs. Perkins quickly pulled Mm-Ma up and said, "Mrs. Hu, we may have a solution. Please sit with me on this chair, and not on the ground, it's dirty."

Unsure if Mm-Ma understood her accent, Mrs. Perkins continued, "Mrs. Hu, your child is far too young for Dr. Perkins and me to care for. We will support you financially so you can take care of her until she is a little older. Then, we will decide on a date for you to bring her to us. And, by the way, what is her name?"

Mm-Ma grabbed hold of Mrs. Perkins' hands and said; "Pei Tse-Mo, thank you! You have saved this child! Her name is Tren-Hwa."

"Spring Flower, eh?" Mrs. Perkins chuckled, and gave me a big smile.

Mm-Ma was elated; the problem of my future was solved! Although not what she had intended, it would have to do. She was profoundly satisfied knowing that her baby girl wouldn't starve to death. Mm-Ma hurried home to tell Mr. Hu, who she knew could use some good news.

The money Mm-Ma received from Mrs. Perkins to support me went to rebuild our home and buy food to sustain the family. So, I stayed skinny and malnourished. To them, I was still just a girl. They wouldn't consider spending money on me when there were other, more critical needs. The flood had left us with virtually nothing to eat. Sadly, the government did little to help, and winter was fast approaching.

3

It was on one of those cold winter days that I was taken across the river for the last time with Mm-Ma and Mr. Hu. No one explained why I was dressed in a new Chinese gown lined with padded cotton after wearing the same rags every day since I was born. I had no idea that rags meant we were impoverished or why other children wore bright-colored clothes. I was too little to notice the difference. But that day, I was aware of my new clothes and sensed something out of the ordinary was underway. It was doubly puzzling that my head had been shaved like a boy's with only a tuft left on the top. Because it was cold, Mm-Ma put a colorful knitted hat on my head, one of the handouts she'd gotten at the refugee camp.

Suddenly, all our neighbors, many of whom were relatives, crowded into our mud hut and began to whisper aloud as if I weren't there or couldn't understand. Of course, they were right; I couldn't.

A raggedy woman said, "Is it true? Is she really going to the foreign devil's home?"

A woman standing next to her added, "I wonder if she'll be frightened?"

Then a man shouted, "I'd say she's lucky!"

And the raggedy woman snickered, "Poor child, she won't understand a word they say! I wouldn't live with foreigners—they're barbaric devils!"

"Yes," another woman murmured, "I bet she'll cry her heart

out and want to come home."

I turned my head from side to side, trying to figure out what they were saying, so much that my neck began to hurt. Mm-Ma looked at my puzzled face and shouted at the gathered crowd, "Stop all this talking! You're frightening her."

A hushed silence prevailed. I looked at Mm-Ma curiously. She held my hands and said, "We're going to be guests at the foreigner's home today. Remember we used to get milk for you from them? You always smiled at them?"

How could I remember? I was still a baby. But as a young child, I accepted her explanation.

Finally, Mr. Hu, Mm-Ma, and I headed toward the river. We got on a raft, and Mr. Hu rowed in silence. Mm-Ma was in deep thought, and my murmurs and prattle fell on deaf ears. Suddenly Mm-Ma heaved a huge sigh and asked, "Lao Hu, are we doing the right thing? Will she be okay with these foreigners?" Mr. Hu did not even attempt to reply. He was still deeply disappointed I wasn't a boy.

Mr. Hu had no idea that girls can bring a lot of joy. He paid no attention to his daughters, even the one who grew up with them to the age of three before being sent away to her future mother-in-law. However, little Tren-Hwa was different. Each time he came home from the rice field tired and hungry, Tren-Hwa would give him such a sweet, innocent smile it was impossible for him to resist picking me up and playing with me for a little while. That was something he rarely did, even with his sons.

I was his child, but when he thought of their poverty and that girls eventually would eventually have to leave home, Tren-Hwa might as well go to the foreigner's home. Perhaps she would have a better life. So, in his mind, the case was closed.

Then at that moment, he caught Tren-Hwa's eyes and her smile, and he quickly looked away.

JEAN TREN-HWA PERKINS

Impatient with her husband's silence, Mm-Ma repeated the question. Appearing annoyed, Mr. Hu shouted back, "Yes!"

That was the second-most extended conversation I ever heard from them. I looked from Mm-Ma to Mr. Hu, trying to grasp the content of that brief exchange. When they noticed I was aware of their conversation, they fell silent once more.

Mm-Ma may have been silent vocally, but her mind was in turmoil with last-minute misgivings. She must have wondered why she was not feeling happy or relieved, even though this was the fruit of her efforts for me to survive. Instead, she was reluctant to let me go. Suddenly Mm-Ma tightened her grip on me. I looked up, and a tear dropped onto my face.

Innocently, I spoke. "Mm-Ma, cry?" I reached my arm out to touch her face. Those might have been my first real words.

"No," she said as she pushed away my hand. "Ma-ma is fine. The cold wind is making my eyes watery."

Satisfied with her answer, I looked at Mr. Hu, and again he averted my gaze. I guessed he had to concentrate on rowing.

Although the flood had been receding and the river width began to narrow, the wind was still cold and stiff, blowing across the water creating whitecaps. Rowing that day was a challenge. The boat had to cut through the waves. Finally, we reached the other shore.

The floodwaters had disappeared from the streets of Kiukiang. Mm-Ma squatted to lower herself so I could slide down from her back. At the age of ten months, I could already walk well enough, and the three of us walked silently, straight along the main street toward the foreigner's home. When we arrived at the big gates, I looked up at them in awe. Mm-Ma lifted the knocker and pounded it against the door, and a gateman swung open the iron gate. He showed no surprise at seeing us. He had been told to let a child and her parents in when they arrived and to take them to the kitchen to warm up. It was about noon, and the foreigners had not returned from the hospital. So we sat in the kitchen while the cook graciously poured tea for my parents.

As we waited, all the Chinese servants came by to take a look. Some came individually, others in small groups. Many of them were amahs (female domestic servants), nursemaids, or nannies. One held a Chinese child, looking well-fed and well-dressed, in her arms. Mm-Ma looked at me then back at the other baby girl. With a sigh, she said, "The difference between them is like day and night. My Tren-Hwa is so skinny. She's had nothing to eat."

The amah with the child replied quickly, "Now you can rest your heart. Your child will be in good hands."

"Where did this child come from?" Mm-Ma asked, wondering why we had had to wait so many months before Mrs. Perkins would let her Tren-Hwa arrive.

The amah replied, "Her mother gave birth unexpectedly at the Water of Life Hospital, which is for men only. She had to go to the Danforth, a Women's Hospital. But she couldn't. Her younger son was at the Water of Life Hospital, too sick to be left alone. So the Ploeg sisters, Poo-Da and Poo-Er, assisted with the emergency delivery at the Water of Life Hospital. Since the baby's father had already passed on, there was no way her mother could take care of a newborn and two small boys with one in the hospital. Without hesitation, the American sisters agreed to bring this baby up."

Mm-Ma was fascinated by what she had just heard. She became braver and asked, "How old is the child?"

The amah answered, "Not quite nine months."

"Then Tren-Hwa must be two or three months older than this girl," Mm-Ma murmured, never quite sure how old I was.

Putting the child on the floor, the amah said, "Don't worry, this baby is big for her age. Yours will be fine."

JEAN TREN-HWA PERKINS

After staring at the little girl, I wobbled over to her. She was holding onto the edge of a chair, trying to stand up. When she did, she was taller than I was, even without standing up straight. Then before any of the amahs knew what happened, the kid swiped me across the face and knocked me down like a feather. I looked up in disbelief but managed to stand and backpedal to where Mm-Ma was sitting, eyes focused on this little bastard, fearing she would come over and whack me again. The young amah, whose name was Wang (王), who I later called Wang-Ma, swiftly picked up the little girl to keep her away from me.

The front gate squealed, and the servants all went back to their posts. The amah, holding the child in her arms, went to the front door to greet the foreigners, leaving only Mm-Ma, Mr. Hu, the cook, and me in the kitchen. Upon learning that I'd arrived, Mrs. Perkins rushed down to welcome me. Mm-Ma and Mr. Hu stood up immediately.

Pushing me toward Mrs. Perkins, Mm-Ma said, "Pei Tse-Mo, this is my Spring Flower. She is here to see you. Thank you!" Mm-Ma was alert enough to know that Mrs. Perkins might not

My new home with Chum, and her amah, Wang-Sao (王嫂)

be able to understand that many Chinese words and that saying too much might confuse her.

Mrs. Perkins smiled at me and said, "Welcome! Little Tren-Hwa." She then walked straight toward me, picked me up, hugged me, and gave me a kiss.

I was shocked and a little frightened. Chinese people never show emotions or kiss and hug openly, even with a child. That being said, it wasn't long before I'd be calling this woman "Mudder," affectionately, or sometimes "Mar-Mar."

Mrs. Perkins seemed to be sizing up the situation. She quickly assigned Chang-Ma (常媽) to be my nanny. Chang-Ma nodded and took me to her quarters at the back of the compound, where the Chinese servants lived. There, in her room, she fed me my noon meal. I was already able to feed myself, because children in places where their parents don't have time to pamper them learn to be more independent earlier.

Mm-Ma and Mr. Hu were having their meal in the kitchen while waiting for Dr. Perkins to come home. The front gate creaked once more, and in came Dr. Perkins, who I would soon call "Day-Day," which, in my mouth, was a way of saying Daddy (爹爹 in Chinese, pronounced like "dee-eh dee-eh"). After finishing their meal, Mm-Ma and Mr. Hu stood up just as Dr. Perkins entered the kitchen. Dr. and Mrs. Perkins both wanted to know more about my abilities and my health.

To the question of whether I could talk, Mm-Ma answered proudly, "Tren-Hwa talks a mile a minute; she even knows enough words to curse!" Mrs. Perkins did not comment but vowed to herself that curse words would never come out of my mouth again. And to this day, I have never uttered a word that was a curse.

Mm-Ma then told Mrs. Perkins, apologetically, that my feet were not bound because neighbors had told her the government had discontinued the practice. Mrs. Perkins looked aghast. It had never occurred to her that Mm-Ma would even think of doing such a thing. What a relief! Although I wasn't happy that Mm-Ma had shaved my head, I knew, even then, that hair grows back but once feet are bound, there's no way to undo the harm.

The Perkinses asked whether I'd had measles, whooping cough, or other children's diseases. Looking at this skin-and-bones child, they were sure Mm-Ma wouldn't know anyway. The conversation ended with Mr. Hu presenting a signed statement that, "On December 22, 1931, both parents are willing to give their daughter, Spring Flower, for adoption to the Perkins family…"

From my Mm-Ma and Mr. Hu's perspective, this statement was sufficient to make the adoption legal and official, and they left without saying goodbye to me. Perhaps it was purposeful. I don't remember what my emotions were that day, nor was I ever told. Whatever they were, they didn't last long because my new mother had thought of everything to make my adjustment smooth and happy.

I also had Chang-Ma. She was in her early fifties, more like Mm-Ma, and I instantly bonded with her and came to love her very much. Chang-Ma never tired of telling others how touched she was when, one day, I found her crying silently.

"Why do you cry?" I had asked.

"My husband has died," she said, "leaving me with only a son who is now very sick. I have such a sad life." Chang-Ma then heaved a big sigh.

"Don't worry," I said. "When I grow up, I'll buy you a bed like the ones the foreigners sleep on, and I will take care of you."

In my childish mind, a comfortable bed would solve all her problems. I never forgot my promise, but Chang-Ma did not live to see me reach even the age of eleven.

SPRING FLOWER: A TALE OF TWO RIVERS

I had come to my new home at the busiest time of year. My second day there was my American mother's birthday, December 23. The next day was Christmas Eve, with Christmas Day that year falling on a Friday. A week later, it was Western New Year's Day, and Chinese New Year came on February 6. With never-ending celebrations and fireworks, it was a whirlwind of confusion.

It was during these months that I had my first memorable mishap. There were no bathrooms in country homes, only a big wooden bucket in the corner of the hut for grownups. The material in that bucket was a valuable source of fertilizer for the rice fields, but even that bucket was a luxury. Most of us used outhouses made of straw. Toddlers and children my age wore pants with a slit in the back so that we could relieve ourselves anytime, anywhere, mostly on the rice fields.

Looking around this big house with wooden floors and carpets, I had a vague sense that I shouldn't just pull open my pants and squat on the floor. And there were all these carpets everywhere. I searched everywhere for a place that seemed right, but the urgency affected my judgment. When I spotted the fireplace, I exhaled in relief. "Perfect," I thought.

It was a bumpy start to a lifelong relationship. I like to think that my American parents welcomed me into their home during the busiest time of year because I was both their birthday and Christmas present.

4

BEYOND THE LOUD and scary noise of firecrackers on Chinese New Year's and learning to pee in the right place, 1932 was mostly a blur to me. I understood only about half of what was going on around me, but it didn't take me long to settle happily into my new American home and to adore my American parents, especially my mother. I trailed after her everywhere, so much so that the servants began to joke that this "Spring Flower" had become an extension of Mrs. Perkins's coattails, or that Mrs.

Growing up and gaining weight fast from all the good eating, ca. 1932–1933

SPRING FLOWER: A TALE OF TWO RIVERS

Perkins had a doll she dragged around.

This house had been a quiet place, where one could only hear the light footsteps of the Americans and their quiet conversations. Now the house reverberated with sounds of children's giggles, laughter, and song.

By the following summer, 1932, the toddler who whacked me when we first met opened her mouth and began to talk. Gone were the days of sign language when she pointed to the things she wanted, even the moon, which I'd bet her aunties (or her two mothers) would have given her if they could. That kid was the apple of their eye. So, I thought, "Hey, brat, what took you so long to speak?"

That kid became my little sister, and we turned out to be "two peas in a pod." Her American aunties gave her a beautiful English name, but in this book, I will call her "Chum," because we were best chums. I was also close to her two guardians, Auntie Dee, whose nickname at the Water of Life Hospital was Poo-Da, and Auntie Bessie, nicknamed Poo-Er. We six became a family.

With two toddlers racing around the house, windows began to shake. My bedroom was on the second floor, and I would dash down the wooden steps to join Chum playing in our massive backyard gardens, while she would walk daintily down—step by step—like a princess. I'd trip and tumble in my haste, causing the stairs to creak, and I'd howl with pain, only to pick myself up and give a sheepish grin to any grownups who were nearby, despite bruises and a bloody nose. Poor Chang-Ma had to run after me on her tiny bound feet to clean me up before the blood would stain my new white dress. One day Chang-Ma stood at the bottom of the stairs holding two big pillows, anticipating my tumble.

On rainy days, when we were forced to be inside the house, I'd sit on the giant rocking chair and rock back and forth as high as I could. One time I rocked so high, the chair toppled over, and I flew across the room into a coat rack, before landing on the rug. The landing was relatively soft, and I'd missed poking my eye out by less than an inch. I wore my black eye as a badge of honor, and everyone asked what had happened. Auntie Dee, the sterner of Chum's moms, did not laugh. She scolded Mother and Chang-Ma, and even growled, it seemed to me, for not watching me more closely. If the house could speak, what stories it would tell!

I was a few months Chum's senior and felt responsible for her. I hovered over her like a mother hen, hoping something would make her cry so I could comfort her. She was not a crybaby (neither was I), so one day I purposely pushed her, just so I could offer consolation. Chum slumped to the ground face down, but still no sound. So I dragged her to the wall to sit her up. Just then, Wang-Ma, Chum's amah who had been watching us like a hawk, came charging out and, with one swoop, swept her up and inspected her from head to toe. Chum had scraped her knees severely when my amah, Chang-Ma, hearing the commotion, came running in to rescue me, fearing what Wang-Ma might do.

Two peas in a pod, ca. spring 1934

Suddenly, I realized I'd done something horribly wrong, and I stood there meek as a lamb. Fortunately, Chum wasn't seriously hurt, and neither of the amahs had the heart to scold me. I narrowly escaped being in the doghouse when the aunties and Mother came home.

Chum and I were both stubborn as mules. There were two little dogs in our house. One was called Pow-Pow (跑跑), which means "Run-Run" in Chinese. He looked like a miniature collie and was Day-Day's pet. The other was my Mother's pet, a little Pekinese called Pe-Ke. I've never been a lover of animals, and I'd avoid them whenever I could. But Chum loved to hold and pet them. One day Pow-Pow was not in the mood to be petted, and he turned on Chum and bit her hand. Even then, she didn't cry. She stood against the wall with her hand behind her back and said nothing. I didn't know what had happened, and for what seemed like hours, I tried to get Chum to play with me, but she stood there, showing no fear or pain. Finally, I grabbed her arm and asked, "You okay? Something wrong?"

Chum showed me her hand, reluctantly, and I was shocked. She was still bleeding. I cried quite loudly to alert the grownups, and Chum had to have a rabies vaccine. Pow-Pow didn't live long after that, and Chum's hand bore the scars of Pow-Pow's tooth marks for the rest of her life.

It didn't take me long to notice a stark difference between us. Chum had a fair complexion, uncommon among Chinese, while I have a more typical East Asian look. Even within the confines of the Water of Life Hospital compound, servants, workers, and staff were in awe of her fair skin. The aunties were particularly proud of it, and I was quite jealous.

But things have a way of evening out. Whenever she had insect bites, they would cause lesions requiring treatment, especially when she scratched them. During the summer months,

Chum's legs would look ugly, covered with bandages. Even still, I envied her, and I began to scratch myself with a vengeance. But no matter how hard I scratched my legs, nothing happened, probably because my nails weren't long enough. I was too little to be grateful for having healthy skin, and I longed for the day when I, too, would have Band-Aids on my arms and legs.

Finally, I accidentally caught my arm in the door and a tiny piece of skin came off. I was so happy; I'd be wearing a Band-Aid. But to my great disappointment, Mother assessed the situation and concluded, "It's a small wound and doesn't warrant a Band-Aid."

So, I decided to peel the scab off so it would bleed, and then I'd get to have a Band-Aid. But despite my earnest efforts — I peeled it off many times — the wound barely bled and refused to get infected. It did leave behind a tiny, triangle-shaped scar on my right arm, which to this day reminds me what a silly and stubborn little girl I was.

By the time the "super holidays" (Mother's birthday on the 23rd, Christmas on the 25th, then New Year's Eve) of December 1933 arrived, Chum and I were old enough to speak in sentences, and for some reason Mother was anxious to know whether we were capable of singing. She began to teach the two of us children's hymns in both Chinese and English, even though neither of us was quite three years old. To Mother's utmost joy, I was able to follow a tune, although the words I sang included incoherent syllables and mumbles. Thus began our "career" singing for the Sunday English service, mainly for all the missionaries and English-speaking Chinese. Day-Day was often the preacher.

Chum showed musical talent early and was an instant soprano singer. In later years, she also became an excellent pianist. I had a low voice, which landed me in the alto range, but I was not at all gifted. And my worst drawback was being painfully shy in front of an audience, another contrast between Chum and me. Poor Mother never knew what to expect of me. More often than not, I'd get stage fright and run off without notice or bury my face in her lap, embarrassing her. The days I was able to stay on stage, I would turn my body away from the audience and not utter a note. Chum had no stage fright at all. She would calmly sing to the end, to the delight of the audience. I was a tomboy with stage fright, an unfortunate combination.

At home, it was a different story. There was nothing shy about me and I sang out of tune at the top of my lungs. My favorite songs were "Jesus loves me hmmm-hmmm I know, something-something, hmmm-hmm-hmm for the Bible something so…." I would connect each song to my next favorite song without stopping, as if they were all one song. Rocking away on my favorite rocking chair I'd belt out, "I have food to eat and clothes to wear…. hmmm-hmmm, something-something…—hmm-hmmm—"I am more precious by far than the sparrows…."

I felt carefree. I was happy, and most of all, I felt loved. Despite my horrible voice and inability to keep a tune, Mother always smiled with pleasure whenever I sang these songs. It was a great comfort to her that this child she had adopted, for better and for worse, had accepted Jesus so readily. Perhaps the experience of hunger, cold, and the lack of love in my short life made me more receptive to anything that offered love, care, and warmth.

5

MOTHER LIKED the name Spring Flower, and I seemed to be blossoming into one since arriving at her home. Still, the urge to give me a proper English name became stronger in her with each passing month as she watched me growing up right before her eyes. Besides, the Chinese staff and servants reminded her that Tren-Hwa, "Spring Flower," has a not-so-hidden meaning in Chinese, implying promiscuity and even prostitution. So, Mother decided that on the day of my baptism, she would give me a new name.

"Little Spring Flower," she said to me in Chinese, the language she frequently tried to speak to me, "this Sunday, we're going to

Hi, my name is Jean Perkins! ca. spring 1935

give you an English name. From now on, we will call you Jean."

"Why?" I asked, confused, and even terrified.

"Jean is an endearing name to me, and I want you to have it." After a pause, she added, "I was going to tell you this story when you get older, but you're so bright I want to tell you now. Before I was born, I had an older sister named Jean."

My eyes grew big.

"You were born?" I blurted out. I thought only children were born, that grownups have somehow always been here.

Mother chuckled, "Yes, Mother was born just as you were, except it was a long time ago." She continued, "My older sister Jean had severe stomach pains, and our father took her to see a doctor."

"Like Day-Day," I interjected, feeling proud that I could call my father by a real English word, *day*.

Mother nodded patiently and said, "Yes, dear. And this doctor told my father that Jean had worms in her stomach. He gave my father a small package of ground glass for my sister to swallow to kill the worms. In those days, the ground glass solution appeared sensible because there weren't many medicines to choose from.

"As soon as they got home," Mother went on, "my father told my sister to swallow the ground glass. My sister pleaded that she didn't want to, but my father insisted. Finally, she did. She was an obedient child. But instead of killing the worms, the ground glass cut up the inside of her stomach, and she died almost instantly. My father has blamed himself ever since."

"So, Mother, you want me to be called Jean to make my grandfather happy?" I asked.

Mother gave me a big hug and a kiss and said, "You are a brilliant and intuitive child."

This entire conversation was in Chinese. I wasn't sure I understood what she was talking about because she had such

JEAN TREN-HWA PERKINS

a thick accent, but I did see tears in her eyes. I was confused in my later years, because the name of her mother—my maternal grandmother—was also Jean. Was I named after her? Was there another Jean who died young, or had I misunderstood the whole story? I never found out. As a child, even life's essential questions would only bother me for a moment. My name was settled on that day.

I skipped off to tell my dolls the great news. "From now on, you must call me Jean."

At last, in April 1934, the day of baptism came. When I came home from the church, I told everyone, with great pride, "They washed my hair in church today, so from now on, you must call me Jean." When the chuckles subsided, the Chinese folks still called me Tren-Hwa (春花). So I became Jean Tren-Hwa Perkins.

A few days later, two Chinese teachers from the Rulison Girls High School came to visit. Mother knew them well. Rulison Girls High had been built by missionaries, and Mother taught Bible classes there for seniors. The teachers were curious to see how I was getting along in an American home. They couldn't believe their eyes when they saw how much I had changed! Instead of the skinny child of a year earlier, they encountered a healthy, rosy-cheeked, bright-eyed kid. But I was still timid, and I hid behind Mother's skirt. These teachers called me "Spring Flower."

Hi Mom, my new Japanese dolls, ca. 1935–1936

"Tren-Hwa, how do you like it here?" one of them asked.

"Do you like your American mother?" the other added. They both spoke in English.

I shook my head in response to their questions, because I was shy and unsure of my English. When Mother interjected and spoke to me in Chinese, I responded quickly in Chinese. The teachers looked amused, as though holding back laughter. At last, one of them said, "Mrs. Perkins, did you know that Spring Flower speaks Chinese with an American accent?"

"No, I wasn't aware of that," Mother replied, a little embarrassed, and she asked, "Do I speak Chinese with an accent?" After an awkward moment that went on forever, the other teacher suggested, "Why don't you speak to her in English? Then she will learn Chinese from others without an accent. She already understands quite well."

"That's an excellent idea," Mother said, adding, "I spoke to her in Chinese because I wanted her to learn her native tongue. I didn't realize I have an accent."

So, my bilingual training officially began. And Chum's as well, after Mother told the aunties what the Rulison teachers had said. The aunties were already speaking to Chum in English. Perhaps, not knowing which language she was supposed to speak had caused the delay in her starting to talk.

From that day on, the Americans spoke to us only in English, and instead of learning Chinese from the staff and servants, my Chinese language skills deteriorated, American-accented or not. Mother began to read children's books to me instead of the complicated hymnals she'd been using. These had been sent to us by my American grandparents in Yonkers, New York.

Mother told me a little about her parents. Her mother stayed home with her while her father was building some buildings in a big city called New York. She also told me about Day-Day's parents. His father passed away when Day-Day was very young, and his mother died a long time ago, too. Then she told me that

Day-Day has a brother named Henry, and they were very close. Although Henry was just a little older, he was like a father to Day-Day. I was happy to know I had grandparents, even though I didn't exactly understand the concept. I was especially curious about this Uncle Henry, who had visited Kiukiang before I came to my new family. I secretly hoped he would come to Kiukiang again, so I could meet him.

The books had colorful pictures and rhymed sentences. Mother read "Mother Goose," "The House That Jack Built," "Three Little Kittens," "Old King Cole," "Itsy Bitsy Spider," "Tom the Piper's Son," and of course, "Twinkle, Twinkle, Little Star" and "Little Red Riding Hood." There were others, too; I can't remember them all. Mother was an expressive reader, and many of her expressions made me laugh. These books were much more fun than hymnals.

One day, Mother joyfully picked up another book that had just arrived from Yonkers. She flipped open to a page and began to read aloud.

"Nip, nip, taes,
The tide's comin's in
If ye dinna rin fast
The sea will tak' ye in..."

She began to cringe

"Goodness gracious," she said. "Why did my mother send this?"

"What's wrong, Mother?" I asked.

She took a closer look at the cover, and said, "It's is a book of Scottish nursery rhymes. We are not going to read this book, Jeanie Precious. You're going to learn American English, not Scottish English. You're not going to sound like a Scottish lassie! I'm already ruining your Chinese." Mother shook her head and picked up another one from the box. "This is a good one. It will get your tongue straightened out and help your pronunciations." And she began to teach me "Peter Piper Puts Pen to Paper." Mother grinned widely and nodded in satisfaction. I failed to understand the difference between the two English pronunciations. Only years later did I learn that my mother was Scottish.

With such intensive training in reading and listening, as well as recognizing letters and words, within eight months I was able to express myself in English, mixing in only a few Chinese verbs! Both Day-Day and Mother were encouraged by my progress in spoken English with precise pronunciation. Day-Day suggested, "Let's enroll Jean at the English-speaking kindergarten affiliated with the Ku-Ling (牯岭) American School. She'll be three-and-a-half this fall."

"That's a terrific idea!" Mother agreed, and added, "Edward dear, I have a suspicion that Jean is gifted with languages. Maybe she'll be a writer someday."

Day-Day chuckled, "Okay, Georgie, maybe. But I'm talking about preschool; let's not get ahead of ourselves here."

Looking from one to the other, I wasn't sure I wanted to be with another group of strangers, especially when I had finally become so comfortable with my foreign family. But of course, I wasn't given a choice, and Mother began to drill me right away about what to say when I met my American teacher.

"Now," said Mother, "I'll pretend to be the teacher, and I will say these words to open the class. 'Well, here we have a new little girl in our class. What is your name, dear?' And then you answer, 'Jean.'" Mother stooped down, put her hands on my shoulders, and said, "Now remember, Jean, that question will be your cue. And the next question will be, 'How old are you?' and you say, 'Three-and-a-half years old.'" Mother repeated this dialog several times, then asked me to perform the sequence by myself.

JEAN TREN-HWA PERKINS

I spoke in what I thought was a grownup tone. "Well, here is a new little girl in our class, and what is your name, dear?"

"Jean!" I answered myself.

Mother was pleased, "Now, Jean, practice the next question!"

"How old are you, dear?" I said, adult-ly, to myself, and then nodded my head—"Four," proudly holding up four fingers.

"Okay, four is close enough, and simpler to say. Wonderful! You're ready for school!" Mother was proud, and she gave me a hug and a kiss.

The day finally came. In September, I began attending

Bathing in the glory of my new red gown, ca. spring 1935

an English-speaking kindergarten, which was preparatory for the well-known Ku-Ling American Primary and High School, located on Ku-Ling (牯岭) Mountain, also known as Lu Shan, or Mount Lu (廬山). Mother went with me until we were across the street from the school's front door. She thought I was now big enough to be on my own from there. As I walked into the building alone and found the classroom, I was immediately greeted by my new teacher.

She promptly asked, "How do you do, Jean?"

I panicked and my mind went blank. That wasn't what she was supposed to ask. It took me a second or two to recover, which felt like an eternity. The teacher was looking straight at me. She was friendly, but her eyes were firmly planted on my face, expecting a swifter reply, I supposed. Finally, I blurted out as quickly as I could, "Jean and four-years-old!" I then tried to hide, as the room full of American children burst out in laughter. How I wished Mother had come in with me!

I was relieved that later, when Mother heard about this, she didn't scold me. She thought I handled it pretty well, considering I was only four, and this was the first time I was ever in a school. And despite my blunder, the teacher and the American kids took a real liking to me. Because I was smaller than my peers, they gave me a nickname, "Teeny-weeny Jeanie."

Mother said, "Jean, you've made friends already. I guess they all like you."

"Yes, Mother, I did! And I like them too. I'm fascinated by their blond hair and blue eyes—just like you and Day-Day. They look completely different from Chum and me."

Mother squeezed my hand and held on to me tightly, without replying.

I enjoyed my kindergarten days a lot, and more importantly, I learned English quickly. From then on, I answered Mother's

Thriving in kindergarten with extra tutoring, ca. 1936

requests by saying, "Okay," which amused the Chinese grownups who were not used to me speaking English.

Mother reported to Day-Day with pride, "Jean is linguistically talented." Of course, I was so little that it was easier to learn new things, but later I convinced myself I might indeed have a talent for languages.

6

OUR BIG house was at the top of a hill facing a street called Ta-Ling Nan Lu (塔玲南路) or South Ta-Ling Road. *Nan* is south and *Lu* means road. Across from our front gate was Da-Sheng Ta (大胜塔). *Ta* (塔) means pagoda, and this ancient pagoda provided the name for our street. The pagoda, viewable from everywhere in our house, sat at the center of the Neng-Ren temple compound (能仁禅寺), an old Buddhist temple. Our house was relatively new, built around the same time as Day-Day's hospital. There were many missionary homes scattered throughout Kiukiang, but ours was the only one on this hill.

Day-Day's Water of Life Hospital (WLH) was at the foot of the hill. Whatever modern amenities his hospital did not have, Day-Day's home also went without. The house was built of wood. We had indoor plumbing but limited access to electricity, so we

Our Kiukiang home on the hill. Mother called it "The Wayside Inn."

relied on candles and kerosene lamps. Grownups cautioned Chum and me to be careful not to set the house on fire, but they were too busy to tell us what to do in case there was a fire.

One evening, as Chum and I were engrossed in some game, her head got closer and closer to the candle, and the next thing we noticed was the stench of Chum's hair ribbon burning. There were no grownups around. "What should we do?" I thought, and Chum and I began to panic. I knew we had to do something

Ceremonies, events, and Sunday gatherings at our garden with Kiukiang foreign missionaries

quickly, as the fire was already spreading to her hair. I saw a pillow and began to pound Chum's head with it, unknowingly smothering the fire. We were both screaming at the top of our lungs, and our amahs, our aunties, and Mother came running. They were shocked to see what had happened, but Mother was also pleased and impressed that she had such a quick-thinking, coolheaded kid. I was still only four.

Later, in school, I learned that the 1871 Great Fire of Chicago revolutionized fire codes and the rescue process in America. But this was rural China, and if there had been a big fire, no amount of water could have saved our house.

Our water source was a well at the back of the house. The gateman was also the gardener, and it was his job to fill the earthen urns that were in the kitchen and all around the house with well water. A family as big as ours used lots of water, and drawing water was backbreaking. Since we never knew his name, Chum and I called the gateman Grandpa Shui (水爷爷). *Shui* (水) means water, and Grandpa (爷爷, pronounced "ye-ye") is the way to address any elder. Grandpa Shui was a stern but friendly man who always wore a smile on his face. He would wave as he passed us in the garden, but mostly he was down to business.

There were no hoses or sprinklers, so he had to water our two big lawns with a watering can. Mother loved flowers, and we had countless varieties blooming in both the upper and lower gardens every season, especially springtime. There were also camphor trees, a couple of cherry trees that bloomed beautifully in the spring, and two Japanese maples whose leaves turned bright orange-yellow and fiery red in autumn. One was big enough for Day-Day to mount a swing on it for Chum and me. And poor Grandpa Shui had to take care of it all—the lawn, the flowers, and the trees.

JEAN TREN-HWA PERKINS

On Mondays, Grandpa Shui had to carry four large wooden buckets of water at a time on two shoulder poles. He would take the water first from the well to the laundry room, providing water for the butler, who was the laundryman on Mondays. I would watch the laundryman for hours. He would scrub each item with a brush, then thrash and pound it with a heavy, wooden paddle, and finally stamp with his bare feet for the rinse. Like Grandpa Shui, he was a strong man, not just washing our family's clothes, but those from the hospital as well. He looked younger than Grandpa Shui, so Chum called him Uncle Paddle (大板叔叔) because of the way he'd use the big paddle to beat the wet clothes. He did it like drumming, and his body swayed back and forth rhythmically, at the same time easing the stress on his torso. Uncle Paddle made laundry look like fun, but later at the age of ten when I was assigned to help him, I found it no fun at all.

On sunny days, Uncle Paddle would hang the laundry outdoors. The clothesline was next to the bank of a pond that was deep enough for us to drown in, so Chum and I were forbidden to go there. Day-Day put up a fence around the area. Always curious, I followed Uncle Paddle to the forbidden zone and watched him hang the laundry. He'd do it for hours, very skillfully. He began by sticking as many clothespins as he could on his waistband or shirt, and even some on his ears, nose, and lower lips. He didn't say much to me—he couldn't with clothespins all over him—nor did he smile much. But he did allow me to sit and watch him.

I loved sunny Monday afternoons watching the snow-white sheets flap furiously in the wind as if to say, "I want to be free—free—free!" On rainy days, the laundry had to be drip-dried in the damp basement, which created a musty smell instead of the sweet fragrance of sun-dried, windblown clothes and sheets.

SPRING FLOWER: A TALE OF TWO RIVERS

With other missionary families and children, ca. January 1936

Just as life with Mother and Day-Day seemed to be carrying on merrily, Mm-Ma made a surprise visit! It had been more than three years since she and Mr. Hu handed me off to my new parents. Seeing me so radically transformed, Mm-Ma was in disbelief. "Tren-Hwa, you're like an angel," she said, awestruck. "You have become a different person. You must be living in Heaven! (春花，你像一个神仙一样，你变了一个人，你在过着神仙一样的生活)." And she was right. I was.

Mm-Ma was disappointed that I didn't recognize her immediately and that my name was now Jean. It was an awkward moment, but Mother was present. Always fast on her feet, she said to me, "Jean, you have two mothers." Pointing to Mm-Ma, she said, "She is the mother who gave you birth. Since she lives in the countryside, she is your 'country mother,' who is always welcome to visit you from time to time." After a pause, she added, "I am your mother now, and you will always be living here with us. You are Day-Day and Mother's most precious daughter!"

Understanding, I smiled and waved at Mm-Ma, still keeping my distance.

JEAN TREN-HWA PERKINS

I responded to Mm-Ma's subsequent visits similarly, although there weren't that many, and Mr. Hu never came with her. As time went on, I felt almost no emotional attachment to her. She was simply someone I was supposed to know, like a relative. The family I'd been living with was the only family I knew and loved. It didn't matter to me who had been my birth mother. What mattered was that Georgina Perkins was my mother now.

During the first few years of my life, the Angel of Death took a liking to me. Unhappy to lose me to the Great Flood, she visited three more times before I reached age six. Each time was more vicious than the one before. Had I remained in the home where I was born, I would surely have left this world long ago. But with me in my new home, the Angel of Death had more of a challenge.

His first visit came when I was four—shortly after Mm-Ma's first visit. Our amahs not only took care of us, but they also tidied all the bedrooms and emptied the toilets into a cesspool at the back of the compound. Farmers would come once a week with huge buckets to take the excrement away for their rice fields and vegetable gardens.

Chum and I loved to watch our amahs eat their meals, hoping they would give us a taste of the fermented vegetables or tofu they had with their rice, or even some hot peppers they'd pickled. Their food was salty, spicy, and tasty. Most of the time, the amahs were frightened to give us anything for fear we'd get upset stomachs, and knowing they'd be blamed if we got sick.

Upset stomachs and diarrhea were common during every child's first five years of life in rural China in those years. And these brushes with death were especially sinister, not because of anything I ate from the amahs, but because of worms, a common malady at that time, which I probably got from the soil of the rice paddies. Midway through my first year at kindergarten,

Day-Day suspected I had worms, and lab tests proved him right. Fortunately, with Day-Day as my doctor, I wasn't given ground glass, but modern drugs. I was grateful for the advancement of medicine in the early twentieth century or the name "Jean" would have been seen as cursed in my family. One drug had the name "Worm Destroyer," or something like that. Unfortunately, my worms weren't affected by the medications, and I became gravely ill from the drug. My stomach couldn't handle Western medicines, and I lost a lot of weight in a very short time.

Day-Day made sure that Mother and Chang-Ma kept me hydrated, and Aunt Bessie checked on me once a day. Wang-Ma, Chum's amah, brought chicken broth mixed with rice porridge to be sure I'd have nutritious input. So I got well, winning that battle with relative ease and holding a 2–0 lead against the Angel of Death. I'm not sure if modern medicine killed the worms, but I do know they learned a lesson. If they didn't treat me well, they wouldn't have much of a life themselves. If they were as smart as Day-Day seemed to think, they needed to develop a good relationship with me.

At Kiukiang Bund with WLH staff: Aunt Bessie leaving for America. I am standing by Aunt Dee, and Chum by Aunt Bessie

The next encounter was much worse. I was four-and-a-half and had a high fever. Mother had left me home while she went to church, and then, uneasy about me being alone, hurried back. My forehead was hot to her touch, and when she took my temperature, it was 104 degrees. The routine for high fevers in those days was an enema. While Mother was getting things ready, I said under my breath, "When I go to Heaven, I want Mother to come with me."

My mother replied, "Silly kiddo, you're delirious."

And I said, "It's getting dark, Mother."

I thought dark clouds were passing by, and Mother proceeded with the enema. A few minutes later, Mother wondered aloud, "Why is Jean so quiet?" Then she screamed in horror. My face had turned blue and my lips were colorless, with foam coming out of my mouth and my body limp. Mother was alone except for Chef Tian (the cook) and Grandpa Shui. Dropping everything, she rushed to the kitchen and said to Chef Tian in Chinese, "Quick! Please go to get the doctor now!"

Chef Tian passed this urgent duty onto Grandpa Shui. Grandpa Shui never expressed emotion and was never in a hurry. He had to be steady not to spill water from the buckets he had to carry. He went to the hospital at his usual methodical pace, although Mother wished he would fly. When he found Day-Day, he said, "Your child is not well, Mrs. Pei thinks perhaps you might want to go home soon at your earliest convenience." Not realizing the urgency, Day-Day continued to see patients before heading home.

In the meantime, Mother continued giving me cold compresses, praying, and waiting. Aunt Dee had just brought Chum home from church, and after assessing the situation, she called for an additional enema. Finally, Day-Day arrived and instantly recognized this was an emergency. He knew small children are vulnerable to fevers and could go either way within seconds. "Quick! Give her a hot bath!" he ordered, as he ran to the tub. Aunt Dee immediately bathed me in hot water for half an hour. When I became conscious, I was carried back to my bed, where I slept for twenty hours. Later I learned that Chang-Ma, sitting next to my praying mother, cried silently. She loved me so much and knew I could go just like that, after all the efforts

I am alive and well with Mother and Day-Day, hospital staff, schoolteachers, and evangelists, ca. November 1936, at a conference in Kiukiang

rescuing me from the flood and famine.

Word traveled quickly throughout Kiukiang and then to other cities nearby that Day-Day had saved my life with a hot bath! Mm-Ma even heard about it, and she hurried across the river to see me. That time, I remembered her better and found it interesting that this woman never seemed to forget me. By then, I held a commanding 2-0 lead on death: the Great Flood, an adverse pharmacokinetic reaction to the Western deworming medication, and a high fever. But the battle was not over. My last childhood brush with death would be the most frightening.

7

IT BEGAN with whooping cough, a common childhood disease. The Chinese name for it is "hundred-day cough" (百日咳), because symptoms can last that long. Whooping cough generates a noise at the back of the throat that sounds like a "whoop," and the sheer force of the coughing can rupture small blood vessels and lead to nosebleeds and hemorrhaging around the eyes, as if the child has been punched. In the spring of 1936, when I had just turned five, I had a rare complication of this.

After whooping for a week, I had the most miserable night—crying in my sleep, choking from coughing, and running a high fever. Mother got up and was surprised to see my face covered with blood. My nose wouldn't stop bleeding.

She woke up Day-Day, who placed a cold compress on my face. After a while, the bleeding stopped, and we all went back to sleep. At three in the morning, I called out, "Mother! I have a bump on my lip."

Poor Mother got up again and lit the candle. Sure enough—my lower lip was swollen. She thought it might be a spider bite but didn't voice her opinion for fear of frightening me. My eyes were wide open as I lay in bed. Finally, I said, "Mother, please don't go to sleep." She lifted me from my bed and into her big one and cradled my head in her arms as she continued to observe me. By six in the morning, my upper lip had swollen too. So she woke my father again.

By now, my whole face was swollen and my eyes almost shut.

Day-Day put antiphlogistine ointment on my face, then covered it with gauze, leaving only my mouth and eyes exposed. To this day, I can still smell the camphor and menthol of the ointment! By now, my whole body was swelling up, from my feet up to my legs, followed by my hands and arms. I was unable to pee. Mother cut the sleeves of my nightgown because my hands were so swollen. Day-Day was afraid a kidney shutdown might be imminent. I was a very sick child.

Day-Day feared that I might have a *streptococcus* infection or *cellulitis,* against which he would have been helpless. There was penicillin at the time, but it was scarce and usually reserved for adults at the hospital. Mother asked Day-Day to get some, but he resisted. As much as Day-Day loved me, I think he was balancing out the needs of hundreds of others with mine.

They tried enemas, pushing fluids, and hot baths with bicarbonate of soda. So a hot bath was not a magical solution to everything. Mostly, they prayed. It was going to take a miracle because the diagnosis was unclear beyond knowing I had whooping cough.

In retrospect, it might not have been an infection at all. It was probably a severe allergic reaction to something. Every hour, Day-Day listened to my chest and the rhythm of my breathing. He gave me some barbiturates, pentobarbital, to calm me. He also used quinine to fight possible fungal infection or malaria. I drank cough syrup from a pretty bottle that Aunt Dee brought over. It had the name Dr. Shoop on it, manufactured in Racine, Wisconsin. Because the syrup was from America, we assumed it must have been okay, but we now know that some early twentieth-century medicines to suppress coughing and fever were rather dangerous.

No one knew why, but the swellings began to recede in the order they had appeared, followed by enormous welts like hives on my legs and buttocks. Then they too slowly went away, but not before turning into huge puss bubbles that I loved popping. I was left with dark, scar-like patches of skin, which eventually disappeared under the summer sun.

This is from Mother's letter to her own mother:

"I do feel prayer brought about the change in Jean last night. She has always been so good getting through everything. She is such a survivor! But pitifully, one had the feeling that she was not going to make it through this time, although Edward has given everything he could think! Then, by the grace of God. Well, Mother, I keep praying so..."

Survive I did! Flood, famine, fever, worms, and what was probably an infection or an allergic reaction. I began to understand that I lived only by the grace of God and my loving family, and so I stopped keeping score with the Angel of Death.

On June 18, 1937, at the age of six, I reached an important milestone. I walked up onto the platform and bowed the way our teachers had been teaching us to do for days. With a beaming face and outstretched arms, I received a diploma from the

Kindergarten graduation, summer of 1937

principal for finishing preschool, and I was eligible to become a first-grader at Ku-Ling American School! I felt so proud!

Day-Day watched with paternal delight and whispered to Mother, "There's no form so neat as the sprightly form of our own darling!" Mother nodded in agreement and smilingly added, "Everyone is out of step, but our son Willie!" I didn't understand what they were talking about—evidently with a Scottish accent—but I knew they were both happy and proud.

Mother was an amateur photographer, and this was the perfect occasion to practice. There were fifteen of us, and many were missionaries' kids. I distinctly remember one little boy called "Ming-Ming" who stood next to me in the photo. He was shorter than I and had a baby face so cute. No one, of course, realized he would someday be my husband!

Dark clouds were settling over Kiukiang. Rumors of an invasion by the "Island Imperialists," the phrase grownups used when referring to the Japanese, began to stir in the air. I never fully grasped what was going on, but I did sense that something ominous was about to happen. There was a change in grownups' conversations, especially at the dinner table. I loved to listen to what they talked about and would often add my opinions, to their great amusement.

One Sunday, Day-Day was serving roast chicken for dinner. I looked at the chicken and said, matter-of-factly, "That chicken will never crow again!" The adults all began laughing so hard tears rolled down their cheeks. It took a few minutes for them to compose themselves and eat without choking. To me, these grownups were acting like children. Finally, I piped up, "I don't understand." A hushed silence prevailed. It turned out not to be a joke at all. The grownups were simply anxious. They didn't know how to explain to a six-year-old that war was probably on

SPRING FLOWER: A TALE OF TWO RIVERS

Gathering of missionary kids, summer of 1937. In the middle of the top photo, my best friend, Mollie (daughter of a Danforth woman physician). Below, with children of Seventh-day Adventist missionaries.

the horizon.

For us kids, life seemed usual. I was preoccupied with the excitement of going to Ku-Ling Resort. We had a summer home on the famous Ku-Ling Mountain, which rises to nearly 5,000 feet high. It is northwest of Poyang Lake (鄱陽湖), at the doorstep of Kiukiang. Our home was part of a resort nicknamed Methodist

JEAN TREN-HWA PERKINS

Valley, where Methodist missionaries would go for rest and recuperation stays. Mother had lots of photos and postcards showing people going up the mountain toward what was known as Lions Leap. Other Westerners lived up there too, some staying year-round. Day-Day went up the mountain before the rest of us to make the rounds for Westerners there who needed medical attention.

At last, on July 17, 1937, we started on our trip. It was about six miles to the foot of the mountain, and then up the steep path with its many sharp twists and turns, including some narrow and treacherous stretches. We went up in an impressive procession of seven rickshaws, which were pulled by *coolies*, a general term used at the time for men who earned their living by bitter, taxing work. It comes from the Chinese word *kuli* (苦力), which literally means "hard labor." I searched first for a children's sedan chair that seated two and would have been perfect for Chum and me, but there were none. Then, I hoped for a rickshaw that could seat four, facing each other. That would be fun, I thought, but those were all taken. So Chum and I had to sit on grownups' laps.

It was nearly fifteen miles up the mountain path, sometimes hanging perilously above deep ravines, before we reached 4,000 feet. I held tightly onto Mother, looking eerily over the edge. One slip of a coolie's foot could be the end. Luckily, these were experienced climbers. As if a sign of events to come, it rained in torrents, soaking the coolies inside and out. Because it was summer, the rain did have a cooling effect and perhaps was even refreshing. But it created a muddy and slippery path. Mother told me that, when necessary, these carriers would climb in winter when the mountain was covered with ice and snow. Day-Day went up Lu Shan year-round to make sick calls to foreigners.

Before reaching the top, there were a few thousand stone steps to climb. This was the hardest part. We could hear the coolies panting and gasping, so I decided then and there that when I became old enough, I would walk up the mountain by myself. As they climbed higher, our ears began to pop, and the chorus of cicadas went silent. Their melody resumed when our eardrums readjusted, and we heard the final crescendo as if they were welcoming us to Methodist Valley.

"We're here!" Mother said, pointing to the sign. I jumped off the rickshaw and ran halfway up the small hill that led to our summer home.

On hearing all the commotion, Aunt Adelaide, our good neighbor, came out. Chum and I called her Aunt *Ah-de-lay,* since Adelaide was too hard to pronounce. We were sure she was at least a hundred years old with her snow-white hair. Actually, she was in her forties! We loved the delicious cookies she'd always make for us as a treat. Aunt Adelaide was really happy to see Mother.

"Welcome back, Georgie!" she said, giving Mother a big hug. "Edward left this morning to make rounds." Then she shouted at Chum and me, "Come with me, kids. See what Aunt Adelaide has prepared for you…"

This journey to Ku-Ling Resort was only my second time on this ancient mountain. The last time I'd been there, I was just three. I was too ill to travel in either the previous summer or the summer before I'd started kindergarten.

JEAN TREN-HWA PERKINS

Trips to our home on Ku-Ling Mountain, 1934–1935

8

UNLIKE THE HOT and humid summer down in Kiukiang, it was refreshing in the mountains. I hardly slept that night and was up bright and early the next day, bubbling with boundless energy and excitement.

Mother and Day-Day had decided to send me to Ku-Ling American Primary School in Methodist Valley, founded for the missionaries' children and other foreigners' kids who lived right there. I'd be boarding year-round. As much as I loved being with Mother, the idea of living in Ku-Ling was intriguing.

At last, Mother, Chum, and I left our house and headed to Ku-Ling American School to register me for the fall semester. And I was to start their preparatory summer program immediately. I kept feeling sorry for Chum. She had to wait another year to be able to attend this English-speaking primary school. I was skipping and jumping, happy as a lark, running way ahead of Chum and Mother, and I ran right past two gentlemen in spiffy uniforms.

They were startled by my skidding past them, and they stopped and chatted with Mother, and Mother introduced Chum to them. Mother shouted and waved me back. So, I rushed back toward her, but by then the conversation was over, and I ran past the two military men again. One of them gave me a big, friendly smile while tipping his cap. I saw that he was bald. It turned out I missed meeting Chiang Kai-Shek (蒋介石, Jiang Jieshi), the president of our country, known as the Generalissimo, and his Commander-in-Chief, Marshall Feng Yu-Hsiang (馮玉祥司令). Looking at Chum and seeing me from a distance, they were both amused and surprised. There weren't many Chinese girls in Ku-Ling Resort in the 1930s, let alone two dressed like foreign children.

Although the district was called Methodist Valley, many esteemed cabinet members of China's Republic Government took family vacations there too. In 1912, Dr. Sun Yat-Sen (孫中山先生) and his Nationalist Party (国民堂: Kuo Min Tang or KMT) established the first Republican government in the history of China. President Chiang succeeded Dr. Sun. Chiang and his internationally renowned wife, Song Mei-ling (宋美龄), would frequently visit their home at the resort.

After Mother told me what I'd missed, I asked, "Are they the people who say 'Come!' and we come; 'Go!' and then, we go?"

Mother nodded her head.

"I'm sorry I missed meeting them!"

"Oh, don't worry, dear, we'll see them on Sunday. He and his wife are coming to church. We've been attending the same church on Ku-Ling Mountain for years. Mrs. Chiang's father was a Methodist minister."

Mother was distracted. She was wondering whether there was an urgent meeting with all these Chinese leaders on the mountain.

This encounter was my second brush with history. The first was being born during the Great Flood, and this concerned the start of World War II. It was July 1937, seven months after the Xi-An Incident (西安事變), when President Chiang's subordinates, Generals Chang Hsiao-Liang (Zhang Xue-Liang: 張學良) and Hu-Cheng Yang (楊虎城), detained him. Before the coup, President Chiang had been focusing on combating the Communist Party (CPC) and its Red Army (紅軍) within China rather than facing the external threat from the Empire of Japan. The incident forced the ruling KMT to align with CPC to fight against the Japanese invasion in what eventually became World War II's Pacific Theater. Ku-Ling Resort was where Zhou En-Lai (周恩來), a vital leader of the Communist Party, met with President Chiang just a few weeks before we arrived, to discuss details of their alliance. The Declaration of Alliance was published and broadcast throughout China from Ku-Ling Mountain during our time at the resort.

We were silent the rest of our way to the school. After meeting the principal and the first-grade teacher, Mother said, "Jeanie, since this preparatory summer session is a half-day program, Chum and I will wait in the library and do some reading. Then, I'll take you both home."

I nodded, and off I went to my classroom—ready to become a first-grader!

The only thing I didn't like about Ku-Ling American Primary School was the noon nap. To me, it was a waste of time. I could hear the streams and brooks gurgling outside my windows, whispering, "Come! Come! Bring your shovels and pails. Let's have fun!"

I also heard the songs of the cicadas, "See–see–eee, if you can catch me-eeee—me-eee! I only live three-eee month-zzz after a hundred year-zzz of hatching-eeee…"

I would if I could, I told them. So I lay there thinking about how to get through the two miserable nap hours. The excitement of living and studying at Ku-Ling was bubbling through my mind, but leaving Chum, my best friend and playmate, really troubled me. Then, I thought about having to live apart from Chang-ma and Mother, and it was impossible to sleep.

During the summer, Mother stayed mostly in Ku-Ling, but she also went to Kiukiang a few times. She had to attend to the business aspects of the hospital, and of course, to see Day-Day. Day-Day rarely vacationed in Ku-Ling during the hot summer months, but he would give Chinese doctors time off for their vacations. Even when he showed up in Ku-Ling, it was for medical needs.

Every few years, though, he and Mother, and sometimes Aunt Dee and Aunt Bessie, would go far away to Japan in September or October for total relaxation—completely away from everything. Sometimes they'd even include a trip to Hong Kong, which they also loved. They would travel throughout the islands of Japan—Mother even learned Japanese. I got to see photos of Mt. Fuji and Lake Ashi near Hakone (はこね) in Honshu, the sacred deer in Nara (なら), and Lake Onuma in Hokkaido way up in the north of Japan. I got to see these beautiful and interestingly dressed Japanese women and girls. Day-Day and Mother adored Japan.

Those were happy occasions for them, but for me, no matter how long or short, being separated from them was painful, and actually for them too. Without Mother, I felt so insecure. Tears trickled down my cheeks every time I bade her goodbye, even if only for a day. My tears would break Mother's heart, so to avoid it, she would sneak out the door before I woke up, and then confess that she did hear me calling her. Whenever I woke up and found her bed empty, I would cry my heart out and feel like an orphan. I did not know which was worse, watching her go or waking up and finding her gone. After a while, I'd tell the two aunties, "I'll stop crying now to save some tears for tonight."

The bond between Mother and me couldn't have been closer if I had been born to her. I would tell her, "Mother, I love you so, you just don't know how much I love you—please don't ever leave me, will you not?!"

Lying there wide awake, I became uncertain. I was almost a big girl now and felt I should be less anxious about Mother's

With other missionary kids at Ku-Ling Resort, 1937

leaving. At the same time, I'd soon be living away from her when school started. I felt empty.

Life can be complicated for a six-year-old, but it's also carefree. Some afternoons, the breeze rustled through the pine needles outside my window, and I could hear them sighing in sympathy, for I couldn't play under their shade or feel their coolness. These were the same sounds that lulled me to sleep for many of my midafternoon naps. After those sweet dreams, there would be more playing with Chum and the missionary kids, hiking, picnics, and singing hymns while watching the sunset.

On a patch of flat land near the hilltop stood a cluster of rocks that looked like a cradle. To those who lived in Methodist Valley, it was known as Cradle Rock. We'd often go there for a picnic supper during the early hours of twilight and watch the colorful sunsets on the western horizon while singing our favorite hymns. We'd always end with our favorite, "Day is dying in the west, Heav'n is touching the earth with rest, Waiting and worship while the night, Sets her evening lamps alight, Through all the sky…," while marveling at the beauty of it all. It made us feel even closer to our great Creator.

JEAN TREN-HWA PERKINS

Days before we were bombed, 1937

Little did I know that as a six-year-old, those major life decisions would be made for me. The serenity of my life would soon be shattered, and some of the happiest times of my childhood would soon be interrupted.

On that unforgettable morning in late August of 1937, while we were still vacationing in Ku-Ling, we were awakened by sirens wailing. Church bells then followed, and the echoes of the bells and the sirens resounded throughout the valleys, warning everyone that enemy planes were nearby. Within minutes, we heard the thunderous roar of bomber planes overhead. There were no telephones or radios in our Ku-Ling home, so it was not until the next day that we received a message from Day-Day, who was in Kiukiang, telling us what had happened.

No longer satisfied with just colonizing China's northeast

provinces, Japan had begun a full-scale invasion of our country. The Imperial Japanese Armies had overtaken Peking and the port city of Tientsin, and were advancing rapidly toward the Central Yangtze River valley and along the east coast. Ferocious battles were already being fought in Shanghai.

The Japanese dropped bombs along the Yangtze River banks as far west as Hankow (漢口, part of today's Wuhan). Eleven bombs were even dropped on our little town of Kiukiang. Twenty wounded men and women turned up at the Water of Life Hospital, where Day-Day spent the day removing shrapnel from their skin. When they received Day-Day's message, Mother and Aunt Dee went down the mountain right away, leaving Chum and me with our amahs.

It was up to me, I decided, to take charge of the daily morning worship. Chum and I chose the hymns and led in singing. Although we were beginning to read the Bible in English, we were nowhere near proficient without our parents. The amahs didn't know English, so we decided to use the Chinese Bible. None of us, including the amahs, knew enough Chinese characters to read it, so we hemmed and hawed our way through, figuring God knew we were trying. After struggling with the reading, we prayed in a simple-minded way, "Please—God Bless all of us! Please—no wars." War to us children was a vague concept, but we knew it was bad.

Days later, Aunt Dee came back, closed our summer home, and took Chum and me down the mountain. I wasn't sure we'd ever return. So much for being a proud first-grader at Ku-Ling American School.

Two months later, in October, the schools in Kiukiang opened despite the chaos. Mother and Day-Day enrolled me at Rulison Girls Primary School, which was part of Rulison Girls High School in town. So, I was a proud first-grader again, while Chum

JEAN TREN-HWA PERKINS

began her last year of kindergarten. I loved my teachers, and I loved arithmetic, but the joy of schooling was short-lived. Shanghai fell. Then in December 1937, the capital Nanking was sacked, followed by a historically brutal massacre. The West stood idly by watching the atrocities, while the Chinese forces fought bravely alone.

A seething mass of humanity soon began moving from China's east coast toward the central and western parts of the country. Most would migrate along the Yangtze River. Riverboats overloaded with refugees were going upstream on the Great River, and many trips ended in tragedy, as the boats capsized from their heavy loads, drowning countless people in the raging river waters. When river travel wasn't an option, migrants would go by train and some even found small planes while others fled on foot, hundreds of them passing through Kiukiang daily. Schools closed for good, including those run by American missionaries. Some schools began moving westward, taking Chinese staff members with them. Americans and British citizens started to consider leaving Kiukiang.

Entering first grade, ca. 1937

War is so terrible, affecting both the rich and the impoverished, and many of the migrants were dazed amid the chaos, not knowing where they were heading. They knew only that they had to get as far as possible from the Japanese invaders as the Chinese armies progressively retreated.

Other foreign missionaries, especially those who had children, unsure where they could hide, left for their homelands. But the war was massive, and eventually worldwide. The once-large missionary community in Kiukiang quickly became small. No more lawn parties at our home, or Christmas and Thanksgiving dinner gatherings. Instead, the wounded continued pouring into the city by the hundreds and soon by the thousands. Day-Day kept his hospital open, as did some other missionary hospitals in nearby towns and cities. Mother and the aunties were busy attending to the wounded day and night. With the increasing numbers of wounded civilians and soldiers, our Chinese servants and amahs were called on to help at the hospital too.

Kiukiang had fallen into chaos and become a war zone, even though the front was still far downriver from us. Air raids and bombings became more and more frequent, even after dark. We were instructed to place American flags on rooftops or paint the roofs with a Red Cross, and to mark the hospital and church boundaries with white crosses, so that these properties would not be bombed. Or, so we hoped.

As children, we couldn't fully understand the seriousness, and so we enjoyed being in the dugout because we got to eat puffed rice while waiting for the all-clear siren. By then, everyone was rationed to two meals a day, so when there was an air raid, it was like getting extra food. After the all-clear siren wailed, we'd scramble out of the dugout, eyes blinking to adjust to the sunlight. For us kids, it was like a sport.

Then the weather started turning cold, and when the sirens began blasting at night, it was getting harder for the grownups to wake us up and get us dressed in the dark. They'd drag Chum and me to the bunkered basement of the hospital a couple of blocks down the hill. Day-Day had had the wisdom to design and build a bomb shelter for the hospital—in 1929!

During one air raid, I woke up already half-dressed by Mother. In a daze I asked, "What are you folks doing?" After that, we all slept at the hospital every night. I told Mother, "I don't like this," and then asked, "Will it all end by Christmas?"

When Christmastime came around, not only had the war not ended, but there were rumors the invaders would flatten Kiukiang! Luckily, it didn't happen, but twenty bombs did land on the nearby airfield on December 22, 1937.

9

BY THE SPRING of 1938, things had gone from bad to worse. We finally moved all of our belongings to the hospital and stayed there as a temporary home. Bombs were dropping ever so close to the hospital compound despite Day-Day and his coworkers putting up as many American flags on the top of the hospital and painting as many Red Crosses as they could. Mother and others even painted thick white lines using limestone to mark the hospital boundaries. Japanese troops were, at the same time, pushing their way up the Yangtze River toward Kiukiang. Kiukiang had always been one of the China's critical inland river ports, and the adults knew an invasion would be inevitable.

Chinese families seeking refuge inside the WLH Compound, ca. 1938

JEAN TREN-HWA PERKINS

By summer, hundreds of Chinese who hadn't fled westward began pouring into missionary compounds. The Water of Life Hospital was already filled with wounded soldiers, but Day-Day opened the big iron gates to let in those seeking refuge. The wards quickly turned into refugee homes, just as they had during the 1931 Great Flood. Multiple families squeezed into rooms designed for two or three patients. Many of these refugees were church members, or the families and relatives of hospital staff. Some were teachers who hadn't gone westward with their schools. Finally, when the Water of Life Hospital could hold no more, Day-Day closed the big front gate, reluctantly. By then, more than a thousand people were living on the hospital grounds.

On July 24-25, 1938, bombs dropped on Kiukiang for thirty-six straight hours, and gunboats anchored on the Great River shelled us continuously. We stayed in Day-Day's lifesaving dugouts, but with all the bombing, even the dugouts shook violently. Dust filled the air, and we wondered if our shelters would hold. The air raids continued for a couple more days. Then, an eerie silence came over us.

Rumors had it that the Japanese Imperial Army was going to take over the city the very next day. The owners of stores and shops that hadn't been bombed put up boards and locked their doors while seeking refuge in the countryside until the worst was over. The hospital gates remained tightly closed. No one dared venture onto the streets.

Always curious, I wanted to take a look at these terrible enemies. I pressed my face to the tiny slit between the gates, and I peered out. I heard marching feet and saw a white flag with a big red ball in the middle. Later I learned it was the Japanese national flag, which all of China came to hate. I saw the troops wearing pointed hats with flaps hanging from the back covering their necks.

Just as I was taking it all in, I was yanked away by a mighty hand, and I heard a voice that sounded both familiar and strange. The tone was angry, "Get away from that gate, Jean! You want to be caught by the Japanese!?"

When the hand loosened, I turned around and saw Day-Day as I never had before. His rage would subdue anyone. I meekly followed him back to the safety of the hospital building. Suddenly, I felt the meaning of war. We were no longer a free nation but ruled by invaders. And my father was acting a little differently.

Japanese troops took over the city, and no one knew what they would do, or not do. The refugees and we remained inside the hospital grounds. Day-Day's hospital was considered American territory, and since Americans were not at war with Japan, the hospital grounds were considered safe. But we didn't know for sure.

Hundreds of children were running around the compound — wildly and aimlessly. So Mother and Day-Day decided to round up all the adults who could be teachers and started a makeshift school for grade-school-age kids. Chum and I both entered the second grade of this temporary school. After nearly seven months with no school, Mother wanted to be sure I got an education despite the war.

Then she went above and beyond. In addition to these makeshift grade-school classes, she asked one of the Chinese teachers to tutor me in Chinese reading and calligraphy. For reasons I don't understand, I disliked this teacher from day one, and I guess the feeling was mutual. He wore glasses that made him look like an old owl. I was rude, impudent, and fidgety, especially when I could see my friends playing happily outside, while I was stuck writing Chinese characters and listening to this man's monotonous voice.

One day, perhaps being fed up with me, he said, "If you keep on being inattentive, I will use the ruler!"

"Go ahead!" I retorted, thinking he wouldn't dare.

Well, he did. I held my hand out, and he whacked me with all his might until my hand was red and swollen. I bit my tongue and didn't even flinch. Nor did I let any tears come, since I was not a crybaby! As soon as he was satisfied, I ran out of the classroom and never went back.

We continued living at the hospital compound for another half a year. This was the first time I mingled with Chinese children of all backgrounds, and it brought me closer to my roots, and it also brought out the tomboy in me. I played marbles with the other kids and a game of throwing a penknife from all heights and angles to stick it in the ground. The loser had to kneel in the dirt to pick up the winner's knife with their teeth, to the dismay of Chang-Ma, who had to wash my muddy clothes afterward.

As the sun was going down, we played "the hawk catches the chicks." One child was the mother hen and another the hawk,

Playing with Chinese kids inside the WLH Compound, ca. 1937–1938

with the remaining kids as baby chicks. The chicks would line up, each hanging onto the waist of the one ahead, and the first would hold onto Mother Hen's waist. Meanwhile the hawk tried to catch the last chick by getting past the outstretched arms of the mother hen and all the other chicks. We'd all yell and scream, wiggling behind the mother hen. I was usually the hawk or the mother hen. This game required teamwork.

We also rummaged through the garbage searching for cloth or wool to make clothes for little dolls we made out of sticks and twigs. Or we tied all the yarn into a big ball and knitted colorful scarves.

One day, Chum and I watched a play that included a traditional Chinese wedding, during which thieves stole a trunkful of the couple's things. One of the thieves was caught and a judge held a makeshift court, but the judge was one of the thieves too. Chinese people can find humor in times of stress.

We children hated the war. With only two meals a day, our stomachs growled with hunger. Then we got down to one meal a day, and starvation felt palpable, especially for us children. I guess that's how poor people have always lived in China.

Perhaps the most frightening experience was when drunken Japanese soldiers barged into the hospital compound, sometimes half-naked. They would stand on the terrace near the front gate, shouting goodness knows what. Some officers had their sword drawn, and others would be thrashing their bayonets. Most of us hid indoors, but some stayed to gawk. Altercations happened more than once, and Mother always came to the rescue. She was a brave woman. She would walk up to the drunken soldiers and speak to them in Japanese. Her Japanese wasn't proficient, but she always managed to get their attention. After a long conversation and much persuasion, they'd put their swords back into the sheaths and put on their clothes, and Mother would escort them

JEAN TREN-HWA PERKINS

out the front gate. You could hear sighs of relief ripple through the compound. Afterward she told us she was just as frightened as we were, but she prayed silently for courage and wisdom.

By the end of 1938, things in Kiukiang began to calm down. Because America and Japan weren't at war, Day-Day skillfully negotiated with the local Japanese commanders, with Mother as de facto translator. Soon Japanese gunboats brought us supplies of much-needed medicines, food, and water. In exchange, Day-Day agreed they would have access to the hospital, as long as it could remain open for Chinese people, too. Within a few months, gunboats with American flags and considerably more supplies began to dock at the Kiukiang Bund, as the riverbank area was called.

After being cramped in the hospital for more than a year, some Chinese refugees and hospital workers cautiously began returning to their homes. Others then followed, and soon the hospital had almost no refugees. When we finally came out too, to our collective surprise, most everything was intact. Day-Day believed this was because there were so many American missionaries and other foreigners whose countries were not at war with Japan, or at least not yet. The city of Kiukiang was in good order, quite unlike the pillaging and looting that had wrecked the capital Nanking, but farming areas outside of Kiukiang were still badly bombed.

On a hot September day in 1939, Mother, Day-Day, and I moved back into our big house. How wildly comfortable it was to sleep in our beds and what great fun to play in the garden and in our spacious yard for the first time in a year and a half! I rushed out the backdoor to climb my trees and swing away under my favorite tree, ironically a Japanese maple. I missed Chum, though. The aunties wanted to stay at the hospital a little longer, so I played and climbed by myself.

Life in Kiukiang seemed to be returning to normal, even though the war was far from over. In fact, it had only just begun. At the dinner table, the grownups seemed increasingly depressed and they whispered about things going on in Europe. I overheard them saying Germany had invaded Poland, while Red Russia and Great Britain were busy with their imperialistic ambitions in northern Europe.

As much as the grownup conversations made us kids nervous, we were delighted that Rulison Primary School would reopen with the teachers who hadn't fled to Sichuan Province (四川). Many had fled to Chunking (重慶: Chongqing in pinyin) on the upper reaches of the Yangtze River. Rulison High School remained closed because there were no high school teachers.

A few months after moving back home, I entered the third grade, even though I hadn't attended much of the first or second grade. Chum and I were in the same class for the first time.

A rare quiet moment in the Water of Life Hospital compound

10

IT WAS THE fall of 1939 when we began attending grade school. The routine gave us a false sense of normalcy, although we did grasp that peace was elusive. I would soon learn the word *invasion*.

So that we'd be safe, our amahs escorted us to and from school. Japanese guards were posted along the streets of Kiukiang to protect each building they occupied. We had to salute and make a ninety-degree bow to each of them as we passed. If we forgot, we would be searched or beaten or threatened by a fearsome police dog. I decided to protest this indignity, and no one could stop me.

One day I told Chef Tian's daughter Sarah, who also attended Rulison Primary School, "Let's not bow to them today."

Chum had left early with Wang-Ma, so Chang-Ma was escorting the two of us. After Chang-Ma bowed and passed the guards, Sarah and I walked by with our heads held high. We heard nothing for a split second, and I thought we'd made it through. Wrong!

The next thing I knew, Sarah was screaming as a massive police dog was chasing after her. She was running in circles out of her wits. My response to the same blinding fear was to stand absolutely frozen, trembling. Luckily for me, dogs don't chase people standing still, even when they sense fear.

Chang-Ma kneeled on the ground and pleaded with the Japanese guards in Chinese, "Sir, please, I beg you, please restrain the dog! They are only children, eight years old, and they don't know any better!" While not understanding what she was saying, they probably guessed from her body language, and they laughed as they kicked Chang-Ma viciously, then pushed her flat to the ground so the dog could sit on her back.

When the guards had had enough "fun," they let Sarah and me pass, but not until we made the proper bow. I was saddened and furious by what I saw, but I couldn't do a thing except pray they would let Chang-Ma go too. Sarah was crying while I couldn't seem to cry out, even though I wanted to. I continued trembling with fear, realizing I had screwed up royally, and Chang-Ma was paying the price. What was I thinking? That was not brave or patriotic. It was pure stupidity, and I had unwisely put others' lives at risk. I now understood what it means to live in a land that has been invaded and occupied.

Japanese soldiers roamed the streets atop huge horses and found pleasure stopping us on our way to school and using the bodies of their horses to press us up against the wall. The bellies of the horses were suffocating us, and the soldiers found that amusing. The horses would get agitated and stamp their iron-shod hoofs in the dirt, kicking up dust. I was frightened a horse would kick me. With a cruel laugh, the soldiers would trot away, leaving us terrified, our faces covered with dirt.

I started to think about revenge. Chum and I decided to throw chewing gum into the trucks for transporting horses that were parked outside the hospital. We hoped in our childish way the soldiers would step on the gum, and their rubber boots would stick to the truck bed. But we couldn't throw them far enough, and most of our gum landed on the dry ground, turning it into dust balls. After many tries, a few reached the truck, and when we saw them prying the gum from their shoes while shouting at one another, some of our pent-up rage in us was released.

Across the street in their barracks, we saw perfectly good

white rice being dumped on the ground while hungry Chinese children waited for a chance to salvage some. That made Chum and me doubly furious. I suggested we make up words that sounded Japanese, like "We hate you!" and "Get out of our country!" We tried, but only got grins and amused looks from the soldiers, so gave up our creative Japanese.

I pleaded with Mother to teach me some Japanese. She looked at me for a moment, then smiled and shook her head. "Language is sacred," she said. "It's complicated and takes time to learn, appreciate, and respect."

Life under the imperialistic regime frequently included curfews, often without notice. The penalties for being on the street after curfew were harsh. Once Chang-Ma and I were one step away from the school gate when suddenly a curfew was imposed, but we didn't know. The guards rushed over and grabbed us. No matter how much Chang-Ma pleaded that we were going into the school right there, they turned a deaf ear or perhaps didn't understand what she was saying. We were pushed at the point of a bayonet into the temple across from the school. There were already several Chinese men there stripped to the waist, being searched by the soldiers. Some were kicked, others were beaten with fists, depending on which the invaders enjoyed more. As I sat on my heels waiting for my fate, suddenly I stood up ready to run, and a hand firmly grabbed my clothes. I struggled to get away, and I heard Chang-Ma's voice whisper, "Child, don't run! They will shoot you on the spot."

I hadn't been trying to run *away*. I had spotted Mother and Day-Day entering the temple gate and had spontaneously stood up to run toward the safety of their arms. Chang-Ma was cautious and quick. She noticed that the Japanese soldiers had their backs to the gate and were unaware of the Americans walking in. Luckily, one of the soldiers did see my parents, and after much talk, Mother got them to understand I was related to these Americans and so we were allowed to leave.

On our way out, Mother and Day-Day held my hands tightly and said, "We are grateful to the milkman who saw the guards take you and Chang-Ma into the temple. He ran as quickly as he could to the hospital to tell us." Mother had tears in her eyes. After that, when I finally got to class, the kids in class cheered for me.

Following such a terrifying experience, you might think I'd leave curfews alone and wouldn't put others at risk again. But no, I still had to push boundaries. The next time a curfew occurred, I was in the safety of my home. Chef Tian told me to get away from the window, but my curiosity got the better of me. I wanted to know why we had so many curfews without warning. So my face was pressed against the kitchen window in full view of the street. What was it we were not allowed to see? Suddenly, I spotted one of the guards heading in our direction. There was a high wall protecting our house, so I felt secure until suddenly we heard an urgent pounding on the front gate.

Chef Tian said, "Tren-Hwa, quickly—run and hide! I think they're after you for watching them!" Frightened, I hid in the basement. Soon I heard heavy footsteps of Japanese guards walking through the whole house with Chef Tian anxiously following them. I held my breath, and to ensure there was no sound, I covered my mouth.

Then I heard one of the guards saying in broken Chinese, "Little girl, no peeking!" Chef Tian said something to him in response, and the footsteps began to fade away. I sighed with relief as the big gate latched with a clang and ran back to the kitchen. Chef Tian wagged his finger at me and said, "When are you ever going to learn, Tren-Hwa? That was too close. If they catch you next time, they could execute you on the spot, and there will be nothing your American parents can do to save you!" I gave him a big hug, then a sheepish grin, and Chef Tian shook his head and walked away.

To this day, I'm grateful to him for saving my life. He was brave. They could have killed him. However, the incident only added to my fury. "When will we be free?" I wondered.

My joy knew no bounds when we received a letter from my American grandfather on Christmas Day, 1939. I read the whole message in English without any help.

"Without any help?" I thought. "Something's wrong."

"Mommy!" — a term I'd learned from the American kids on Ku-Ling Mountain.

"Yes, honey?"

"Why didn't Grandpa write the way grownups do?"

"So you can read it all by yourself," she answered.

Well, I guess I wasn't grownup after all. With a sigh, I wondered how long it would take an eight-year-old to be considered an adult.

A few months later, a telegram arrived with the shocking news that my beloved American grandfather had died suddenly. It meant no one would ever call me "the Kid" again, and I would never receive another letter from him. It was my first encounter with a loved one dying. My heart felt heavy and sad. Sorrowfully I asked, "Mommy, do all people die when they get old?"

"Yes, dear, they do," Mother answered.

"Well, I'll have to get to Heaven soon," I muttered.

"Why?" Mother asked.

"Because I cannot live apart from you!" She wondered how old I thought she was.

Then one day Day-Day and Mother announced they were heading back to America. It all made sense with Grandpa passing away, and shortly before they left, my grandmother broke her hip, so they needed to be with her.

I stood on the Kiukiang Wharf with tear-filled eyes and a broken heart, my world shattered. I waved mightily as the fast-disappearing river steamer took Mother and Day-Day away. I had pleaded in vain to go with them. Although I understood why, I couldn't bear yet another separation.

Before leaving, Mother tried to cheer me up by saying, "We won't be gone for long, Precious, and when we come back, we'll bring your grandmother to live with us. Won't that be wonderful?"

What could I say? I nodded my head, but the sobbing wouldn't stop. I thought I was old enough not to feel such separation anxiety, like the time when I was just a toddler, and they left for a trip to Japan. A gentle touch on my arm made me look up. Through my tears, I saw Aunt Bessie, and she said, sympathetically, "Jean, we can't see them anymore; let's go home." Home? What is home without my parents? The thought brought fresh tears.

To add to my misery, with the construction to our house not yet complete, the aunties and Chum had to live temporarily at a place called *Mao Cha Han*, another missionary compound that housed American female missionaries. Losing my parents and now having no aunties or my pal Chum either, I felt lost. I would beg Chang-Ma to take me to visit Chum, as we children weren't allowed to walk on the streets alone.

Chang-Ma and I made several visits to Mao Cha Han. We had fun, and Chum missed me too. She showed me how the electric lights worked, which fascinated me. But Chum never seemed happy there, as if something was on her mind. Maybe she didn't understand why she and the aunties had to stay at Mao Cha Han. Perhaps she thought Mother and Day-Day didn't want them to live with us anymore.

When I was leaving after my last visit there before they all moved back home, Chum stood on the terrace watching me at the foot of the garden. As I reached the front gate, she directed a torrent of anger at me. I can't remember what she said, but it had to do with their staying at Mao Cha Han, and called me a "pig," one of the most degrading terms in Chinese. I lost my temper, and called her a pig too. The "battle of the pigs" had begun.

Pig this and pig that were flying like a thousand daggers, with more colorful words for emphasis. Soon, there was fist-punching and hair-pulling, and a group of Chinese children who lived on the compound gathered to watch us tear each other's hair out until a shocked Chang-Ma rushed out and dragged me away. She was in tears, and asked me, "My Tren-Hwa! What has gotten into you? You are always such a loving child!"

I felt ashamed, and could never forget the disappointment on Chang-Ma's face that day.

11

WHEN THE NEW wing of our house was finally completed, the aunties and Chum came home. I was happy to have Chum back, and our quarrel was put to rest when she realized how wrong she had been. We had rooms next to each other and shared a balcony. A tree branch from the upper garden stretched onto our gallery, and each spring, a pair of pigeons would make their nest there. We loved to watch the little blue eggs hatch and see the tiny baby pigeons flapping their wings.

The aunties lived downstairs. The rooms where they'd stayed before were now for Grandmother. I finally understood why we added a new wing to the house. As Mother had promised, Grandmother would indeed leave Yonkers and come live with us in Kiukiang. And she brought her Scottish companion, Aunt Katty.

While my parents were still in Yonkers, Chum became a diligent student, while I, on the other hand, was like a kite without a string, or a dog without a leash. Teaching and learning in China still followed ancient traditions, and we learned history and classics by reading them aloud over and over until we memorized every single word. Most students didn't understand anything

Back to grade school in sailor suits, ca. 1940, during the war and occupation

they'd read. By the time Chum and I were in grade school, due to Western influence, some of these old methods changed, but we still had to memorize our lessons. Although the style of writing Chinese characters was becoming plainer and easier to understand, I found memorization extremely boring. Even the modernization of the language was like updating the Aramaic Bible to the King James version, still pretty old-fashioned.

I not only hated memorization, I was terrible at it. Perhaps my memory suffered some damage when the living room rocking chair slammed me against the wall, or perhaps was affected by my malnutrition as an infant. But I was only bad at memorizing texts I couldn't understand. Ever since Mother and Day-Day began speaking English with me and after years at American schools, I had become awful at Chinese and clueless about China's history. Now, with no one watching over my studies, I would read for about ten minutes and then fly down the back stairs and go to the lower lawn, where we had a pond, to see if the hundred-year-old turtle would appear. I swung high in our Japanese maple tree, nearly reaching the top of the tree. And I would climb the maple tree and play house up there, while Chum was faithfully memorizing her lessons.

Chum was not a tree-climber by nature, but it was still more fun when she was with me. I would help her climb up to a spot where she could stay before I leaped from branch to branch like a monkey. We were both happy when Day-Day built a chicken coop, because it was like a playhouse. When the chickens finally came, we didn't want to share the coop with them until Chang-Ma explained, "It will be fun to watch baby chicks come out of their shells, so share the house with them." And so it was.

With all play and no study, my grades plummeted. That was when stern Aunt Dee began to take an interest in my report cards. She'd been a teacher at a one-room school in Michigan before becoming a nurse, and she seemed to relish comparing Chum's grades with mine each month.

"Ah," she'd glower, "Chum got a 90 in Chinese and, let me see, Jean got a 60!"

Or she'd say, "Chum is doing well, Jean not so well." This unforeseen academic calamity was taking place while my parents were in Yonkers and Aunt Bessie was in Michigan on vacation. I was left without a mentor.

As my academic slide continued, others began to comment. My best friend's mother, a Chinese obstetrician, would say, "All those girls Mrs. Perkins has helped don't seem to do well in school. And Jean is no exception, she's perhaps the worst." Then she'd sigh and continue, "Strange, no one dares to tell her to straighten up." One time the whole class failed an arithmetic test, and the teacher was so upset, she whacked all our palms with a wooden ruler, except me.

A student sitting nearby protested, "That's unfair!" and another voice echoed her words: "It's because Tren-Hua is Dr. Perkins's daughter." Without a word, the teacher marched to my desk, took hold of my writing hand, flipped it palm-up, and proceeded to give me ten lashes, each harder and louder than the last. I gave her neither a tear nor a sound.

While my parents were gone, Mm-Ma made a couple of visits. her visits were becoming increasingly embarrassing for me as I had no feelings toward her. I just missed my American mother so much. To make the matter worse, each time Mm-Ma had left, Chef Tian would make fun of her accent. He wasn't trying to be mean. He was just amused at her country dialect, seeming to forget he was from the same rural district. Being reminded of my roots added to my misery.

I flunked third grade. Although the school gave me a chance to make it up, there was no one to help me, or even anyone who cared. I began to feel inferior, especially when Chum, my junior, would be entering fourth grade in the fall, while I had to repeat third grade.

My world was crumbling, and I began to wonder whether Mother and Day-Day would still love me. They had been away for six months, which to a lonely child was an eternity. My ninth birthday came and went, and I yearned for them. Only my pillow knew, as it was soaked with tears many a night. I felt stupid and I began to act stupid. And I was becoming depressed. "Mother always made me feel important. Look at me now; I'm a disgrace."

My woes finally ended on October 14, 1940, when Mother and Day-Day returned and brought my grandmother and her Scottish companion, Aunt Katty, to Kiukiang. They'd been away for eight months! I was so happy I began following Mother everywhere, afraid she might disappear again. To add to the excitement, Aunt Bessie was on her way home too. Perhaps Aunt Dee would now stop reading my grades aloud!

My eighty-five-year-old grandmother and I bonded instantly.

Meeting my grandma for the first time, ca. fall 1940

SPRING FLOWER: A TALE OF TWO RIVERS

She recognized me at first sight at the Kiukiang Bund. She'd seen so many photos of me from Mother, she couldn't make a mistake. Grandmother was hard of hearing, and we spoke using a small loudspeaker. Despite being frail and in a wheelchair, she adjusted well to living in a strange land whose language she couldn't understand. A few days after she arrived, she began to prefer her Chinese amah, Lo-Ma (罗妈), to Aunt Katty. Lo-Ma was nearly sixty and had a gentle touch, and she was much more patient. They communicated well through signs and body language, with occasional help from Chum and me.

Chum and I felt sorry for Aunt Katty, as there was nothing for her to do except sit in her room and come down for meals. So we'd drop by to visit her, mostly out of curiosity. She had so many things we'd never seen before, like lipstick, makeup, curlers, and nail polish. Mother and the aunties never used these things, and we wanted to know what they were for and how to use them. What fascinated us most, though, were her false teeth, which moved up and down as she spoke. We knew it was rude,

Day-Day's idea of wearing glasses to help me study, ca. 1940

but we couldn't help but giggle. Aunt Katty was a kind soul. She took it all in good humor, although there must have been times she would have slapped us if she could.

Mother and Day-Day took the news of my flunking third grade seriously. Day-Day examined my eyes to see if my vision might be part of the problem. He dilated my pupils, and I could hardly see for a few days, and found that I was hyperopic (far-sighted), so he fitted me with a pair of glasses. He believed I would do better in school after that. What a genius!

I put them on reluctantly and wished I'd get sick so I wouldn't have to go to school with glasses on. No such luck! I was as healthy as a horse. On a late fall day in 1940, my head hung down as low as possible, walking two steps behind Chang-Ma, I sauntered toward school. My face was red as a beet when I entered the classroom. As I slid into my seat, someone shouted, "Look, the flunked-out kid has four-eyes!" I prayed the floor would open and swallow me up.

A few months later, I transferred to the Dragon Hill Primary School, also a missionary-run school but English speaking for many missionaries' kids. A few of the students there had been my classmates in kindergarten. Mother and Day-Day thought a change in school might bring back my confidence, and it did. I caught up in no time, at least for the academic standards at Dragon Hill Primary School. By the summer of 1941, I was deemed ready to skip ahead to fifth grade in the fall.

I was much more comfortable in an English-speaking environment and learning American literature than memorizing the boring Chinese classics. Mother and Grandma both tutored me with reading and writing daily, and I knew the main factor was that I felt secure and loved again with Mother and Day-Day back at my side.

Just as I was moving ahead and enjoying the fall semester

of fifth grade, we were cruelly reminded that war was going on. On December 7, 1941, news of the bombing of Pearl Harbor in Hawaii sent shock waves throughout the world, including in the Central Yangtze River Valley American missionary community. War was declared on all fronts by all sides. It was sudden and unexpected. Even the Chinese who had worked closely with the Americans were wondering what would to happen to them. If the Japanese turned hostile toward the Americans in Kiukiang, there would be no one to protect the Chinese coworkers or us. An old Chinese proverb says, "Troubles never appear in ones (禍不單行)." It couldn't have been more accurate.

Suddenly Grandma became bedridden and was in constant pain. A rash on her lower back slowly spread around her waist. Day-Day thought it might be herpes. "Difficult to treat," he said, shaking his head.

Lo-Ma whispered to me, "There's a dragon on your grandmother's waist. It means pain and death, but death will not come until the head and tail meet." I looked at her wide-eyed. No one knew how long the process might take, but we watched daily and could see the lesions advancing, slowly but steadily.

Meanwhile, the Japanese occupying forces, who had been friendly with Americans while colonizing China, turned visibly hostile. American flags on roofs no longer assured protection. Japanese guards standing at the hospital gates began checking people randomly and creating havoc inside the facility, preventing normal functioning. Going to school became impossible.

A handful of American missionaries, including my parents and Aunt Bessie, had no intention of leaving China. They had made their life's work to serve the Chinese people, and they intended to stay and do so till death do them part! But finally Japanese commanders ordered all Americans to evacuate from occupied areas immediately. The deadline to leave Kiukiang was May 1942. My tiny world was hanging in the balance.

Last Sunday gatherings of the remaining Kiukiang missionaries, ca. 1941

12

AFTER A WEEK of wondering what would happen to me if Mother and Day-Day were forced to leave, I walked into the study unannounced. This was the room where my parents would get their business done and sometimes study the Bible. Only grownups were allowed, but on that Sunday afternoon, I didn't care. "Mother, are you going to take me to America this time?"

Mother was calm, and she glanced at Day-Day, who was typing away at his big wooden desk. Day-Day looked up and gave me a broad smile. Then he nodded his head toward Mother, and she waved me to come closer.

"Darling," she said, "I know you were upset when we went to America without you. We didn't have a choice. Other than the paper your birth parents signed stating that they gave you up for adoption, we didn't have any official American documents affirming your adoption by us. So, while Day-Day and I were waiting to leave for America last year, we made your adoption legal through the US Supreme Court for China in Shanghai. You are now legally our daughter, recognized by American law!"

Mother paused as though waiting for a reaction from me. When I didn't seem excited, she continued, "We told the aunties, and so when Aunt Dee went on vacation, she did the same for Chum. Now Day-Day and I, along with Aunt Bessie, have applied to the Japanese officials for permission to take you and Chum with us to America. We are waiting for the final approval."

I was speechless, so excited to hear this news. I didn't exactly understand what Mother meant by adoption papers and why being their daughter needed all these approvals from some court in Shanghai. I always thought as long as they loved me, that was more than enough proof. But I did understand that Mother and Day-Day were planning to take me along, that they would not leave me behind this time!

"But," Mother added, "in case you and Chum are not allowed to go with us, we have asked Dr. and Mrs. Cheng to take care of you while we're away. We have packed two trunks full of clothing, books, and other necessities, and sent these items to their home." Dr. Cheng was a member of the hospital staff.

I was far less enthused about that option, and I told Mother, "I don't want to live with them. I want to be with you, Day-Day, and Grandma! I want to go to America."

Mother could only smile and say, "Well, Precious, that is what we are praying for."

Not long after that, the great news came. Japanese officials in Kiukiang granted both Chum and me permission to leave with our American parents. I was so happy I nearly burst. At the mere thought, my heart would thump wildly. I climbed onto the swing and flew up as high as I could, shouting at the top of my lungs, "America! America! Whoopee! Whee-eeee!" The tree shook and leaves fell as I swung upward toward the deep blue sky. I'm sure Chum was just as excited, but she rarely showed emotions. She was probably in her room studying for finals.

After knowing that Chum and I could leave with them, Mother began telling us about America. "Now Jeanie, you'll get to see the stores where your grandmother and grandfather got the clothes, books, and toys they sent you, like 5-and-dimes and Woolworth's." My mind began to drift to that faraway land. I felt I was going to a fairyland, or heaven.

But back on earth with just three weeks before our departure, everyone was concerned about Grandma. She was eighty-seven years old and gravely ill. She couldn't possibly take this journey to America. Nor could we leave her alone. We could only pray that God would relieve her pain and suffering. One day while Mother and I were in Grandma's room, she suddenly threw up her arms and with a radiant smile called out, "William!"

William was the name of my grandfather.

Then just as suddenly, her arms came down, and her smile was gone. With difficulty, Grandma told Mother, "I saw your father coming toward me. I was so happy, but as soon as I called his name, he stopped and gave me a disappointed look and walked away...."

With two weeks left before we were scheduled to depart Kiukiang, the rash around Grandma's waist was closing in. Lo-Ma whispered to me, "It won't be long before the head and the tail meet...." And sure enough, a few days later, the relentless dragon's head finally caught up with its tail, and Grandma died peacefully in her sleep.

"When we prayed, we did not want you to die, Grandma," I thought as I looked at her face. "But we didn't want you to be in pain either...." She looked as though she was asleep.

Chum and I led the funeral procession, wearing flowery dresses and carrying baskets full of flowers. In China, when elders die at an advanced age, it's an occasion to celebrate the deceased's long life. My Grandma had a Christian funeral and was buried at the American Cemetery in Kiukiang on the banks of the Yangtze River.

It was quite an experience for me to watch the grownups bury Grandma. I will always remember her face. She looked peaceful and natural in her coffin, and I knew she and Grandpa were together in their Heavenly Home, perhaps looking down and smiling at me.

JEAN TREN-HWA PERKINS

The day finally came. On April 21, 1942, under the watchful eyes of Japanese guards, we left the house we'd loved so much. Our procession filled several rickshaws, and it took eleven more coolies to carry the rest of our luggage, which included a gray metal suitcase with copper trim where Mother kept all her photographs from the past half-century. Our procession made quite a sensation as we went down the main street of Kiukiang toward the Bund to board a Yangtze River steamer to Shanghai.

To add to our already heavy hearts, Mm-Ma and Mr. Hu got word of our leaving and rushed across the river to see me off, wondering if they'd ever see me again! Mm-Ma wiped the tears from the corner of her eyes and held my hands for a moment, and then she said, "Tren-Hwa, after you leave, I am not sure we will ever see you again." I didn't know how to respond, so I gave her a grin of hopelessness. Mr. Hu stood a few feet away, watching without saying a word. It was the first time in ten years that I'd seen him.

Our best friends from school were clinging to the rickshaw Chum and I were in, crying and shouting for us not to forget them, ever! Weeping uncontrollably, I assured them I'd never forget them. Chang-Ma did not come, as she had already left Kiukiang with her son's family to go far away to the countryside. Wang-Sao, Chum's amah, became my de facto amah after that.[1]

Wang-Sao had so much more

The day before we left Kiukiang, 1942

---

1   We had begun to call her "Wang-Sao (王嫂)" because she was much younger than Chang-Ma and Lo-Ma. The word "Sao (嫂 or 阿姨)" is an equivalent of "aunt," whereas the word "ma (妈)" refers to an older woman and is an equivalent to "grandma."

fun with us. We loved her stories, jokes, and riddles. Although uneducated, she had a brilliant mind. And she was also more agile than Chang-ma or Lo-Ma because she had "liberated feet," which meant her feet were not bound. She was one of the lucky ones whose feet were allowed to grow freely! On that day, Wang-Sao wept silently and was the last one left standing on the dock.

The last goodbyes said, we walked up the plank. Unlike a decade earlier, when I crossed this ancient river on a small wooden raft, it was my first time going downstream on a real boat, with decks and cabins! As an eleven-year-old who had only known the people we were leaving and had only lived in Kiukiang, the excitement of exploring the wonders of a river steamer overwhelmed my sadness almost immediately.

The next day, we reached the famous Shanghai Bund (上海外滩). As soon as we landed, the Japanese hustled all the Americans into waiting buses that took us to the Columbia Country Club, which had become an internment camp for evacuating Americans from China. We were among the first evacuees to arrive. Being a kid, I didn't feel the anxiety grownups had about the living conditions there, the food, or having to sign out whenever we left the camp, describing where we would be going and when we'd be back. To me, it was exciting to be crowded into an enormous lounge with hanging sheets separating the women and children from the men. Families were not allowed to be together. For each meal, we stood in a long line with empty plates waiting for food. I don't remember what we ate, but it was not Chef Tian's homemade food. It didn't matter. I was much interested in everything going around us.

I used a flush toilet for the first time. Mother told me that after I was through, I needed to pull on a chain I could hardly reach. So, on my tiptoes, I got hold of it and yanked it as hard as I could. The thunderous roar sent me running out for dear life. After that,

JEAN TREN-HWA PERKINS

I tried to hold it in as long as possible. Sometimes, I waited for one of the grownups to go with me.

We did get out of camp and went to a big department store, where I took my first ride up an escalator, which I called "walking stairs." It was fun, but I was afraid my feet would get caught. I was overwhelmed by the vastness of Shanghai, the tall buildings, and the urban rush.

Three weeks went by, and I continued to enjoy our life at the Columbia Country Club. But soon more Americans were brought in, and the Japanese guards became physically and emotionally abusive to some of them. I still remember the name of one, Bishop Ward. The Japanese guards pumped water into his stomach, and then punched and jumped on him. We were shocked, as we were being treated pretty well. Perhaps it was our luck, or maybe because our group had more children. Mother said, "We may never understand. There's a war going on."

A few weeks later, we were summoned for an announcement. A Japanese official spoke to us in English: "Tomorrow, you will get up at 3 a.m. This is top secret. Do not communicate this information to a single person outside of the Club." We had no idea what was going to happen. The grownups began to pack silently, while we children were sent to bed early so we could wake up on time.

At 3 a.m. on June 7, 1942, half asleep, I crawled out of bed and we all stumbled out the big gate of the Columbia Country Club. To my amazement, Mother and Day-Day had many Chinese friends who lived in Shanghai who were waiting at the gate to see us off. They stood motionless, but their eyes were saying, "Goodbye!" I think they also wondered if they would see these Americans again. Somehow, they had gotten word of our departure and were determined to let the Americans know how much they appreciated all that these missionaries had done for China.

We were whisked into a long line of waiting buses and began a ride through the streets of Shanghai that I will never forget. Although it was foggy and dark, through the windows I could see bodies lying everywhere—on sidewalks, roadsides, and doorsteps, men, women, and children, young and old. I had forgotten my beggar days and had no idea such poverty existed. "Mother," I whispered. "Are they all dead?"

"I don't know, honey," she whispered back. "Some might have starved to death or died of some disease. Perhaps a few died of old age or the horrors of war. I'm sure many froze to death in the winter."

"When I grow up, Mommy, I'm going to do something so that Chinese people do not starve or freeze to death." Mother gave my hand a gentle squeeze and seemed happy by what I said.

Then she said in a low voice, "War is a terrible thing—for everyone." I will never forget that statement. After that, there was silence. Mother continued to hold my hand, as our bus ambled through the dark streets heading back to the Bund, where we'd landed a month earlier.

The sun was rising on the eastern horizon, foreshadowing the historic journey we were about to take.

Part II

The Hudson River: My Home

13

THE YANGTZE RIVER steamer had been exciting, but it was nothing compared to the gigantic Italian Ocean Liner, the *SS Conte Verde,* that we boarded in Shanghai. My heart was ready to leap out of my chest with excitement. "What it must be like to ride on that great beast!" I whispered to Mother. This storied ocean liner was built in Scotland and had its maiden voyage in 1923. Scotland, of course, was Mother's homeland. It had just sailed from the Port of Yokohama under the name *Teikyo Maru*. A Japanese ocean liner called *Asama Maru* escorted us for a while, then it headed to Southeast Asia to transport Americans who were there. Both the *SS Conte Verde* and the *Asama Maru* were already carrying Americans gathered in Japan. We were called the "Shanghai group."

I couldn't wait to explore this beautiful ship. But with six hundred adults and children, we had to wait patiently, as everyone boarded alphabetically. Clutching my bag of dolls, I shifted from one foot to the other, wishing our last name began with A.

At long last, our names were called. Mother, Day-Day, and I were ahead of Chum because our family name began with "Pe" and Chum and Aunt Bessie's with "Pl," Ploeg. My parents and I had a stateroom all to ourselves, while Chum and Aunt Bessie had to share theirs with a stranger. Stateroom (or cabin), I learned, is the word for a room on a ship, and they're smaller than most hotel rooms.

SPRING FLOWER: A TALE OF TWO RIVERS

During the voyage, the lady rooming with Chum and Aunt Bessie almost lost an eye when an electric fan swirled off its hinge and hit the side of her face. I believe God planned for Aunt Bessie to be there. As a professional nurse, she gave her emergency treatment until a doctor was able to come. I think the doctor was my father, but it was so long ago I can't remember for certain.

With my dolls safely on my bunk, I was off to explore the *Conte Verde*. The first thing that caught my attention was an Italian band playing, something I'd never seen before. They struck up the tune of "Dixie Land" to welcome all the "Yankees" aboard. The lounge was huge, especially for a small kid from Kiukiang. After that, I climbed to the top deck and was thrilled to discover a swimming pool. Soon I'd be spending hours a day in this beautiful pool. That was where I learned to swim. Someone accidentally knocked me underwater, and I struggled to get my head up above the water. It seemed like there was a heavy object pressing on my head, and I thought I was drowning. When my head suddenly popped out of the water, I could breathe again! I looked around and realized that no one had even noticed me. This near-death experience brought about a positive effect. I would never again panic about going underwater. After a while, I learned to dog-paddle, and felt less vulnerable. I was proud of myself because I was able to succeed in something that I had failed to master during our summer on Ku-Ling Mountain.

On the deck, I peeked through a window and saw a big screen with life-sized people on it, like a photo but they were moving and talking, and I could hear music. I couldn't imagine what this was, so I ran to our stateroom and told Mother.

She didn't seem surprised. After a pause, she said, "It was probably a motion picture."

"A what?" I asked, still bowled over with excitement. Before Mother could respond, I asked, "May I watch one?"

"No," she answered firmly, and the concept "motion picture" went unexplained. Later that day, Day-Day offered a softer reply, telling me that in a year or two when I was older, he would take me to a play at a theater. I didn't know what a play or a motion picture was, but thought it best not to ask. It was enough, I felt, that Mother was letting me roam the ship on my own, a lot of freedom for an eleven-year-old.

One Italian sailor waved to me and took off his cap every time I walked past, muttering a few words in Italian. I would greet him in return with a "hello."

The flushing toilets on the ocean liner were even scarier than the ones at the Columbia Country Club. I'd pull the chain and run for my life.

When the ocean liner was about to set sail and leave Shanghai, an emergency siren sounded. Later we learned that our ship had nearly been torpedoed due to mistaken identity. The grownups were visibly shaken, but we kids had no idea what had happened.

At last, on June 18, 1942, I left China for the first time. From my heart, I shouted, "Hello, America, here I come!" We voyaged onto the East China Sea and southward, hugging the coastline and threading through Taiwan Strait toward the South China Sea, stopping for two days in Hong Kong to load more Westerners. Most newcomers from Hong Kong boarded the *Asama Maru*. We weren't allowed to get off, and so I only glimpsed the curvaceous shape of Hong Kong island from Victoria Harbor. After that, we passed some small islands of the Philippines and Indonesia. We may have picked up more people there, too; I don't recall.

When we arrived at the port of Singapore, again we could only watch from the deck, as still more Westerners came on board. Most of them were Americans, but I learned that some were Canadians. Soon we waved goodbye to the coast of Malaysia and then Indonesia, as we sailed through the Strait of Malacca.

SPRING FLOWER: A TALE OF TWO RIVERS

Once through the strait, this grand ocean liner sailed out onto the open sea, cutting across the Indian Ocean and heading toward our first destination: Mozambique in Africa. We were at sea for more than a month.

Aunt Bessie and Chum were nauseous and dizzy with cold sweats from seasickness most of the way, and were barely able to leave their stateroom. These gigantic ocean liners go really slowly, so slow that missionaries from the city of Wu-Hu (芜湖) would, in jest, greet those of us from Kiukiang by saying, "We are mossing along to Moss-am-beek," Some even said that moss grows faster than the pace of the ship.

Although I didn't get seasick like Chum and Aunt Bessie, I did start feeling a little woozy by the third day after we went through a rough patch of huge waves that rocked the ship. I lost my appetite for the Italian breakfast rolls I'd loved so much at first, and never ate them again. I did manage to steal a few rolls to feed the seagulls that seemed to be following us. I wondered where they lived, since there was not even a rock sticking out of the water once we entered the Indian Ocean.

I was too shy to make friends with other children, and so I roamed the ship pretty much on my own, a lone ranger without adult supervision. After a few weeks, someone shouted, "Land, land!" and we all scrambled to the decks, and sure enough, we could see a shoreline in the distance. On July 22, 1942, our ship reached the Port of Lourenço Marques. Mozambique was still a Portuguese colony. Today, Lourenço Marques is Maputo, the capital city of Mozambique, 6,721 miles from Kiukiang. After gathering more Americans from Southeast Asia, *Asama Maru* also arrived and docked nearby.

Unwittingly, I took part in a historical event. It turned out we were the first group exchanged for so-called Japanese "prisoners of war," which included Japanese Americans, who had been rounded up in America and arrived in Mozambique from New York via the Swedish ocean liner *MS Gripsholm*, nicknamed the "Mercy Ship" during World War II. As I learned later, this was a civilian equivalent of a POW exchange, and it was top secret. The US State Department and the Japanese Department of Foreign Ministry negotiated the exchange to bring back prominent American officials, diplomats, businesspeople, journalists, mission workers, and those of other professions who had been trapped in Japan-occupied Asian territories after Pearl Harbor.

Because there were fewer Japanese personnel in America, to make this an equal exchange, the US Government rounded up hundreds if not thousands of Japanese Americans, many of them second- or third-generation Americans. They had been in internment camps (called War Relocation Camps) before being shipped to Mozambique. Japan agreed to take them because their ability to speak English would be valuable during the war.

To prevent the Axis Powers (Germany, Italy, and Japan) from moving into South America, the US and fifteen South American countries allied. Consequently, many people of Japanese ancestry who had been living and working in South America were deported to New York, where they were deemed illegal aliens and thus qualified for the Mozambique exchange. Some had been picked up by the *Gripsholm* in Brazil.

This exchange was mediated by Switzerland (representing America) and Spain (representing Japan), both nonparticipants in the war at that time. The transfer took place at a neutral site, and it turned out that ours was one of only two such exchanges between Japan and America. The other took place a year later, in September 1943. A third one never came to pass when talks broke off between the US and Japan. A specific list of "prisoners" was compiled for both sides, and our names appeared in the Sunday *New York Times* on June 28, 1942:

SPRING FLOWER: A TALE OF TWO RIVERS

Perkins, E. C., Yonkers, New York
Perkins, Mrs. G. M. P.
Perkins, J. H.-T.
....
Ploeg, E., Grand Rapids, Mich.
Ploeg, E. L. [aka "Chum"]

Chum and I might have been the only Chinese nationals in these two exchanges.

Most of these events eluded my comprehension, and I had no sense of their magnitude. I did hear that our *Conte Verde* and the *Gripsholm* were docked bow-to-bow. The exchange of thousands of people between them, including hundreds of children on both sides, took days. There were precise lists of individual names. I saw many Japanese children my age who looked confused and terrified. Some were crying. Some kids were noisy. As we lined up, a few Japanese children thought they could come over and play with us. Of course, that wasn't allowed. One of them shouted, "Is there a pool onboard?" Another giggled and said, "The food was terrible on *Gripsholm*." No one from our side responded, but I could tell that they were speaking flawless American English. Now I understand they were Americans of Japanese ancestry.

Our side had a sense of suppressed jubilation, but we could feel the tense atmosphere as we lined up to walk onto the *Gripsholm*. Mother held my hand tightly throughout, while Day-Day walked just ahead of us, looking pensive. Aunt Bessie held onto Chum. They were a few people behind us in the line. I looked back a few times to make sure they were still there. Mother would whisper calmly, "Jeanie dear, focus straight ahead. They are coming right along just fine, don't you worry." Shortly after the exchange, the *Conte Verde* and the *Asama Maru*, carrying those exchanged Japanese, including North and South American citizens, left the piers and headed for the Port of Yokohama.

The war was far from over, and millions were still to die. No one at that point could predict winners or losers. For many of the exchanged Japanese, the anxiety was about leaving the only country they had ever known and heading to the one where they didn't even speak the language.

I wondered, "What must that feel like?" I remembered again what Mother had said, "War is a terrible thing — for everyone."

14

AFTER THE *Conte Verde* and *Asama Maru* departed, everything became spacious and quiet. Before we set sail for New York, we were allowed to have a day visiting the city of Lourenço Marques. Disembarking, I walked on solid ground for the first time in more than a month; it felt as though the earth were coming up and grabbing my legs. I was as unsteady as a drunken sailor. When I told Mother, she explained, "You have sea legs, dear! You'll be fine in a bit." Sure enough, in half an hour I began to feel normal.

My parents and the other missionaries decided to visit a native Methodist church in town, and Chum and I went along. I found walking along the city streets, seeing men, women, and children with really black skin, breathtaking. At home in Kiukiang, we sang a song in church, "Jesus loves the little children; all the children in the world; red, yellow, black, and white; all are precious in His sight...." and now I understood for the first time that people have different color skin. Mine is yellow, Chum's is whiter, and Mother's, Day-Day's, and the aunties' is white.

After the African minister shook my hand, I stared at it for a second, and to my surprise, shaking his hand had left no color on mine!

Color aside, I found the Africans to be so friendly. They invited us on a motorboat to watch a live hippopotamus, the first time I saw this large and strange creature. The docile animal reminded me of Chinese water buffalos because both enjoyed being in the water, even though they didn't look alike. We were warned not to bother them, that they sometimes overturn boats!

There was sand everywhere, and buried in the sand were tiny red seeds with black tips (they were likely *Abrus precatorius*, also known as rosary pea or jequirity bean) that we gathered. I kept mine for years. I remember the events of that day vividly, even now.

On July 28, 1942, we left Mozambique on the *MS Gripsholm*, passing by Cape Town, South Africa, toward the majestic Atlantic Ocean. Mother was excited when pointing out the Cape of Good Hope, but I failed to understand her excitement. On August 10, we came ashore in Rio de Janeiro, then the capital of Brazil, which had been a Portuguese colony until 1822. I was happy as a lark when I learned we would again be allowed off the ship to tour an ancient city.

We were bussed first to the foot of Mt. Corcovado, 2,300 feet high, and then rode up in cable cars. It was scary to look down, and there were stretches we ascended pretty much vertically. I wished Ku-Ling had cable cars to lift people to the top, so the coolies wouldn't have to work so hard. At the top of Mt. Corcovado was a statue of Jesus looking down on the city, His arms stretched out forming a cross, as if giving a blessing to all. It was a breathtakingly beautiful panoramic view; the whole city and bay appeared in a bird's-eye view. A shop on the mountaintop sold ornaments and souvenirs. I was awed by the beautiful butterfly wings embedded in glass. By the time we got back to the ship, it was pitch black, and the lighted city looked even more dazzling. Shanghai seemed dull in comparison.

We left Rio in mid-August and began the last leg of our long journey to America. When our ships had been docked bow-to-bow, one Japanese American boy asked us how the *Conte Verde* was. We said it was great, but now I realized the *Gripsholm* was truly excellent. It was so spacious that it felt like being on two luxury liners. And the swimming pool was indoors, so we could swim even when it was raining. That being said, the fatigue of the long voyage had begun to set in, especially for us kids.

One night, while sailing in complete darkness near the northern coast of Brazil, we saw an oil tanker burning in the distance, lighting up the sky. One of the sailors shouted, "Oil's floating on the water!" The *Gripsholm* made a wide circle around the burning ship, avoiding the oil. The captain wanted to see if there were survivors, but there were no signs of life, so we sailed on.

One constant reminder that there was a war going on was the request for everyone to salvage aluminum foil wrappings from cigarette packs and chocolate bars. I did that faithfully, and I had quite a big ball of aluminum wrapping but didn't know whom to give it to. So I left it on the ship when we got off.

Aunt Bessie and Chum seemed to perk up for the last leg of our voyage, perhaps because the *Gripsholm* was steadier or perhaps because there weren't as many high waves as we had had on the Indian Ocean. Chum and I were mostly together now. When we could, we dressed alike. Aunt Bessie made us identical dresses, and people on the ship asked if we were twins! With the stress of the harsh exchange behind us, our parents thought we should brush up on reading and spelling, much to my dismay. It meant that I couldn't play or roam the ship as much.

But the grownups had a point. If we wanted to enter the fifth or sixth grade in America, we had to be able to read, write, and spell on a fifth- or sixth-grade level. Although I had attended an American kindergarten, summer school on Ku-Ling Mountain before first grade, and the mostly English-speaking primary school where I had to repeat third grade, most of my lessons had been in Chinese. So for the rest of the journey, we studied pretty hard. Aunt Bessie found a geography book and tutored us in reading and spelling.

Unlike Chum, I was not born to study. As we got closer and closer to America, my excitement was mounting to the point where I could no longer concentrate on our lessons. For the Americans on board, including Mother, Day-Day, and the aunties, they would be coming home and be free at last. But what, I wondered, about Chum and me?

Then one day, Mother shouted, "Come quickly and look, dear."

I'd never seen her this excited, nor have I since. She was like a child, and I rushed up to get on deck. Yes, there She was, the magnificent Statue of Liberty, standing majestically in New York Harbor with Her arm stretched high into the sky holding the torch.

As we sailed past the Liberty lady going upstream on the Hudson River, I stared intently at her face. Strangely I sensed a profound sadness in her smile, and I wondered why.

So, this was America, the land of the free and the home of the brave! On Tuesday, August 25, 1942, we docked near Jersey City, New Jersey. I spotted Aunt Dee on the pier. The tall, handsome man next to her with a face full of whiskers and sideburns must have been Day-Day's older brother, who I was to call Uncle Henry. He had been waiting on the pier to greet us, along with the aunties' older sister, Anna Ploeg, and Anna's husband. What a joyful reunion!

Because there were 1,451 people and the FBI and other agencies had to check everyone thoroughly to ensure there were no spies among us, it took three days for us to disembark. Many of the passengers, including Chum and me, were designated for Ellis Island, so we were the last ones to leave.

SPRING FLOWER: A TALE OF TWO RIVERS

Associated Press Wire: August 28, 1942.
"Jersey City, N.J., August 28. — Dr. E. C. Perkins, brother of Professor Henry A. Perkins of Trinity College, is shown with his wife and their adopted 11-year-old Chinese daughter, Jean Hu Perkins, as they were about to leave the diplomatic exchange liner Gripsholm, *which arrived this week. Professor Perkins, who lives at 55 Forest Street, Hartford, met his brother and sister-in-law at the dock and said that they were looking "much better" than he had expected after the arduous journey from Kiu Kiang, China, where Dr. Perkins was a missionary.*

Among the last to disembark, Dr. Perkins and his wife and daughter went immediately to their home in Yonkers."

Well, we didn't quite go immediately to our home in Yonkers. We stayed at the Waldorf Astoria Hotel on Park Avenue in Manhattan first, and Chum and I went to the US Immigration office on Ellis Island the next day. Sensing the consequential nature of what was about to happen, Mother briefed me on what the immigration officials might ask, such as age, name, name of parents, where I came from, etc., just as she had when I first attended the Ku-Ling American Kindergarten.

The next day, we all took a ferry to Ellis Island and entered the waiting room. Many others were already there, and I waited nervously. Finally, hours after Chum and Aunt Bessie went into their assigned room, my number was called. Mother, Day-Day, and I entered a room with no windows. Oddly, I was no longer nervous.

Two officers—a man and a woman—were there. After I triumphantly answered the female agent's questions, such as my name and where I was going, the male officer began to speak. "So, Miss Perkins, do you have when any birthmarks?"

I answered calmly, "No, sir."

Then he pressed, "Well, is there anything by which you could be identified if needed?"

I thought for a moment and saw my right thumb, which ever since I could remember always had a discolored nail. Stretching my right hand toward the officers, I asked, "Will this do, sir?" The man nodded his head.

"How did that happen?" he asked. I shook my head, with a grin, to indicate I didn't know. Mother and Day-Day, sitting on a long wooden bench behind me, must have been feeling proud. I was handling myself well.

I forgot who asked the next question: "Do you have any blood relatives here in America?"

"Yes, Uncle Henry. He lives in Connecticut!" I answered with pride and without the slightest hesitation. Both officers cringed and gave Mother and Day-Day the "I knew it!" look, implying I had lied.

Mother stood up and explained, "Sir, I don't think the child understands what blood relative means."

I turned my head, and she explained that Uncle Henry was Dr. Perkins's brother, and was not my blood relative because Day-Day adopted me. Day-Day was grinning. The officers nodded, understanding now that I hadn't lied.

Later, when Mother told Uncle Henry about this, he laughed so hard his whiskers and sideburns shook. He seemed pleased.

"Jeanie dear, you are not wrong at all," he said. "You are my niece, and no niece of mine could ever be wrong!"

But we were still with the officers on Ellis Island, and next came the bad news. Although Mother had shown my legal adoption papers from the US Supreme Court in Shanghai, I was only allowed to stay for three months!

Mother asked, "Where do you expect a child of eleven to go

after three months? Back to her war-torn country? Aren't we at war with Japan? Isn't the Republic of China our ally?"

The officers looked surprised by Mother's assertiveness, as she had been docile until then. After much discussion between themselves, the female officer told Mother, "Your daughter can stay here 'on parole.' As soon as the war in her country is over, she will have to leave within three months." I didn't understand any of this, but Mother looked angry and began to lecture the officers on the meaning of Ellis Island.

Ellis Island was designated the site of the first Federal immigration station by President Benjamin Harrison in 1890, and until it closed in 1954, any immigrant deemed physically and mentally fit had the right to be naturalized at age eighteen or above. Given that I had proper adoption papers signed by the US Supreme Court for China and that I was coming from an allied country, based on the immigration rules of the time, my entry should have been straightforward. After continued wrangling between Mother and the officers, they informed Mother and Day-Day that for me to become an American citizen, it would require another process that could take place only after I turned eighteen. Chum, it turns out, had had the same verdict. Although Day-Day had a law degree, he was unsure whether they could do anything at this point, so they didn't press the issue, even though they didn't know what it implied for the future.

I, on the other hand, was beyond ecstatic, and the granting of a temporary stay didn't temper my enthusiasm for seeing America for the first time. Mother and Day-Day took us all around New York City. We went to Rockefeller Center and Radio City Music Hall the first night, and I was in awe of everything, especially the glittering lights on Broadway and Times Square. I saw strangely dressed dancers in front of a theater. Mother pulled my arm pretty hard when she realized that I was staring.

JEAN TREN-HWA PERKINS

I fell in love with the city with the skyscrapers — the Woolworth Building, the Chrysler Building, and the Empire State Building on 34th Street, where we went straight up to the top. Chum and me took our first ride in an elevator. It was scary; I had butterflies in my stomach. When we reached the top, we rushed outside, and I was in awe! Our hair was flying in the strong wind. As we looked down, we saw cars so small they looked like toys. As I looked around, I spotted two rivers flanking the island, converging at a distance toward the Statue of Liberty. As twilight approached, I watched lights of different colors coming on, one by one, from all directions. Everything started to look greenish-blue, with a tinge of light yellow. To me, the view was sad, and my mind drifted to the other side of the world I called home, where there was also a river.

The next day, we walked along the East River until both the Manhattan Bridge and the Brooklyn Bridge came into view. What a scenic vista! After lunch, we strolled through Central Park, which I'd heard about from Mother. It was beautiful. Then we hopped on the uptown subway and visited Columbia University, passing St. Luke's Hospital on Amsterdam Avenue, where Day-Day had learned to be a surgeon. After that, we sauntered toward the Hudson River. While the grownups chatted, Chum and I skipped ahead until we reached 79th Street. There, on an old wooden pier, we sat down to watch the sunset. Mother reached for my hand, her face reflecting the orange and red sunlight, and she appeared to be in deep thought. I also saw Day-Day looking at Mother and realized how far I had come from the Yangtze River in central China.

Those remarkable days flew by, and it was time for us to go to home. Day-Day and the aunties took a yellow cab, while Uncle Henry drove Mother, Chum, and me in his 1935 Chrysler. We flew through the streets toward Grand Central Station to see

Chum and the aunties off. They would be traveling to Grand Rapids. Chum suddenly grabbed my hand. We looked at each other, realizing we'd be separated for the first time.

As Chum and the aunties boarded their train, I began to cry uncontrollably. Chum, as always, was in control of her emotions. As tears streamed down my cheeks, the train disappeared from sight. Chum was the only sister I'd ever known, and the aunties were a part of our family all these years. None of us knew what the future would hold. Placing her arms around my shoulder, Mother said, understandingly, "Come, Precious. The train has left, and we too must head for home."

Home, of course! The place Mother grew up in, by the Hudson River, and it would soon be my home, too. Wiping away my tears, taking one last look in the direction Chum and the aunties had gone, I set forth with my Day-Day and Mother to our home: 6 Arthur Place, Yonkers, New York, in Uncle Henry's Chrysler.

15

I LOVED living in North Yonkers, and America became my home. Over the next two years, I became an all-American teenager, attending Yonkers Public School No. 16 (PS 16) on 759 North Broadway. And I fell in love with our house at 6 Arthur Place the moment I approached it from the driveway.

The house sat up on a hill, and my second-floor bedroom had two windows. Out of my favorite window, facing due west, I had a beautiful view of the Hudson River and the Palisades on the New Jersey side of the river. I could watch the boats and barges on the Hudson by day, and on clear nights, I could see the moonlight flickering upon the water. In no time, the Hudson became *my* river. Then, suddenly, a landslide on the Palisades produced a formation that looked like Hitler's face, which ruined my view! Day-Day reflected, "Perhaps it's God's way of reminding us there's still a war going on."

My house on the hill, 6 Arthur Place, Yonkers, NY

SPRING FLOWER: A TALE OF TWO RIVERS

My other bedroom window faced north toward the woods. Thanks to my grandpa, these woods were preserved and no road was ever built through them. Many generations enjoyed the fruits of his petitioning Yonkers City Hall, and it was quiet almost every night, except when we heard cars screeching to a halt, failing to recognize the dead end.

That house was heaven to me. I had a Victorian brass bed, which Mother had slept in as a child, and I even found some of Mother's dolls dressed in nineteenth-century clothing stored in a wooden cradle in the attic. I put them on the windowsill, along with the ones I'd brought from Kiukiang. At times, dolls were my only playmates, especially when it was raining and I couldn't visit friends' homes. I even had *my own bathroom*. I could jump out of bed and waltz into the bathroom to refresh myself any time of the day. I was no longer afraid of flush toilets, and I actually learned to fix them when the tank didn't fill properly. And the bathtub was porcelain, with spigots! I became so used to hot and cold running water, I wondered if I would ever get used to living in China again.

With one of my neighbor's two kids

In the middle of our front yard was a giant crabapple tree. The neighbor's two little girls and I would play hide-and-seek there. The tree had been planted by my grandma and grandpa when Mother was young, so it must have been over a century old by the time we lived there. The tree was especially beautiful in spring when it blossomed. I had never seen crabapple blossoms, and they made me think of the tree-filled garden that I loved in Kiukiang. Our house in Yonkers felt special because Mother had grown up here. I'd never met Grandpa, but there were many photos of him around the house.

The only negative experience I can think of was the neighbor down-the-street's dog. I was afraid of dogs, and this one bit people. Avoiding him became my daily task. I walked around the block to stay away from him, but one day as I came home from the opposite direction, I felt a heavy weight on my shoulders and froze in my tracks, too frightened even to scream. He had been following me. Thankfully, he took off as quickly as he'd pounced but only after licking my neck and ears. My legs were still shaking as I went to the bathroom to clean up. Mother, who was preparing dinner, seemed surprised to see my terrified face, but she didn't say anything.

I enjoyed reading, including *Little Women, Little Men, Heidi, Anne of Green Gables, Uncle Tom's Cabin,* and the Covered Wagon stories. Reading was my favorite pastime in Yonkers before I started making friends. When I began *The Adventures of Tom Sawyer* and *The Adventures of Huckleberry Finn,* Day-Day told me that he and Uncle Henry had lived next door to Mark Twain. I thought he was kidding.

On my first day at PS 16, Mother took me to the principal's office and showed her my report card from the fourth grade at Dragon Primary. The principal had been one of Mother's high school classmates, and she handed the card back to us, laughing, "Georgie, I might need to brush up on my Chinese, but I do recognize the grades. Could one of you translate the subjects?"

I volunteered, "Yes, I can," in a voice so shy it was barely audible.

She nodded in approval and said, "You speak English pretty well for a Chinese." The principal then led me to the fifth-grade classroom. All heads turned as I was introduced to them as Jean Perkins.

Mrs. Hughes, the homeroom teacher, showed me my desk, and as I sat down, the whole class stood up. I scrambled to my feet, not knowing what to expect. Then I heard the words: "I pledge allegiance to the flag of the United States of America," reciited in unison. Before I could figure out what to do, they started singing, "O say can you see, by the dawn's early light, what so proudly we hailed...."

I was perplexed. Having lived under Japanese rule half of my short life, I had a good idea about patriotism—loving your country and its flag, but not that of an enemy. What was I supposed to do? Was America my home now? I soon joined the rituals with pride and reverence, and I even joined Girl Scout Troop 11. I loved my scout uniform, especially the barrette! I felt so proud when I marched with the other Girl Scouts in a May Day Parade at Getty Square in downtown Yonkers.

At first, I struggled in school. My first humiliation came when I couldn't spell *pneumonia* for the life of me. Mrs. Hughes asked me to stay after school till I could spell it correctly, but the harder I tried, the worse it got. I was on the verge of tears when voices of my Kiukiang days spoke inside my head: "The girls Mrs. Perkins helped never seem to be good in studies. This one is no exception." I held back my tears and shouted in my mind, "We'll see!"

Sensing it'd been a long day for me, Mrs. Hughes relented, "Jean, you may go home now, but be sure you can spell it by tomorrow." I was relieved and more determined than ever to do well in English.

During my two years at PS 16, I observed a wide range of personalities. One tiny girl named Heather fluttered like a butterfly from desk to desk, friendly to everyone. Doris, like me, was timid. Joan loved horses and was always shaking her

JEAN TREN-HWA PERKINS

ID bracelet as if it was in her way. Jack would run his fingers through his curly brown hair each time Mrs. Hughes asked him a question. Hampson was gentle, kind, and talented in music. Redheaded Frank with a face full of freckles was the first boy to give me a Valentine's card, on February 14, 1943. The boys wore suits and ties, and we girls all wore dresses. It made us feel we were doing something meaningful and instilled self-respect.

All my classmates were helpful and kind to me. I never heard a single word of discrimination from them, not even "Chink, Chink Chinaman." The only time I felt the sting of prejudice was on my way home from school one day when a kid I didn't know yelled, "Jap! Jap! Jap!"

I turned around and told him, "I am not Japanese! I am Chinese!" He was taken aback by my assertiveness. I walked away, knowing that even if I were Japanese, this was no way to talk.

Then there were Jill and Betty, who befriended me on my first day at PS 16. Each took it upon herself to protect and stand up for me whenever necessary, and we became lifelong friends. The first time we met, Jill came up to my desk and said, "Jean, my name is Jill. Can you please take off your glasses so we can see what you look like?"

Although I didn't like wearing glasses, I was too embarrassed to take them off once they were on. I shook my head no, and my face turned red. Thinking I might not have understood, she took off her own silver-rimmed glasses and said, "See, like this."

Reluctantly, I took them off for a second, then put them right back on. Jill smiled broadly.

Betty had blue eyes with a head full of blond curls that bounced like springs down to her shoulders. A few curls found their way to her forehead, and she'd blow her lips sideways to brush aside the tickling hair. She loved to lick her lips till they chapped and cracked.

We became the Three Musketeers, lots of tomboy play—we all had that streak in us. We loved to climb trees. I even taught them Chinese ways of playing with marbles and the game of flipping an open penknife into the ground from different parts of the body.

One day we were playing near Yonkers Harbor, and I couldn't believe my eyes. There was the *MS Gripsholm*. It turns out it was waiting for its next POW exchange, which took place in September 1943. I told them about my journey, and they both were in awe.

I learned how to ride a bicycle on Betty's bike. One day, I dared her to sit behind me, and downhill we went. I was startled at how quickly the speed picked up. As I swerved onto the wrong side of the road, I saw an oncoming car. I couldn't pump the brake effectively enough, so to stop, I crashed onto the sidewalk. Betty didn't know what had happened, but she knew something was very wrong. Luckily she landed in front of me and wasn't hurt, nor was her bicycle. I had bruises on my right knee and felt warm blood trickling down my leg. I'd worn slacks that day, so no one even saw the blood.

After snowfalls, some roads were closed so kids could go sledding. Day-Day and Mother had bought me a sled for my first Christmas in Yonkers, and we took turns going down the hill. One time, we all piled on and tumbled down to the bottom of the hill. We just loved it! We had such good times together.

My parents and I attended Morsemere Methodist Episcopal Church, now a historic landmark. Mother and my American grandparents had been members of this church. The congregation was thrilled to see a Chinese girl there, and it was there that I met Marie. Marie also went to PS 16 but was a grade ahead of me. Through church functions, we became close, but because she lived further away, we didn't play together as much as I did with Jill and Betty.

When Marie and I did play, she would come to my house, and sometimes she'd even spend the night. We would play with my dolls, pretending we were their teachers. With Marie, I was less of a tomboy, although we both could climb trees with ease. We were content just sitting on a branch and talking—instead of swinging like monkeys as I had in Kiukiang. One day, as we were perched on a tree, Marie looked at me and asked, "Jean?"

Suddenly her face became serious, and I sensed she was going to say something important. "Yes?" I answered.

"I was adopted too."

"Really?" I exclaimed. "Because you were a girl?" That was the only reason I knew why parents gave up their children.

"No," she said. "My parents both died of tuberculosis when I was young. Our neighbors, who were childless, took me in and later adopted me. Before they did, I lived at a Catholic boarding school, where I was so unhappy I didn't know what to do."

"Are you happy now?" I asked.

"Oh, yes!" she answered.

"So am I, Marie, I am so lucky to have my parents."

In those days, adoptions were a family secret. Being adopted became a precious bond between us, and we became lifelong friends.

In our North Yonkers home, no one could be idle. There were no

Marie and I in Bronx Park, ca. 1943

amahs like Wang-Sao, Chang-Ma, or Lo-Ma, and we had no cook like Chef Tian. Of course, we didn't need a Grandpa Shui to fetch water, but Mother had to tend her own gardens and plants. And I had to put into practice what I had learned by watching the servants in China, chores like washing, starching, and ironing, and I even helped Mother clean house. My job was to dust the parlors. Some duties were more complicated here than in China, and the skin peeled off on my knuckles from so much scrubbing.

It was difficult to wash the overalls that Day-Day wore in his victory garden. Victory gardens were prolific during World War II, as there weren't many vegetables in the stores. We used ration coupons. Washing machines were still uncommon, and Day-Day's overalls got so heavy in the washtub, I could barely lift them. I did manage, though, and we had a ringer to squeeze the water out. When I hung the clothes out to dry in the backyard, I felt proud of my accomplishment. I'd sit there and appreciate what Uncle Paddle had done for us for so many years.

The chore I liked least was darning socks, especially Day-Day's! I'd learned to use a needle at the age of four, but those were for big stitches to make clothes for my dolls. Darning socks was time-consuming, as all of Day-Day's socks were old and worn. "It'd be easier to buy new ones," I thought.

In China, I was never fashion-conscious; there was no need. I wore whatever was made, bought, or handed down, with pleasure. But after I entered fifth grade in Yonkers, something happened.

When the weather turned cold, I wore my navy-blue sailor suit. Mother always bought me sailor suits when she and Day-Day vacationed in Japan. She said they were Japanese schoolgirl uniforms, and I loved wearing them. But walking into class that day, my fifth-grade teacher said, "What do we have here? A sailor girl!"

JEAN TREN-HWA PERKINS

Heads turned, and my face turned crimson. I wondered if I had done something wrong. No one was wearing a sailor's suit. I sat through class, feeling really uncomfortable, and when the bell rang, I ran all the way home, rushed to my room, took off the suit, and never wore it again! Not long after, while visiting some of Mother's relatives in Hastings-on-Hudson, I learned that my clothes were out of date, not appropriate for an eleven-year-old. Soon I received two blouses and two skirts, made out of old clothes but in the style that girls my age were wearing.

I learned quickly that for Americans, clothes are not just something to wear. Styles had meaning with judgments attached to them. Anyone who didn't follow the trends was considered old-fashioned or boring. So I began to ask for things my best friends were wearing, like shorts, sweatshirts, slacks, and dungarees. I also wanted a red-and-black checkered flannel shirt. For dress-up, I wanted a suit and a blazer.

I rarely got what I wanted, though; we lived frugally. Whenever I asked for something, Mother and Day-Day would say it was too expensive. They considered things such as a sled, roller skates, ice skates, and even a much-needed winter coat as frivolous. I would only get stuff like that at Christmastime or on my birthday. I asked for a bicycle so many times Mother even pleaded on my behalf, but Day-Day held the line.

Gradually I learned that missionaries live on a meager salary. Despite being a licensed physician, Day-Day was considered unemployed when we were in America. We had no real income besides family savings and the money Day-Day earned from occasional emergency calls or substituting for doctors on leave. Most of all, Day-Day figured that our time in the US was temporary, so even when he was offered a position at St. Luke's Hospital, he declined, thinking it wasn't necessary.

We almost never ate at restaurants, and Mother wasn't much

of a cook. One day, she invited some of my classmates over for a Chinese lunch, and her idea of a Chinese meal was rice with boiled vegetables and overcooked turnips in soy sauce. It was horrible, nothing like the food I had in China. I missed Chef Tian, but I also appreciated that my mother was trying, even if what she served was an utter disaster. She was reminding me not to forget China.

So, I never learned to cook, although Mother did teach me how to make delicious Scotch shortbread and peanut butter brittle. I often wondered what my classmates thought of that "Chinese" meal. We had cake and ice cream for dessert, so I assume all was well.

16

I LOVED the fact that I was able to spend more time with Mother and Day-Day. My father realized he hadn't played with me much in China; he was so busy caring for patients. "Why not make it up now," he decided. So one day, he got down on his hands and knees growling like a bear and crawled into my room. Frightened by this odd show of parental affection, I screamed and tried to escape. Mother heard us and came immediately. And when she saw what was going on, she laughed uncontrollably and chided Day-Day, "Let me remind you, Edward, Jean is eleven years old and will soon be in the fifth grade. She's too old for this kind of child's play."

Day-Day stood up, hung his head down like a naughty boy, and the three of us laughed really hard. It was the first time I saw Day-Day's playful side. He was always strict and focused on his work. Still, I knew in my heart of hearts that he loved me; he just had a different way of showing it from Mother, and on that day, he was so relaxed that his love was on full display.

Enthralled by this unexpected expression of his love, I stared at Day-Day lovingly as he headed for the kitchen, and for the first time, I saw he was getting older. He always tried to hold himself straight, like the young athlete he had been at Yale. But ever since receiving a near-fatal blow to his back by a heavy metal door some years ago, he hunched over more and more. I cannot remember the details of his accident, as it took place in Shantung (山东) in the 1920s, well before my time. He was there to help the American Red Cross with famine relief and an outbreak of pneumonic plague. As I watched him leaning forward, I realized that without Day-Day and Mother, I would not be alive today, not to mention thriving in Yonkers, New York.

Soon Day-Day would be away for days at a time. When I couldn't hear him snoring, I surmised he wasn't at home. He would often go to Manhattan, to an office high up in a building on Fifth Avenue to consult for the Methodist Mission Office and to document mission history in China. He took me along a few times, which I loved. One time, we left the City late, so instead of taking a subway and the train home, Day-Day hailed a cab, and within minutes, we were stuck in traffic on the Upper East Side. The driver yelled in disgust, "Ahh, the game again," and he threw his arms in the air before putting them back on the steering wheel.

"The Yankees are playing?" Day-Day asked. "Are they in the pennant race?"

The driver nodded without turning around.

"Who are the Yankees?" I asked.

Day-Day looked at me for a second, then said to the driver, "We'll get off here." I followed my dad outside.

"Where are we going, Day-Day? Should we tell Mother?"

"We'll be late anyway, and Mother will know to eat on her own, Jeanie dear. Let's grab a bite to eat in the diner over there."

I ordered a Dagwood sandwich and a cold bottle of Coca-Cola. I was starving and thirsty, and I rarely got to eat in a restaurant.

We sat in a booth by the window. I was reading a poster that told the number of billions of gallons of Coca-Cola syrup that had been produced to date when Day-Day tugged my arm and pointed to a well-lit, mammoth structure not far away. "Jeanie, look. That's Yankee Stadium, where the baseball team plays."

JEAN TREN-HWA PERKINS

I was in awe. It was huge, and it looked alien.

"Day-Day, what's baseball?" I asked as the waitress came over to refill my father's coffee cup. She looked at both of us and gave a friendly and bemused grin before walking away.

"Baseball's a game where one man uses a bat to hit a ball thrown by another man, called a pitcher. Then the man who is hitting tries to get to first base. If he goes around all four bases, his team scores a run." Day-Day picked up four wooden coffee stirrers, laid them out in the shape of a diamond, and explained the basics of baseball.

"That sounds like fun. Did you play at Yale?"

"No, Jeanie, I ran track. I would have loved to play baseball, but that was long ago." He was still laughing as the food arrived.

After a few bites, I looked up at him and asked, "Day-Day, would you take me to see a baseball game?"

He nodded. "Yes, Jeanie. That's a promise."

During the next few months, I studied this exciting sport, listening to games on our radio (before we sold it) and reading books from the library. Our memorable evening at the diner was in 1943, which turned out to be a remarkable season for the Yankees. They won their fourteenth American League pennant and then beat the St. Louis Cardinals in five games for their tenth World Series' win. And they did it without Joltin' Joe DiMaggio, who was fighting in the war.

Another remarkable event took place in the summer of 1943 when we boarded the Pullman train and went straight to Hartford, Connecticut. We went to see my beloved Uncle Henry, and I met Aunt Olga for the first time. Uncle Henry had met us at the station and drove us to 55 Forest Street, next door to where Samuel Clemens (whose pen name was Mark Twain) lived. He was a longtime friend and confidant of the Perkins family. Day-

Day hadn't been joking when he told me that while I was reading *The Adventures of Huckleberry Finn*.

Uncle Henry and Aunt Olga's mansion enthralled me—it was the kind you read about in storybooks. So this is where Day-Day and Uncle Henry grew up! During that trip, I first learned about Day-Day's early life before becoming a missionary, dedicating himself to the Chinese people. Uncle Henry told me the story.

Day-Day had been a poor little rich kid, a dashing young man. He didn't know what to do with his life, and squandered away his time and his fortune. After that, he was just lost, even attempting suicide. One evening in around 1904, Day-Day roamed the streets of Kingston, New York, a hundred miles upriver from Yonkers. He had just helped a friend move there and, not knowing what to do, decided to find a church and talk to a pastor. It was pouring rain, and all the churches were closed except one he'd passed earlier that he thought might be too sophisticated. The pastor and his family were there, offering refuge for anyone who needed it on a stormy night.

My father, tall and handsome, in his late twenties, was soaked to the bone. His clothes were so drenched, a puddle formed where he stood inside the church. He was about to retreat when the pastor reached out, saying "Welcome, stranger, we're about to start our family prayer meeting. Do join us."

Hesitantly, he walked to where the family was gathered. The pastor introduced himself as Rev. Philip Watters, and then his family, including his eight-year-old daughter, Hyla Watters. To digress, Dr. Hyla Watters became a missionary physician and was stationed at Wu-Hu General Hospital (芜湖总医院), downriver from Kiukiang. "Hyla Doc," as she was known, always called Day-Day "Big brother (大哥: pronounced *da-ge*)" in Chinese. Years later, I would call her Aunt Hyla.

After that night, Day-Day became a member of the Watters

family. Rev. Watters asked him to attend a ten-day revival service, and Day-Day accepted, adding, "If I don't find what I'm looking for, I will find peace in death." Rev. Watters thought that a bit dramatic.

With this attitude, Day-Day attended the revival. As each day ended, Rev. Watters asked if he felt any different, and my father admitted, sadly, that he hadn't found what he was looking for. As the last day of the revival came to an end, Day-Day was profoundly depressed. He headed toward a cliff along the Hudson River, determined to end his misery. As he walked along the trail, he saw a poster that said, "The Spirit and the bride say, 'Come!' And let him who hears say, 'Come!' Whoever is thirsty, let him come; and whoever wishes, let him take the gift of the water of life," from Revelation 22:17. Day-Day made an about-face and ran to find Rev. Watters. When he saw him, he asked excitedly, "Does 'Whoever' include me?"

Rev. Watters assured him that it did, and Day-Day wept for joy. Then and there, he knew what he wanted to do with his life. He would go to medical school and become a missionary in India. Later a friend convinced him to go to China instead. In 1910, on his first trip to China, he fell in love with Kiukiang and its people.

Not long after, Day-Day met and fell in love with Georgina M. Phillip, a beautiful lassie from Edinburgh, Scotland. Miss Phillip turned out to be Aunt Hyla's Sunday School teacher. Edward and Georgina were married on June 15, 1916, and they sailed to China for their honeymoon. They settled in Kiukiang and built the Water of Life Hospital. Fifteen years later, I became their adopted Chinese daughter.

During that unforgettable visit to Connecticut, a maid in a black uniform with a white starched collar and cuffs answered the door to Uncle Henry and Aunt Olga's house. She looked just like a maid in the books I'd read about little rich girls in mansions. But in the books, the maids were never happy. Books are books, and this was my Uncle Henry's Hartford home, so I was sure their maids must be satisfied because Uncle Henry and Aunt Olga were so kind. Their situation wasn't that different from our life in Kiukiang, with amahs, butlers, and cooks.

As we entered their house, Aunt Olga was smiling and invited us to join her for the noon meal. She was a frail and tiny woman who spoke with a faint Danish accent (I imagined). I knew she'd come from Denmark and had been an actress. Uncle Henry kissed the top of her head, and we went upstairs to freshen ourselves. Then we had lunch with Aunt Olga, and I could tell she wasn't doing well.

Uncle Henry was always full of fun. The twinkle never seemed to leave his eyes. He had been a highly respected physics professor at Trinity College in Hartford and at some point was also the school's president. During lunch, I learned that I had two American cousins, Henry Jr. and Evelyn, both much older than I. Neither was home that day; perhaps they were away at college.

Then, as I was only twelve, they left me alone to amuse myself while the grownups talked about old times and everything else they wanted. So I roamed freely, exploring their mansion. When I entered the library, I came upon rows of photos on the wall and the desk. I looked at them intently and wondered who they were. Some were photos of Day-Day with Uncle Henry, and also Aunt Olga. Then I heard a knock. It was Aunt Olga.

"Interested in those family photos?" she asked as she walked in. "Yes, there's our older son, Harry. We call him Harry instead of Junior. He's an electrical engineer; he lives in Schenectady. You'll love Harry. Like his dad, a very humorous man."

After a brief pause, Aunt Olga picked up another frame and said, "That's Evelyn's family."

"She already has a family?" I asked, surprised.

Aunt Olga chuckled. "Yes, your cousins are much older than you. Let me see, that's her husband, Amyas Ames. He works in Washington, DC, and is helping President Roosevelt with the war planning. And these four darlings are my grandchildren. Oakes is now twelve; he's your age; Ned is three years younger. And these two lovely angels are Olivia and Joanie. Aren't they cute? Evvie takes good care of them. They are living on Long Island now. Maybe one of these days, we'll take you to see them."

Aunt Olga put down the Ames family photo. "Help yourself rummaging through anything you find fascinating," she said. "Otherwise, things are just collecting dust here." Then she slowly walked to the door. It was evident that she was frail. I had just met my entire American family through photographs. I couldn't get over how dashing Uncle Henry had been, and how beautiful Aunt Olga was.

I also remember meeting a pretty young woman named Lucy, I think, who shared her bedroom with me while we visited. She told me she was attending Vassar College, and I was so impressed that I declared to Mother, "I will go to Vassar someday." Mother smiled and told me that my cousin Evelyn had also graduated from Vassar. Evelyn Perkins Ames went on to become a well-known author and poet.

Little did I know that this would be the last time I'd see any of them.

17

IN THE FALL of 1943, I entered the sixth grade at Public School No. 16, and with a new homeroom teacher, Miss Ryan, I began to enjoy studying. She made everything exciting and easy to understand. For geography, we made a map of South America out of cookie dough. Playing with food was fun, and then we had to read and learn more about the countries of South America. We learned without being pressured to memorize. And of course, it helped that I had passed through South America on our journey to America. The American way of learning was much more suitable for me. And most of all, Miss Ryan cared about us as individuals and made it fun to study.

When one of my classmates in sixth grade got a "permanent" wave on her hair, I wanted one too. Feather cuts were in fashion, and I thought they looked pretty and natural, but what I got from Mother was a flat "no."

"Jeanie," she said, "you were born with straight hair, and that is the way your hair is staying. Your straight, black hair is beautiful."

One weekend, when Mother and Day-Day had to be away for fundraising, I told them I was too old to have a babysitter. Although I liked Audrey and she even gave me goodnight kisses, she was only two years older than I was. The whole thing seemed silly. So, Mother asked our pastor's wife if I could stay with them. Mrs. Churchill agreed, and it was certainly an eventful weekend.

On the first night, Mrs. Churchill asked, "Jean, would you let me curl your hair?"

"Oh, no, Mother wouldn't let me, Mrs. Churchill," I answered.

"Don't worry, Jean. The way I do it, your hair will be straight by the time your parents get home." So I consented, with a slightly guilty feeling.

After I washed my hair, Mrs. Churchill tore strips of cloth and twisted my long hair so she could roll it close to my head. As I looked in the mirror, all I could see were big white knots. It was uncomfortable, physically and mentally. That was the first time I knowingly did something I'd been told not to.

The next day, Mrs. Churchill undid the strips of cloth and, lo and behold, to her credit and skill, I thought my hair looked pretty for the first time in my life. It hung down my back and shoulders in long curls, just like Betty's! But I felt so guilty I asked Mrs. Churchill if she could straighten my hair immediately.

"Oh, yes," she assured me. "All you have to do is to get your hair wet and comb the curls out." She patted on my shoulder and laughed as she walked away.

The next morning, I did what Mrs. Churchill suggested, but there were still plenty of waves in it, and when I saw Jill and Betty that Sunday, they noticed a slight difference but couldn't quite pinpoint it.

Later that night, my parents came home. I quickly confessed to relieve my guilt. To my surprise, Mother didn't scold me. Instead, she said, "I guess it's all right if you want to curl your hair, but only with curlers, no permanents."

So I did. The first time I curled my hair with curlers, I got a photo taken at a studio. I didn't do as well as Mrs. Churchill, but it was the beginning of something new and different!

Shortly after New Year's Day, Mother and Day-Day dropped a bombshell. They were selling our home, and we would be moving to South Yonkers to stay at the home of Mother's friend, an old classmate. Later I learned that we were struggling financially, and even with help from Uncle Henry and Aunt Olga, we were unable to make ends meet. After hearing the news, I tossed and turned all night. I tried to think of a positive side to leaving our beautiful North Yonkers home, but I couldn't come up with a single reason, except maybe getting away from the neighbor's dog. Leaving our home would mean leaving PS 16 and especially Miss Ryan, and tears began to fill the corners of my eyes. Moving to South Yonkers would force us to change churches, too. "Where will we store our furniture and all these photos of Grandma and Grandpa when we sell the house?" I thought.

I lay in bed sleepless, listening to Day-Day's supersonic snoring, wondering how Mother could have slept all these years. I didn't dare get up. The house was old and the floor squeaked, so I feared waking Mother up. A flood of memories kept me awake. To a thirteen-year-old, two years is a long time. I thought this would be our home at least till the war was over and we returned to China. Over the past two years, I'd changed a lot. "I'm now an all-American kid," I said to myself. "My life will never be the same again in South Yonkers."

The next morning, sleep-deprived, I stumbled into the study, where we often sat to listen to the radio. I loved listening to the news, which told us about the war, and I looked forward to storytelling programs. I listened to baseball games when I had permission from Mother. She was surprised and mystified by how much I knew about the game. I also enjoyed the music of Bing Crosby, Bob Hope, and Frank Sinatra. The song I loved most was "I'm Dreaming of a White Christmas." These became my parents' favorites too. On Christmas Day 1943, Day-Day had given me two Bing Crosby records, "White Christmas" and "I'll Be Home for Christmas"! We had a gramophone that Mother

JEAN TREN-HWA PERKINS

would occasionally bring out so we could listen to these beautiful melodies, and I would listen to them endlessly.

Just months earlier the aunties wrote that Chum would be singing on the radio during the *Children's Bible Hour,* broadcast nationally from Grand Rapids. Mother, Day-Day, and I huddled close to our wireless and heard Chum's still childish but beautiful soprano voice. We were so proud of her! Mother looked at me wistfully, as if to say, "I wish you could sing a solo someday too!" She tried her best, but I was too shy. I did eventually join the church's junior choir but ended up giggling because I was so nervous.

I presumed the radio would be sold along with the house, so I quietly whispered, "Goodbye, radio. You've given me so much pleasure. I'll miss you a lot!"

I went to the kitchen and gave Mother a big hug. Day-Day always kissed me on the top of my head, never on my face. He hardly ever hugged me, even though I know he loved me just as much. He didn't like to touch females. I thought that's why he had established the Water of Life Hospital only for men. I didn't understand that it was because there was no men's hospital in Kiukiang at the time.

Since no one seemed to care for my presence, I walked back into the living room, thinking of playing the piano. There wouldn't be many more chances to play, because the piano surely wouldn't be coming with us. As I sat on the bench, I thought about how much I had disappointed Mother.

Shortly after we arrived in Yonkers, Marie and I began piano lessons with Mrs. McCracken. We went to her home together. At the time, I didn't realize how rude and ungrateful I was acting. Mrs. McCracken, a sweet, gentle woman, would sit on the piano bench next to me, and I couldn't stand the smell of her perfume. So I asked her to sit further away. She did, but I continued to complain, and finally, she went to the back of the room and shouted the instructions. I was just eleven, but that was no excuse for such rudeness.

Marie quit piano lessons after a year, because she felt she had too much homework. I didn't want to go to Mrs. McCracken's alone, and besides, she asked us to practice two hours a day, which was unfathomable for me. So I screwed up the courage and told Mother, "I think it's a waste of money to give me piano lessons, because I'm not musically talented like Chum."

Mother looked surprised, then hurt, and said, "I am disappointed to hear this, Honey, because I had hoped you might someday do evangelistic work for your people, and knowing how to play the piano or organ would be a great asset. It's not a waste of money when it's for a good cause, and it isn't about talent." What could I say? I had a stubborn streak. To this day, I regret quitting piano lessons and acting disrespectfully toward Mrs. McCracken.

I found myself sitting at the piano, my fingers refusing to move. So I decided to try something I could manage, "Home, Sweet Home." Hearing me, Mother and Day-Day rushed to the living room to join in the singing! Suddenly the cloud lifted, and I realized that as long as we were together, our home would be wherever we are.

The next week at school, Miss Ryan told me, "Jean, I know you're upset about leaving PS 16, so I talked to the principal, and she'll allow you to continue attending and graduate from here, even after you move to South Yonkers."

I was thrilled but puzzled. "How can I get to school from South Yonkers?" I asked.

"I live in South Yonkers, and I'll pick you up every morning and take you home every afternoon."

What a caring person! I felt like hugging her, something I'd never done with anyone outside my family. I refrained because I wasn't sure it would be proper for a student to embrace her teacher. Instead, I said with a big smile, "Thank you, Miss Ryan!" I skipped off to tell Jill and Betty, and we hugged each other with joy!

While the sadness of moving out of 6 Arthur Place lingered, the ensuing months went by quickly. I'll never forget Miss Ryan, as she drove me to and from school every day. On my last day at PS 16, Miss Ryan got the whole class to sign an autograph book for me. I graduated from the sixth grade with the class I had come to know and love so much. Mother had left her camera in Kiukiang, hidden in the attic. Fortunately, Jill's mother took many photos of graduation day. Marie came to our graduation party at Jill's house that evening, and of course Betty was there too. The three of them gave me a Frank Sinatra record, "You'll Never Know," as a going-away present.

As time went on, I often read the childish writings from the autograph book, and Jill's mother's photos helped me remember the faces of my dear classmates. But these were all tragically lost during a life-changing transition later in my life.

My sixth-grade graduation photo at Yonkers Public School No. 16, ca. 1944

18

THE SUMMER of 1944 came too quickly. My room at the home owned by Mother's friend was a cubbyhole in the attic compared to the one I'd had in North Yonkers. My parents' quarters were on the second floor, facing the street. They had plenty of windows, but no river view. I'd been spoiled living in big houses, even in Kiukiang, and this place was suffocating. To make matters worse, we had to share the second-floor bathroom with the landlady's live-in boyfriend. I didn't understand what "live-in boyfriend" meant, and Mother never explained. The man was polite but sharing a bathroom with any stranger was most inconvenient.

My parents' room also served as our living and dining room. We ate breakfast and lunch there, and for supper, we went to a nearby boarding house run by two sisters. I wished we could eat at home and not with strangers, but the people who ate there were consistent and courteous, and we soon become friends. The food was scrumptious, and one woman who ate there turned out to be my math teacher at the next school.

The older of the two sisters was blind. Although she didn't know what I looked like, she took a real liking to me. I was an odd kid, I guess, as I disliked being kissed, especially gushed over with saliva. This blind lady *showered* me with kisses all over my face. One day to avoid this onslaught of lovingness, I stayed quiet as I walked in and sat next to Mother. But nothing escaped the elder sister. Since she hadn't heard my voice, she asked, "Is Jean *not* here tonight?"

JEAN TREN-HWA PERKINS

Mother nudged me, and reluctantly I got up from my seat and walked to her to receive my daily love bath. As she kissed me to her heart's content, my stomach turned somersaults and I lost my appetite. Years later, when boys tried to kiss me, my reaction was the same. I've always been kiss-phobic.

After moving to South Yonkers, we didn't have much of a home life or time to relax. I hated dressing up for dinner. I would have preferred wearing pajamas at home. I saw much less of Day-Day. I worried that he might miss my sixth-grade graduation, but of course, he didn't. He only hugged me once in my life, and it was on that occasion. Day-Day continued working at various hospitals, such as Seaview Hospital, a tuberculosis sanitorium on Staten Island, and New York Post-Graduate Medical School and Hospital, which today is the New York University School of Medicine. He even took classes in public health at Yale twice a week. I laughed when Mother told me, "The last thing Day-Day needs is another degree. He has studied law, religion, and medicine." She smiled and added, "That's your Day-Day, forever trying to learn new things and new ways, especially in medicine. Day-Day never gets tired of that. He's always excited about learning. Frankly, dear, you and I should be more like him." I knew what Mother meant, and I accepted the challenge.

I missed my friends from North Yonkers. "What are Jill, Betty, and Marie doing at this moment?" I often wondered. I lived too far away to know. We didn't have a car, so to amuse myself, I remembered the good times we'd had together. With a sigh, I closed *David Copperfield*, which was my summer reading assignment. I enjoyed this book and read it in bed till two or three in the morning. I didn't understand every word but reading such a big book was an accomplishment for a thirteen-year-old. But that day, I couldn't continue.

SPRING FLOWER: A TALE OF TWO RIVERS

I peered through the tiny bay window of my attic bedroom to see what the weather was. Since Mother and Day-Day sold our radio and gramophone, we had no music, weather reports, or news. I felt flustered and frazzled. I walked down the narrow stairway to my parents' room on the second floor to look out their window. Just as I'd expected, it was dreary out. "What a dumb place to be," I complained.

I went to the living room on the first floor and turned on the landlady's radio without permission. My mood improved as I tried to listen to baseball games, remembering that beautiful night with Day-Day at the diner near Yankee Stadium. Then I looked at the clock and wondered, "Where are Mother and Day-Day? Don't they know I'm starving?" Suddenly, I heard them coming through the door. I leaped from the chair, turned off the radio, and flew to the second floor to wait for them. As they were coming up the stairs, they looked thrilled to see me, even though I was pouting, "Where have you been? I'm hungry."

A family photo at Lake George – Silver Bay, ca. 1943

They'd been raising funds for the Methodist Missionary Society and their beloved hospital in Kiukiang.

"Honey," Mother said, "we have good news. Day-Day has been accepted as the campus doctor for the summer at Silver Bay, just like last summer. So we'll be going to Lake George again!" Working at Silver Bay was another odd job Day-Day took to support us during our time in the US.

"Oh, boy!" I shouted, my face now all smiles. "When do we leave? I can't wait to get out of town!" Then I asked, "Will we be able to visit Uncle Henry and Aunt Olga on our way, like last year?"

"Not this time, Jeanie. Aunt Olga isn't well." Day-Day sounded pensive. The news was disappointing, and Aunt Olga's frail figure flashed before my eyes. But for a thirteen-year-old, going back to Silver Bay was no less exciting.

I began packing, hoping the two friends I'd made there last summer would be back again. One friend, a Chinese girl named Juju, was a year younger than I. It was the first time I was with a Chinese person in America. She had a three-year-old brother they called Di-Di (弟弟), which means "younger brother." It seemed odd to call him Di-Di instead of by his proper name, but that must have been his nickname.

Juju and I got along fine speaking English. I had a hard time understanding her parents, who spoke Cantonese, the language of Guangdong Province and a foreign language to me. Each province in China has a unique dialect. Sometimes traveling twenty miles is like going to a different country, because the language is difficult to understand.

Juju was small, but not shy. She liked playing rough — shoving and pushing. She was even more of a tomboy than I was. We both loved to swim, but neither of us had had lessons. We watched those who knew proper swimming and tried to imitate them, but mostly we just had fun. We threw pebbles into the deep end of the pool and then swam underwater to pick them up. I never mastered the art of diving. Each time I tried, water went up my nose, and it hurt. We enjoyed doing cannonballs from the diving board, making a huge splash when we hit the water.

I had just turned twelve, and I could feel the changes in my body. Sometimes Juju would push me right in the chest, and I'd feel excruciating pain. I was clueless about what it was, so I tried to avoid her pushes as much as I could. I thought I might be getting an infection, but I was too embarrassed to ask my parents.

I investigated myself, and to my horror, two little bumps had appeared on my chest, and they hurt when I touched them. As the summer went on, the pain increased, and these two strange things got bigger. Although I knew Mother had breasts, it hadn't occurred to me that this could happen to me. "They're disgusting," I thought. I didn't dare tell anyone, fearing I was ill and might die young.

I began to hunch my shoulders, hoping they wouldn't show. I wore dresses that were loose in front. I'd always wanted to wear a polo shirt as Betty did, but when I finally got one — with Silver Bay written across the chest — I didn't dare wear it for fear that these things would show. I couldn't resist going in the water, so I still wore my bathing suit, which luckily was the wrinkle type where nothing showed. But I was deeply unhappy with this unexpected turn of events. I'd always wished I'd been a boy, and now all the more so. Mother didn't seem to notice, or if she did, she didn't say anything. So I just kept hunching over more and more to keep these things as inconspicuous as possible.

The other friend I met at Silver Bay was Phyllis. People never got tired of commenting on our contrasting hair colors. Phyllis's was blond and mine was raven black, as the grownups put it. We were both shy, and yet we both loved to act. She was a year older than I. On rainy days we would play in my room, pretending we were actresses, and we were both in love with the same invisible Mr. Bird. We spoke with British accents to make it sound professional, and we'd laugh and have a great time. I decided I wanted to be an actress someday if I could muster the courage. Child stars Elizabeth Taylor and Margaret O'Brien, who had lost her front teeth, were my favorites, although I still had never seen a movie.

JEAN TREN-HWA PERKINS

"Jean, are you daydreaming again? Are you packed and ready for the trip? You're so quiet." It was never a good sign when Mother called me Jean. Hearing her admonitory tone, I stopped daydreaming, which had been much too frequent as of late. Then, suddenly, she walked in. "I knew it, darling, you haven't finished packing yet. We're leaving early tomorrow! Please get it done now so we can head to the boarding house for an early dinner. We need to retire early tonight!" I knew she meant business, so my suitcase was packed within minutes.

The next morning, we were in high spirits as we boarded the Pullman train for Albany. As the train raced along the tracks, my excitement mounted, looking forward to hikes in the woods where, the previous summer, I had learned about wild blueberries, blackberries, and strawberries. I already knew about raspberries because they grew on Ku-Ling Mountain. One time in China, I made a raspberry dessert mixing berries with milk, butter, and sugar. I thought it would be great, but the butter didn't fit at all. In the woods around Silver Bay, I loved chewing the wild peppermint and wintergreen leaves as we hiked.

Besides hoping to see old friends again, I looked forward to attending the crafts workshop where last summer I'd made a pair of moccasins. I pretended they were loafers, which were in style at the time.

My train of thoughts came to a screeching halt when the conductor shouted, "Albany!" The excitement of seeing Silver Bay kept me in high spirits. We got off the train, hopped onto an Adirondack Trailways bus, and the three of us headed toward

Juju and I at Lake George – Silver Bay, ca. 1944

the resort.

Our rooms were the same as the previous summer. I unpacked quickly, put on my shorts, and headed for the log cabin where Juju had stayed last time. Sure enough, her whole family was there, and it was a joyful reunion. I had grown more than Juju had, Di-Di was less of a baby, and Juju didn't push or punch me anymore. We still loved to swim and dive for pebbles and make huge cannonball splashes. Then I went back to the resort motel to search for Phyllis, and indeed, she was there too. It was a joyful reunion, and we continued acting with "Mr. Bird."

Each morning, Mother and I would pick wildflowers and place them on the dining room tables before people arrived for breakfast. I loved breakfasts; there was always melon to savor. I loved the waiters and waitresses when they sang, "We are the Emps of Silver Bay. The place we love so well. The people always shout whenever we go out: 'Here come the Emps of Silver Bay.' Tra la la la la, We are the...." I wanted to be exactly like them when I grew to be their age and I would earn my way through college. I wasn't allowed to dance, but I loved watching the Emps dance and sing at the clubhouse. It was more listening than watching, because they would stay up late into the night and I could hear them from my bed.

Another highlight of being at Silver Bay was watching movies in the auditorium. At last, Mother and Day-Day let me see moving pictures. Most of the films shown were homemade, people on their family trips, but there were some children's movies with Charlie Chaplin and Shirley Temple. Shirley Temple was no stranger to me. I had many paper dolls of her back in Kiukiang. And I got to see one movie my parents wouldn't have approved of, the 1942 comedy *Road to Morocco,* starring Bob Hope and Bing Crosby, my favorite singers. When I began Nathaniel Hawthorne Junior High in September, the assignment for composition class

JEAN TREN-HWA PERKINS

was to write about the best movie we saw during the summer. So, I was lucky that I saw *Road to Morocco*.

Our vacation ended with a big step for me. I'd wanted to be a babysitter for a while, and Mother found a couple near our hotel who needed a sitter for one night. I was thirteen with no experience. Mother took me to their house, then she left. When the baby's young mother was going, she said, "The money is on the shelf above the fireplace. If I'm away for two hours, take fifty cents. If it's three hours, take all seventy-five cents." I watched the clock, and when the mother came home, she'd been gone for just under two hours. but I took all seventy-five cents.

Mother came to meet me to walk me home, and she asked, "How much did they pay you?" I told her the rule. "Well, how much did you take?" she asked.

"Seventy-five cents," I said.

Mother turned right around and said, in no uncertain terms, "You go right back and return the extra twenty-five cents you didn't earn!"

Without a peep, I ran back and knocked on the door. The baby's mother looked surprised. "My mother told me to return twenty-five cents," I explained, "because I didn't babysit for three hours." She was surprised and said, "Oh, honey, it's quite all right, but thank you for your honesty. You can keep it." I laid it back on top of the fireplace and thanked her before running out as fast as possible. It was my first and last babysitting job.

We were always the last to leave Silver Bay, because Day-Day wanted to be sure that no one needed medical care before leaving. Mother suggested, "Before we head home, let's take a ferry around Lake George and enjoy the last of the summer light. We might even see a few colorful leaves on the trees."

"That's a great idea," I said. "Thank you! Maybe I'll sneeze less while we're on the lake." During our last days at Silver Bay, my hay fever had kicked in. I never had hay fever in China.

"Maybe it's the goldenrod," Day-Day suggested while we were on the ferry. "I never noticed goldenrod in China."

"I hope I get better when we get to Yonkers," I said.

"Hopefully, so. The City has fewer wildflowers," Mother said.

"Lake George is so beautiful. I hope we come again next year," I sighed. No one seemed to hear me, so I sighed again. Still no response, so I took one last look at this beautiful lake while the ferry headed back to the dock.

At last, we boarded the Pullman train and rode home, and to our surprise we were on the same coach as Eleanor Roosevelt, the First Lady of the United States.

Mother whispered, "Jean, don't look around, but Mrs. Roosevelt is sitting behind us." Pretending to stretch my neck, I turned my head and caught a glimpse of her. She was absorbed in a book and didn't lift her head. I was awestruck by the experience. America's First Lady was traveling on her own in the coach during wartime. Perhaps she was on her way to Hyde Park. Less than a year later, with the war still going on, the Pullman train was used to transport President Roosevelt's body to his home one last time. I seemed to have a way of running into world leaders, first Chiang Kai-Shek and now Eleanor Roosevelt. I often seem to be in the right place at the right time.

19

I WAS ANXIOUS about starting a new school with a whole class of strangers. But as soon as I met my homeroom teacher, Mrs. Eaton, my concerns melted away. She was the Miss Ryan type. Mrs. Eaton cared about her "brood" of kids as a group and individually. We all came from different elementary schools, where we had stayed in one classroom the whole day, studying all subjects with one teacher. Mrs. Eaton knew we'd be baffled by the junior high school system.

"First of all, welcome to Nathaniel Hawthorne Junior High!" she said, emphatically. I could feel the tension in the air relax at the sound of her motherly voice. "Unlike grade school, classes here are held in different rooms with different teachers," she continued. "As you can see, I've written out your schedule on the blackboard. Please copy it onto the card on your desk. When you finish, I'll take you on a tour of the school."

An arm shot up. "Yes?" she asked.

"Where do we go if there is no class?"

"Good question. You come back to this room, number 215, which is your home room. I'll always be here to answer your questions." Worried faces broke into smiles, and we were invited to introduce ourselves. Again, I was the only non-white. Looking around, Mrs. Eaton spotted me and said, "We have one student from a foreign country. China, right?"

My face blushed with embarrassment, but I did manage to nod my head.

A boy called Jacob immediately stood up, "I—uh came from Poland," he said.

Another girl, who soon became my best friend, called Doris C., said, "My parents came from Czechoslovakia."

Mrs. Eaton said, "Great, children; this is what America is all about. I hope you will all do your very best and become an outstanding class, one I can be proud of."

Hawthorne Junior High was a big school, and we weren't the only seventh graders. Many homeroom classes were part of the seventh grade, and this was true for eighth and ninth grades too. I enjoyed Hawthorne immediately. My eyes opened to new levels of knowledge and a new world I had no idea existed.

Science was fascinating, and the terms hydrogen and oxygen were utterly new to me. Literature and composition strengthened my desire to become a writer. Home economics showed me that cooking can be fun, but sadly, only how to make French toast and peanut brittle stayed in my mind.

Miss Krautz, the teacher who ate her dinners at the same boarding house we did, made math easy to understand. She was strict but for some reason insisted I was talented in math and told my parents so. Every time someone the class couldn't solve a math problem, she looked at me and said, "I'm sure Jean can solve it!" I would then quake in my boots and stare at my desk to avoid eye contact. I was nowhere as good as she thought, and her calling on me made me nervous. I managed to solve math problems for homework because I could take my time, and there was always a feeling of satisfaction when I got the right answer. But talented? No. Hard-working would be more accurate. Suddenly, I began to love to study.

I never cared for gym, though you'd think a tomboy like me would love gym classes, but I never liked running around indoors and I never got good at team sports, even though I was

JEAN TREN-HWA PERKINS

Doris C. and her little sister at their South Yonkers home

always running or walking with a bounce in my step.

Doris C. lived near us, and she'd come by every morning to walk to school together. She had asked me to come to her house many times, but Mother forbade me from going to homes where she didn't know the parents. I felt bad, but Doris C. was a sport, and we got along just fine. As we got to know each other better, I learned she did chemical experiments at home but disliked reading and literature. One day I said, "Let's go to the library. I'll show you what I like to read, and maybe you'll get interested too." She agreed, and I introduced her to *Little Women*, *Little Men*, and *Uncle Tom's Cabin*.

"I'd rather read stories about horses or dogs," she said, after thumbing through the books I'd recommended.

"Okay, let's look for them," I said.

We did, and pretty soon, Doris C. started to love to read, especially books about dogs. Reading broadened her horizons, although she did end up becoming a chemist.

Doris C. was much more independent than I was. One day

she said, "Let's take the subway to Manhattan on Saturday."

"Can you find your way back?" I asked anxiously, wondering at the same time whether Mother would allow me to go. To my astonishment, Mother consented, but at the last minute I declined. I wasn't really sure Doris would know how to get back.

Living in South Yonkers wasn't that bad, after all. We were closer to the shopping center. As a thirteen-year-old, I got an allowance of twenty-five cents a week! I was becoming a real American teenager. I usually spent my money on comic books, which were ten cents each. My favorites were "Bugs Bunny," "Donald Duck," and "Dagwood." I didn't like the violent ones. How did my parents allow me to read comics? Well, it went back to North Yonkers. Each Sunday after church, we'd visit the Wadsworths, who had been friends of my parents and also of Mother's parents. On Sundays, we didn't work, study, or read most regular books, but I could read Sunday school papers, the Bible, and books like *Little Women*.

The Wadsworths always had the Sunday newspaper on their coffee table, in plain sight, especially the colorful comic pages right at the top! The grownup talk was mostly dull, and when I wasn't dozing after a big lunch, my eyes would wander to the comics. Even from afar, I could make out some of the images and words. One Sunday, Mr. Wadsworth noticed me doing this, and he asked, "Jean, do you like to read the funnies?"

My eyes brightened. "Oh, yes!" I answered. I looked toward Mother for approval. Her expression was hard to describe, a mixture of surprise, disapproval, disappointment, and confusion, which I chose to interpret as, "All right, kiddo." Bravely, I picked out the comic pages and soon immersed myself in "Bugs Bunny." From then on, I looked forward to our Sunday visits with the Wadsworths.

While living in South Yonkers, I loved to roam in the 5-and-

JEAN TREN-HWA PERKINS

dimes. I looked at the dresses, visualizing my grandma doing the same when Christmas or my birthday came around. Perhaps Grandpa browsed among the toys to see if there were things I might like to play with. I bought some curlers and even had my photo taken after I curled my hair. Mother and I loved going together to Woolworths, which had *everything*. Life in America seemed grand.

One girl in our class would wear the same dress week after week, then one day she came to the class wearing a new dress, and we were so happy for her. A few weeks later, she disappeared. Her home address was near ours, so Mrs. Eaton asked Doris C. and me if we would visit her to see if she was okay. After searching awhile, we found her apartment, knocked and knocked, and finally a woman cautiously opened the door to a bare and cold apartment. We presumed she was our classmate's mother.

"Our teacher asked us to see if your daughter is okay." Her mother didn't speak English, and we didn't find out anything. We told Mrs. Eaton what we'd seen. A few years later, Doris C. wrote to me that the girl had run away. It was the first time I had a glimpse of less-fortunate people in America. I had thought China was the only country that had poor people.

One morning in December 1944, I woke up to find myself soaked in blood. I was terrified; I had no idea what was going on. Then I remembered when I was about nine overhearing some older girls talking about how scared they were when blood came oozing out of them, and it made a big impression on me.

Mother had bought me a box of Kotex not long before, but all she said was, "Jean, you may need these someday." She didn't provide any explanation. In Mother's generation, you didn't talk about these things. So I locked myself in the bathroom, and with my hands trembling, I tried to figure out how to use one of these things. I had a trillion questions, but I didn't dare ask. How long was I going to bleed like this? Can I go to school without it soaking through my pants? When do I change it? Will it hold all day?

I quietly washed my pajamas and sheets, put them on the radiator to dry, and went off to school in a panic. At school, I couldn't concentrate on anything the teachers were saying. It was such a relief to finally get back home. Mother had guessed by seeing the washed items, and so we did have a talk, which made things much better for me. I decided right then and there that if I ever had kids, I would tell them way ahead of time to prepare them for what to expect, even though I didn't have the faintest idea how children were born or if boys used Kotex.

20

SEVENTH GRADE was much more fun than I'd anticipated. Time was flying, and I had fully begun to embrace new friends and our new home. It was a wonderful school year, and I was starting to believe I was pretty smart, or at least more intelligent than people gave me credit for. I even began to dream of becoming a writer. I enjoyed each of my classes and looked forward to starting drama classes in the eighth grade. Then, suddenly, my dreams and hopes were shattered.

Sunday, April 29, 1945, was an unforgettable day. The Italians surrendered to the Allies and executed Mussolini and his Nazi compatriots. Berlin was on fire, while the Red Army was closing in. The Allies uncovered the atrocities of the concentration camps, and Hitler's full surrender seemed a matter of days away.

In my own little world, I turned fourteen and had one month to go before finishing seventh grade. We had a fantastic lunch after church, and Day-Day offered me a piece of cake with ice cream. After lunch, I was diligently studying at the table when Mother began speaking. "The war will soon be over," she said, "and Day-Day and I have decided to go back to China."

I was speechless. There was nothing I could do or say, and even if I could, it was too late. I hated when we had to leave North Yonkers, but this was far worse.

"We're called to continue our work in China," Mother continued, "and we'll leave sometime in May. Don't tell anyone, not even your closest friends. We'll be going on a naval battleship, and it's top secret."

That night, I wept. "Don't Mother and Day-Day care how I feel? Don't they know I've become an American teenager?" Then I started to feel guilty that I might love my own people less than my American parents did. They were Americans, but they had such strong affection for China and her people. Maybe they were Chinese in a past life, I thought. I'd been reading about reincarnation in some books at the library. And I knew full well that without the boundless affection of Mother and Day-Day, I could never have survived.

Mother said we'd be going via India, that we would fly over the Himalayas and enter China from the west. I felt utterly listless, and the word *India* kept going round and round in my mind. Fear of jungles, snakes, elephants, tigers, and monkeys overwhelmed any sparks of joy I might feel about returning to China and seeing my childhood friends again. "Why India?" I kept asking myself.

It never occurred to me that India might have civilized people. I didn't even think of going to the library to read about India. Instead, I just worried and became extremely unhappy during the days leading up to our dreaded departure. Walking to school with Doris C. became an ordeal; I had to keep this all a big secret. I tried to appear as happy as I could, even as my heart was breaking, but our conversations became shorter and shorter.

Nine days later, on Tuesday, May 8, 1945, I disappeared from Nathaniel Hawthorne Junior High School without a trace. Instead, I was on a huge American battleship—I think it was the *USS Wisconsin* or maybe the *Missouri,* some name from the Midwest—again crossing the vast Atlantic, this time heading to India. From the radios onboard, we learned the world was celebrating the defeat of Nazi Germany. I stood at the rear of the

JEAN TREN-HWA PERKINS

deck leaning against the guardrail, staring in the direction of New York Harbor and my beloved Hudson River. As I watched the land disappear, the sun began to set unceremoniously. By now, Doris C. would surely have found out from our landlady, Mother's friend, that I had left. And soon Jill, Betty, and Marie would receive letters I wrote them from the ship. What a shock this would be for them! I couldn't even see them before leaving.

Tossing and turning on the bunkbed that night, I felt just miserable. Mother sensed it. She tried to cheer me up and gave me a whole dollar to buy anything I wanted at the ship's PX. I bought a dollar's worth of Hershey bars and ate six of them, one after another! Oh, that was a mistake. Now I was both miserable and sick. A few days later, after I felt better, I began roaming around the ship just like three years earlier. But I couldn't begin to compare my emotions now with how I felt on the steamers that brought me to America.

It was a military ship, and there was no swimming pool. Missionary families who worked in India were on board, but most of the passengers were US troops heading out and GI wives with their children going to visit their servicemen husbands. I met one young woman with two adorable children, a boy about three and a girl about two. She was going to Turkey, where her husband's infantry unit was stationed.

After a few weeks' sailing, Mother called to me excitedly. "Jean, come on deck quickly!" I rushed to the deck just in time to see the Strait of Gibraltar, as we began to enter the Alboran Sea, the westernmost part of the Mediterranean. I finally came back to life on this ship. While I was grieving the loss of my life in America, we had crossed the Great Northern Atlantic. There they were—two continents sandwiching our ship. To our left was Spain, and to the right was Morocco. Again, I was reminded of the movie *Road to Morocco*, and I quietly grinned. Such a narrow channel separating two continents!

After days on the Mediterranean, we came to the Suez Canal. Passing through its midway point, we docked at Ismailia and stayed at a place I remember as an Italian prison-of-war camp while waiting for another American naval ship to take us to India. Day-Day suggested we visit Cairo while we were waiting. So we went by bus and saw the Sphinx and the pyramids.

After months at sea, it was now midsummer and boiling hot in Egypt. I was not at all excited by the idea of seeing some ancient stones and bricks piled up in a desert. Seeing my lack of interest, Mother tried to cheer me up. "How often does one have a chance to see an ancient wonder of the world?" So we boarded a filthy, crowded train and ventured forth. The natives seemed used to the discomfort, but my ride on a Pullman train had spoiled me. These seats were hard, and my butt hurt. I didn't like anything about it. Then, all of a sudden, when we stopped at one of the stations along the way, I heard a child's voice outside the window singing "Pistol Packin' Mama." I couldn't believe a native kid in this remote area was singing a song that was still popular in America (even Bing Crosby was singing it)! Had Mother known I could sing it too, I think she would have fainted—and I almost blurted it out. I missed Yonkers so much! Kids don't have to work to learn popular songs. They just pick up lyrics quickly. When I first arrived in America, the first song (by the Pied Pipers) I heard was "Mairzy Doats." Go figure! The world didn't seem so big after all.

We got off the train in Cairo and boarded a dusty bus to see one of the Great Wonders of the World. Boy, was I ever wrong! The poor Sphinx had to have its chin propped up, but it still looked majestic! And the pyramids were breathtaking. We tried to climb the Great Pyramid but couldn't quite make it up.

When we got back, Ismailia was even hotter, so hot that I

went swimming with some American kids in the filthy, disease-infested harbor. Even today, I shudder when I think of it, but it must have been all right because I'm still alive.

The navy ship finally came, and we continued on down the canal, sailing through the biblical Red Sea into the Arabian Sea to complete the last lap of our journey to India. In no time, we docked at the storied city of Bombay. And to my great surprise, no elephants were running wild. There were no jungles either, but sacred cows were roaming the streets and obstructing traffic. It didn't seem to bother drivers or pedestrians. As we walked along the sidewalks, I saw beggars everywhere. And most distressingly, there were hundreds of lepers, many without fingers, toes, or even feet, leaning against the walls. Still-uninfected children crawled all over their parents and played in the dirt. It was shocking. Although I had seen a little poverty in the US, I had no idea there were countries as poor as China. How foolish I'd been to be so scared of India. Now I had only sympathy. And images of China began to creep back into my mind.

We stayed at the Mission House in Bombay. Since I was the only non-adult, the manager of the house told me I could eat ice cream to my heart's content. This trip to India turned out to be heaven on earth! We mostly ate Western food, but sometimes Indian food was served, which I enjoyed.

Even as I was starting to embrace this new world, I was anxious to know when we'd leave India. Mother said we were waiting for a plane to China, over the Himalayas. Then one day, a couple of gentlemen from the Board of Mission asked Day-Day if he could relieve a doctor in India who hadn't had leave in a long time.

They casually added, "The war in China isn't over yet, so you might as well wait here."

As Day-Day walked them out, I became hysterical. "Mother,

why did we leave New York so quickly if China is still fighting Japan?"

Mother acted as if she didn't hear me, so I raised my voice. "What about Chum and the aunties? Have they left America too?"

Mother calmly said, "No, dear, they decided to stay a bit longer."

"Then why couldn't I finish seventh grade?" I began to bite my lips, I was so angry. Mother did not reply.

Before Day-Day first went to China, he'd thought of becoming a missionary in India, so he was glad for the chance to stay in Bombay. Had I known we were going to spend a year in India, I would have begged to spend another year in America. The war was *not* over yet. Later I learned that Aunt Dee and Aunt Bessie had written to Mother: "Dear Georgie, the war in the Pacific is far from over. We hear the Japanese are ignoring calls to surrender and refusing to give up. They have dug their heels in for the long haul with their last-ditch of effort to defend their Mainland, so an Allied invasion of Japan is in play, and that could take quite some energy and time at a terrible cost for Americans. We have no idea where this war is going."

They also told Mother they wanted Chum to complete her junior high and not to have her education continually interrupted. I wished Mother and Day-Day had thought the same for me. Unlike Chum who was in Michigan, I was in India about to enroll in my third school in four years. No one ever asked what I wanted. So, we stayed, and I got to see beautiful fireworks in Bombay celebrating the Allied victory of the war in Europe.

On our third night in Bombay, I had the most severe headache I'd ever had. I thought my head would explode. Mother and Day-Day slept on the only bed, and I slept on the hard floor, which I didn't mind, but with this headache and no pillow, I rolled in agony but made no sound. "What a place to die," I thought. "I

JEAN TREN-HWA PERKINS

left America to die in India. Couldn't I have waited a bit longer to die in my own country?" My mouth was dry, and I did believe I was dying. I began to pray, "Please, God, I don't want to die yet." Finally, I called Mother, "My head hurts terribly, and I am so thirsty." Mother got up quickly and felt my forehead, which was hot to her touch.

"Edward," she said, "wake up! Jean has a high fever." Day-Day got up quickly and, feeling my forehead, he agreed. They put cold towels on my forehead. Mother put her pillow under my head, which made me more comfortable. I drank a lot of water. Day-Day gave me a pill, which was probably aspirin, but the fear of malaria had entered his mind. About then, I decided to put off death and get some sleep. I fell into a deep sleep. Two days later, Day-Day sighed with relief and said it was probably heatstroke or fatigue from traveling. Mother bought me a white hat, and I never had another attack like that again.

One day while we were roaming around Bombay, we noticed people running toward an alley. Curious, we followed the crowd, and we saw an emaciated Indian with legs crossed and hands together in front of him in prayer, sitting on a platform. Day-Day recognized him right away. "That's Mahatma Gandhi," he said. "He's fighting for the rights of the poor, particularly the untouchables, or outcastes.

Walking past Gandhi, ca. 1945

If they touch the food of the other castes or even cast a shadow on it, it will be thrown away, considered contaminated." It was the first time I heard the term *untouchable*. I understood poverty but not the caste system.

Seeing Gandhi was another historical encounter for me. At a later time, we ran into a crowd listening to speeches by Gandhi and Jawaharlal Nehru demanding independence from Britain. Decades later, when I saw the epic movie about Gandhi starring Ben Kingsley, the same chord was struck within me, reminding me of that memorable day.

In late June of 1945, with no sign of the heat letting up in Bombay, the Board of Mission gave Day-Day his assignment in India. He was to begin working immediately at Nadiad, 300 miles north of Bombay. I was to attend the British-run Woodstock School (established in 1854 and still in existence today) in a town called Landour-Mussoorie in the state of Uttarakhand, 700 miles north of Nadiad in the Himalayas and 900 miles northwest of Mount Everest! I'd never been away from home, and Mother was uneasy about my living in a dorm. She got in contact with a family who had been missionaries to China before the Japanese invasion, and they were only too happy to have me board with them. Their children went to the same school. Pleased that I would be in good hands, Mother and I started on our journey to the Himalayas.

21

AFTER TWO LONG days on the train, Mother and I transferred to a muddy bus. Although we'd had a sleeper car on the train, I was exhausted. The bed was hard, and the train rocked all night long. The bus ride was even worse. I got motion sickness as we slowly wound our way up the Himalayas and was grateful I hadn't eaten anything too complicated on the train, mostly just toast. Mother seemed much better. She thought my dizziness might also be due to the altitude. By the time we reached Landour-Mussoorie, we were 7,000 feet above sea level. The view was breathtaking and the campus beautiful, although the air was thin. Woodstock School was only open in the summer and fall. It was closed for winters because it was too frigid in the mountains. So vacation was in winter, when it was warmer on the plains below.

Finally, Mother and I arrived at the home where I would be staying. Mrs. Hall welcomed us and showed me to the guest room, where she introduced her children. Pointing to the boy, she said, "Joe is my second son. He's thirteen."

"Jean just turned fourteen," Mother interjected.

Mrs. Hall smiled. "They certainly grow up fast. Even my baby girl is already nine now. Her name is Phyllis."

Phyllis and I said a casual hello to each other, and soon we became great friends. Joe and I got along well, too. However, the two of them liked to kid me because I wasn't familiar with life in the Himalayas, especially wildlife. A fear of animals gripped my heart when they told me there were bears around.

SPRING FLOWER: A TALE OF TWO RIVERS

"Don't worry, Jean," Joe said. "If they come after you, just run as fast as you can, downhill, because they can't run fast going down, with their big hind legs. They're quick climbing, so don't try to outrun them going uphill."

Luckily, during my half-year in the Himalayas, I never encountered a bear. The one day I did see a pair of shining eyes in the bushes at dusk, I ran indoors in a hurry!

After staying a few days, Mother returned to Nadiad. For the first time in my life, I was all by myself. And once again, I had to adapt to a new school. The system was different from what I had experienced in either China or America, and I can't honestly say I liked it. I resented being placed in the sixth "standard," the British term for grades, which was like repeating sixth grade. And we were in one classroom with one teacher for all subjects except Hindi, which all foreign schools had to teach ever since the independence movement began in India. There was no science or math class. The only useful thing I learned was how to look up references to write an essay. So I wrote about Florence Nightingale.

With friends at Woodstock School, Mussoorie, India, ca. 1945

Home economics was most memorable for me. I learned how to use a sewing machine and made a couple of new skirts, which I desperately needed. We'd left America in such a hurry that Mother hadn't had time to think of getting me larger clothes. I was her first kid, and she didn't realize that I would keep growing. So I hardly had any presentable

JEAN TREN-HWA PERKINS

clothes to wear. After we knew Day-Day was going to stay on in India, Mother and I searched all of Bombay, but we couldn't find anything suitable for a girl my age. Some kids in class knew that I had just come from the "States," and they wondered why I was not fashionable like the other American kids there. The only thing I had to showcase was my blazer, which was still in style.

I remembered my home economics teacher at Nathaniel Hawthorne Junior High saying, "Learn how to sew, Jean. It will be useful one day." At the time, I thought it strange. I planned to be a writer, not someone who could sew clothes. I was beginning to receive the lesson of the ironies of life.

And again, I was the only Chinese in class, but not the only non-white, as there were Indian kids too. I didn't get to know my classmates well, although I still remember a few names. I tried to make friends, but it didn't come as easily as in Yonkers. That was surprising because most of the kids were Americans. Only a few were from England. Perhaps it was because I didn't live in the dorm, so I had less contact with the other kids. Whatever the reason, it wasn't that big a problem because I had joyful times with Joe and Phyllis. I even used rags to curl Phyllis's hair, just as Mrs. Churchill had done with mine.

While in the Himalayans, I saw people dressed in native garb, and they weren't Indian. I asked Joe and Phyllis, and they told me they were Tibetans. I had only a vague idea of where Tibet was.

My half-year at Woodstock finally ended, and although I enjoyed being with the Hall family and playing with Joe and Phyllis, I was ready to leave. I knew I'd miss waking up each morning with the panoramic view of the mountains hiding behind white clouds and the expansive lush, green terrain, not unlike upstate New York. I had become familiar with high altitudes, the outdoors, and the many stairs one had to climb going from building to building.

Mother and I wrote almost every day. This was the last letter I wrote to her from Woodstock:

> My Dear Mother,
>
> The school will be out in one more week, and I will be coming home soon, and I will travel with Nancy and her brother, Patrick. You know them — they are the children of the missionary doctor Day-Day took the place of. They signaled me out a few weeks ago and told me who they were. So, they asked me to tell you not to come here to get me, as they have to go to Nadiad anyway. They believe they know the way well.
>
> I can't wait to see both of you, and where you live in Nadiad! Lots of love and kisses to you both!
>
> Jean

I bade Joe and Phyllis farewell at the bus station and journeyed back to Nadiad with Patrick and Nancy, proud to be traveling without Day-Day and Mother for the first time.

"What a cute little house!" I exclaimed as I walked into our home in Nadiad for the first time. Unlike the pointed roofs in China, these were flat, like pictures I'd seen of houses in Jerusalem. The cook was Indian; I don't remember his name but he was as delightful as Chef Tian and much taller. He understood enough English to know what we

Mother and I in Nadiad, ca. 1946

wanted. He gave me a big, broad welcoming smile. I kidded him by asking, "So, you're the one who was frightened by the big cobra?" He grinned sheepishly.

Indian people believe in reincarnation, so they won't kill anything alive, no matter how dangerous, because it might be one of their ancestors. For white people, killing dangerous animals, or even non-dangerous creatures like deer that eat their crops, is all right. In one of Mother's letters to the Himalayas, she told me how Day-Day had bravely and singlehandedly killed a cobra, and that the cook, as dark-skinned as he was, looked pale watching the struggle between Day-Day and the snake. When I read her letter, I thought, "Mother, how old do you think I am?" I doubted that my father would ever have killed anything except perhaps a fish, and even that was when he was a small boy.

Myth or truth, this house had only two rooms. The smaller half was the living room, where the front door was. The larger half was the bedroom with two beds, the smaller one for me. Connected to the bedroom was a bathroom with a flush toilet, which was something we didn't have in China. The shower had cold water, which was drained directly through a hole into a gutter outside. The bathroom had bare cement floors, and there was a dim light bulb on the ceiling. I always showered before dark, so I could watch the hole, ready to run and scream if a cobra or any snake crawled in. Luckily, during my five-month stay, the snakes stayed away!

Nancy and Patrick lived nearby, and we went biking along the narrow streets of Nadiad, sometimes at dusk. I wasn't a good biker, especially when I rode the grownup's bike that belonged to Nancy's father. Surprisingly, I didn't knock anyone down or fall off, despite the rough roads. When I think of it now, I'm amazed I managed to stay on that tall bike. Being young and adventurous helped.

A picnic trip, ca. 1946

One event did frighten me, though. It was one of those bright, sunny days on the Indian plains, and Nancy invited me to a picnic on the outskirts of town. We all piled into Nancy's car and drove down the dirt road. I sat in the car more concerned about where we were heading than about the picnic. Would there be wild animals? What if we met up with a tiger or a lion? These fears gripped my imagination again. Then, as Nancy stopped the car, I looked out the car window and saw a huge banyan tree full of monkeys!

Reluctantly, I got out of the car. While the other kids joked and laughed, I was tense inside and out. I sat gingerly on the blanket they had spread, fearing there might be a snake beneath us. Then I looked up into the tree, hoping all the monkeys would stay where they were. When the sandwich plate came around, Patrick joked, "Be careful — don't let the monkeys grab your sandwich. If they do, don't fight with them!" He didn't intend to frighten me, but he did. I ate everything that came my way as fast as I could, so there would be nothing in my hands to attract these creatures. Nothing happened, but I was greatly relieved when Patrick and Nancy decided to head back home.

Monkeys in India are as used to people as squirrels and pigeons are in America. If you don't aggravate them, they won't bother you. Some are as cautious about us as we are about them. I was told by one kid how they clamp down a monkey's head and open its scalp to eat its brain, while it would still be kicking and alive. Real or fanciful, I shuddered.

When Christmas came around, Nadiad had no snow. To add insult to injury, we decorated a shrub instead of a fir tree. It was not the same at all; it didn't seem right. Fortunately, even then, I understood that the true meaning of Christmas was not the tree, but that it was the day Christ was born. So, we decorated the slender shrub, and just as in China, the cook and his family joined us in our morning family prayers.

Our makeshift Christmas tree in Nadiad

Mother and Day-Day gave useful gifts as well as money to the cook and his entire family. They, in turn, brought us some native delicacies and two pretty saris for me, which they draped over me right away. I still have a photo of me wearing that sari. I look kind of Indian. The three of us—Mother, Day-Day, and I—didn't have much to give each other. I had made handkerchiefs for Mother and Day-Day at school, and I was promised a bike when we got to China.

Day-Day's year-long contract finally ended. It was May again, the time of the year that always seemed to signal changes. Word had come months earlier that the fighting in China had officially ended and that the Japanese had surrendered to the Allies, which included China. While I was up in the Himalayas, I heard teachers talking about some otherworldly bombs that were dropped on Japan, killing hundreds of thousands, or even millions. So it was time for us to be on the road again—perhaps this time, we'd finally head back to China.

Spending a Christmas with our Indian friends. The sari was my Christmas gift

In May 1946, when I had just turned fifteen, we bade farewell to our new friends in Nadiad, Indians and missionaries alike. Much as I had resented coming to India, after staying for almost a year, I had come to love the Indian people. They were amiable and civilized, and many were just as impoverished as the Chinese.

It was a long, weary trip from Nadiad back to Bombay. Then we headed to Calcutta. As the train crawled across the plains, which looked very, very dry, monkeys played, jumped, and climbed up and down trees. There were wild peacocks everywhere, some spreading their fan-shaped tail feathers as if to overshadow the old, dilapidated train cars. There was other wildlife, but to my disappointment, I never saw a wild elephant or a tiger.

We shared a sleeper with an Indian couple. They spoke limited English, and we struck up a few conversations, learning more about their unique customs. They did not use chopsticks, knives, or forks. They ate with one hand, while reserving the other for toilet purposes. That was not the hand with which they contacted others, and they carried a jug of water with them for hygiene. They liked to chew betel nuts, which made their lips red (and later I learned, can cause oral cancers). Finally, after traversing nearly the width of the Indian subcontinent on this dusty and rumbling train, we arrived in Calcutta.

It was much like Bombay. Sacred cows were everywhere, and there were even more beggars on the streets. From where we stayed in Calcutta, I could see a Chinese flag waving in the breeze, and it stirred something inside me. Perhaps I was a bit homesick for China. Or was it that my country was at last free from oppressors and invaders? Whichever it was, I felt a twinge of patriotism, and suddenly I longed to return to my Chinese school and greet the people I knew. For the first time, I felt proud to be Chinese, and was glad we were going back.

After waiting for a long time, we were finally allowed to board an American military ship docked on the Hooghly River, which is a tributary of the Ganges. Interestingly, Mother had told me that we could be flying over the Himalayas to enter China from the western end. Well, I was really looking forward to my first flying experience. So much for that. The military vessel, already was full of GIs, was allegedly heading to Hong Kong. As I watched Calcutta gradually disappear from sight, a Chinese girl around my age came up to where I was standing, my arms hanging over the ship's rails.

"Hello," she said, with a slight British accent.

"Hi," I responded. "What's your name?"

"Grace," she answered. Then, she warmed up and started to tell me more of her story. "I'm on my way to Canton to visit relatives. Then I'll go to England for further study."

"I'm Jean," I introduced myself. Then, while not knowing exactly where Canton was, I asked in a surprised tone, "Why England?"

"I like England better than America," she replied.

I couldn't believe anyone would like England better than America, not that I knew anything about England. I'd met a missionary from England called Aunt Edith. She was a very close friend of our family, and she spoke with a British accent. I had the idea that the British people are more solemn and don't get jokes quickly. These were traits of Aunt Edith.

"It must be pretty dull there," I said, a matter-of-factly.

"Why do you think that?" Grace asked with a surprised grin.

"The British don't have a sense of humor. I knew an English missionary," and I began a long-winded ramble: "This Englishwoman often came to our home. Whenever something funny was said at dinner, my friend Chum and I would double over with laughter, while her face remained expressionless, which made us laugh even harder."

"I prefer their seriousness," Grace responded, clipping my wings. Our conversation ended there, and from time to time since I have wondered how Grace did in England.

The next day when I was on deck again, a handsome GI with blond hair and beautiful blue eyes came toward me and began to talk. I think his name was Benjamin.

"I'm from Iowa, and I'll be stationed in Shanghai," he said. "I want to buy a camera and tour all of China before returning home." He said much more, but that's all I remember. My heart was beating faster and faster, and my face felt red and hot. I was becoming tense and stiff, and my mind started to drift. My fingers and lips were quivering as I stared into this GI's bright blue eyes beneath his beautiful, wavy blond hair. I was mesmerized, and I wondered if Day-Day looked this handsome and tall when he was younger.

As I collected myself, I realized the sun was setting, and we'd reached the open sea on the Bay of Bengal, heading toward the Andaman Sea and the Strait of Malacca. Perhaps as soon as the next night, we would arrive in Shanghai.

Part III

Anguish of Separation:
My Awakening

22

THE VOYAGE was rather uneventful, except that Day-Day decided to introduce me to a new language. I had the choice of German, Russian, or Latin, and when Mother chuckled as Day-Day offered to teach me Russian, which he'd learned on a train ride in Siberia, I chose Latin. Learning this ancient language was fun but hard to remember.

Again, our ship cut through the Strait of Malacca, and this time we hugged the coast of Malaya. We stopped briefly at the Port of Singapore to drop off hundreds of GIs, refuel and restock, and we were allowed to get off for a few hours. Mother and I walked along the harbor side and managed to get a glimpse of Singapore, an exciting mix of colonial affluence and extreme poverty. "Singapore isn't that different from China, perhaps worse," I thought.

We made another brief stop in Hong Kong to dispatch more GIs, before rushing full-steam-ahead toward the Shanghai Bund. When we went through Hong Kong, we weren't allowed to get off at all, and then, finally, Shanghai was within view.

The Shanghai Bund looked nearly the same as when we left four years earlier, except instead of a Japanese flag, the flag of the Republic of China was flying. Since Chiang Kai-Shek (蒋介石: Jiang Jie-Shi) and the Chinese armed forces were allies of the Western forces that had defeated Japan, the flag was a symbol that China was once again a free country. Or was it?

Poverty was still everywhere. Beggars roamed the streets,

perhaps worse than before. Seeing this dampened the joy of returning, and at the same time, reminded me of the pledge I had made when we left for America that I would try to help China rid itself of poverty. Having now seen America, I had a blueprint. I would replace all the mud huts with little white houses with green shutters, a fifteen-year-old's plan for wiping out poverty.

In Shanghai, we stayed at the Blackstone Apartments with my parents' friends. Day-Day needed to make arrangements to take some orphans back to Kiukiang from the Shanghai orphanage, where they had to stay when Americans were forced to leave China. Among them were two little girls my parents had intended to adopt but were too young to take with us. One was named Jessie, the other Elizabeth. There was a third baby named Ruth who was too small to be in an orphanage, so during the war, she stayed with her wet nurse outside of Kiukiang.

I had looked forward to having three little sisters. I could teach them English, and we'd have lots of fun. But Jessie's natural mother reclaimed her, furious that her daughter, now nine years old, was undernourished after living in the orphanage. Then Elizabeth was adopted by someone from another city. And when Ruth's wet nurse brought her to our home, she wept at the thought of giving Elizabeth to us, as she'd become attached. Understandingly, Mother let the nurse adopt Ruth. So I was without any little sisters. Looking back, they probably were better off in their new homes. The situation in China was about to take a turn.

While we were in Shanghai, Day-Day didn't forget his promise. He took me to a bicycle shop and let me pick out the bike I liked. I was so excited, I hardly knew which to choose. Then I spotted a powder-blue girl's bike, and that was it. At last, I was a proud bicycle owner. I couldn't wait to ride it, but for now, it had to be crated for shipping to Kiukiang.

After a week in Shanghai, we finally got on a Yangtze River steamer. Leaning against the rail, staring at the river, I thought about my early years living in Kiukiang. Would my childhood friends remember me? Would I recognize them? Suddenly I became nostalgic. The sparkling reflection of the sun on the water was mesmerizing, and I remained in deep thought.

An image of the Hudson River outside my bedroom window in South Yonkers flashed before my eyes as the steamer pierced through the riverbed, creating huge splashes against the side of the ship. As I watched the water flowing eastward, I remembered an old Chinese saying: "Only the waters of the Yangtze River surging east can understand my heart."

We had to spend one night aboard the steamer. When I went to see my cabin, a young lady hailed me by my Chinese name, "Tren Hwa." I looked at her with surprise, then smiled politely as I didn't recognize her. She walked over and started a conversation in the Kiukiang dialect. To my dismay and embarrassment, I grasped for words, but only English came out. I had to lead her to my parents' stateroom. Mother put me to shame, as she talked to the young lady in Chinese better than I could. Now I realized why Mother had tried to make conversation with me in Chinese while we were in America. She was concerned I might forget my native tongue, and sure enough, I had! Unless people spoke slowly, I barely understood what they were saying. And I could hardly respond unless I mixed English with it.

The next day we arrived, and for the first time in my life, I had a perfect view of Kiukiang from the middle of the river. First, the River Lock Tower (鎖江樓塔) came into view, then the Kiukiang Pagoda, the city's proud, ancient landmarks. Soon I saw a huge crowd waiting to welcome us. Firecrackers went off by the hundreds, perhaps thousands. The old staff members of the Water of Life Hospital, the Rulison Girls High School students and faculty, Danforth Women's Hospital faculty, and many church members were all there, along with missionaries who had returned before us. There were strange faces as well, probably curious onlookers.

I squinted and finally spotted Wang-Sao! She saw me too and she began to run along the riverbank, waving, as our ship was being maneuvered towards the dock. It was a great moment. People asked me all kinds of questions, and all I could do was to grin and nod my head. Occasionally a few sounds of "Oh" and "Ah" mixing with some "yeahs" would escape my mouth to acknowledge that I heard them and that I understood. "It's a matter of time before I have to let the cat out of the bag," I thought. "This is so embarrassing! Suddenly, I cannot communicate with people in my native country. I don't remember the Chinese language!"

Our first stop was Danforth Women's Hospital. Day-Day's staff told us we would stay there for a month while our house was being fixed up. It was in terrible shape, as we'd been away so long. Construction workers were whitewashing the walls and repainting the woodwork. We were thankful that whoever lived in our house had installed electricity, so we wouldn't have to use candles or kerosene lamps anymore. But there was still no flush toilet. More importantly, Day-Day was happy to learn that Danforth and his Water of Life Hospital finally had electricity, which meant he could install a much-needed X-ray machine.

When we reached the Danforth compound, Mollie, one of my best childhood friends outside of Chum, rushed over to see me. She had grown much taller than I, and she dragged me to her home full of excitement. Mollie's mother, an obstetrician at Danforth, had always thought little of me, especially when I was flunking the third grade. But seeing me and hugging me now,

JEAN TREN-HWA PERKINS

she was impressed by my fluent English. Then she heard me try to speak Chinese, and she and Mollie laughed till tears rolled down their cheeks. They kept asking questions so they could hear me mix Chinese and English. I was so embarrassed that I was determined to recover my fluent Chinese with or without an American accent. I didn't want to be a foreigner in my own country.

It turned out to be immensely challenging. I had long forgotten so many Chinese words, not to mention that my pronunciation was terrible and I was misusing many words even before I went to America. Including the semesters at the Dragon Hill Primary School, when I spoke mostly English, I had been in English-speaking schools for nearly five years, a third of my life. So the laughter continued. Weeks after we came back to Kiukiang, I went to one of my classmates' homes for dinner, and I ate quite a lot. It had been four years since I'd had real Chinese food. After eating as much as I could, I remarked, "I am so full I could die (我饱的快要撑死啦)!" My classmate immediately said, "Jean, please don't use the word *death*, especially at this time of the year. It brings bad luck!"

It wasn't just the language. I had forgotten my own culture.

Wang-Sao was excited to see me back. After the whitewashing and repainting were complete, she meticulously cleaned the whole house for us. About six weeks after we arrived, we finally got to sleep at home. But for some reason, we still went to the homes of Danforth staff members for dinners.

After we moved home, the first thing Mother did was to search for her camera. In 1942, she had hid it on one of the rafters, because the Japanese forbade cameras leaving the country. Consequently, we had no photos of our journey on the *Conte Verde* from Shanghai through Southeast Asia to Lourenço Marques, and then on the *Gripsholm* to Rio de Janeiro and the

Hudson River. Amazingly, the camera was still there! But because of the attic heat, it didn't take photos as sharp as before.

Just as everything seemed to be calming down after we moved back into the house, I noticed an onslaught of rashes on my arms and legs, and then on my face. I was itchy all over. When Mother said something, Day-Day shrugged his shoulders and said it could be skin allergy from the fresh paint. Then I got dysentery, a cruel reminder that this was not Yonkers, but rural China. Thinking it was temporary, no one took my condition seriously and it got much worse. Soon I was too weak to get up for meals. Mother brought me lunch from the missionary home each noon in the blazing sun, dripping with sweat, her dress soaked to the hems by the time she brought it to me. But she never complained, she loved me so much.

Three weeks later, Mother was struck by typhoid, a disease she had encountered before. This time it was nearly fatal, and Day-Day took her to the Danforth Women's Hospital. So we all moved back to the dorm of the Women's Hospital to give Mother our full attention. And I was left to struggle with my dysentery alone, until one day I was so weak, I fainted in the bathroom with a thud. Wang-Sao heard the noise and came quickly to the door. She called my name—no response. Then she knocked frantically, and her loud knocks finally woke me up. I was on the floor, clutching the heavy porcelain toilet cover broken in half. I somehow managed to put the broken cover back on and stumble out of the bathroom, only to collapse into the arms of Wang-Sao waiting anxiously outside the door. All this commotion alerted Aunt Clara, an American missionary nurse at the Danforth Women's Hospital.

On learning that I'd had dysentery for more than a month, she suggested to Day-Day that I should try the new antibiotic drug called Sulfaguanidine (a sulfa drug). Lo and behold, my dysentery cleared in a few days, and I was back on my feet. I had no idea why Day-Day didn't give me the medicine earlier. Perhaps he was too busy trying to get his hospital in order and manage the many repairs that were needed. He didn't even know I was sick until Mother became ill. Years later, I discovered that it was because antibiotic drugs were so rare and valuable, and so many people in the hospital needed them, and Day-Day always thought about others before his own family. Fortunately, unlike when I had whooping cough and he was determined to let me get through it on my own, this time he relented. I was well now, but Mother was near death with typhoid. I felt guilty that I might have been the cause, making her work so hard to take care of me. I wasn't allowed to be with her, though, because it was so contagious.

Before I got sick, Mollie and I had watched from a window outside the contagion ward, and we saw a Chinese nurse dying from typhoid she had contracted from a patient. The nurse's mother stood at her bedside day and night. With great effort, the patient raised her trembling arm and waved it weakly, gesturing for her mother to leave. Despite her daughter's efforts and with tears streaming down her face, the mother refused to go until the ordeal was over and the nurse finally lay still. It was a terrifying sight. Would my mother go through all that, too? Tears began to stream down my face at the mere thought.

In some Chinese folklore, it is said that after someone dies, their spirit roams to all the places they had been in life, beginning three days after death. Being a Christian, I wasn't superstitious, but the thought of such a possibility haunted me and preoccupied my mind. So on the third night after the nurse died, just as I turned off the light and was about to doze off, I felt the presence of someone or something in my room. This being, which appeared to be the nurse who had just died, leaned over me, pressing slowly onto my chest so I could hardly breathe. I screamed with fright, but no sound came out. Quickly I fumbled for the light and turned it on, but there was nothing there. I left the light on the rest of the night. The experience unnerved me.

Now if my mother was going to die, I couldn't even go see her and tell her how much I loved her and how sorry I was she got sick, perhaps from caring for me. I wondered if Day-Day blamed me, because he barely showed signs that I existed during Mother's illness. Then came that critical night when all medications had failed. They had already given her valuable doses of penicillin, and had been vigorously trying to keep her hydrated with salt and sugar water, considered state-of-the-art treatment at the time. Now she was on her own. "Will Mother survive, or will she die?" we all pondered. Day-Day was on his knees praying, and he prayed the whole night through, not leaving Mother's bedside. I stayed outside the room all night, and when I wasn't crying, I prayed quietly. It was more like begging God not to take Mother away. I made a promise to the Almighty that I would do anything He asked in exchange.

By dawn, Mother stirred. Her vital signs were weak, but still there. We had prayed for a miracle and God had answered our prayers. Tears of joy streamed down all our faces. We hugged whoever had been waiting outside her bedroom. I was most relieved, as Day-Day came out and kissed me on my forehead, lightening the guilt. I wanted to rush in and hug her, but that was not allowed, as she was too weak and frail. We didn't want her to relapse.

Slowly but surely, Mother recovered. However, her right leg continued to suffer from elephantiasis and was twice as big as her left one. She couldn't walk well, but it was so great to see her alive. With Mother slowly recovering, Day-Day decided that she and I would go to our resort home on Ku-Ling Mountain for the rest of the summer. To my great delight, Wang-Sao came with us. She was always fun.

The fresh, cold air did Mother a world of good. Her health progressively improved, and I couldn't have been happier. We took many walks together, including a return visit to Cradle Rock, where a group of boulders took the shape of a cradle. From there, we would watch the beautiful sunset. It had been ten years since we'd been there. In the fall of 1937, I was supposed to attend Ku-Ling American School, but then the war came. Our summer home was in surprisingly good shape despite not having been used for a decade. Aunt Adelaide, our neighbor, had passed away, and we had new neighbors, Mary T. and her mother from Nanking. Mary invited me to join her on a three-day hike to the other side of the mountain to see famous temples and an ancient college called White Deer. A male Chinese friend of theirs would be the guide and take care of us. Mother gave me permission, and off we went.

We hiked by day and slept in temples at night. We bathed in springs after dark while wearing our clothes. Then we changed to dry clothes in the temple and went to sleep. It was a little scary to be in these mysterious temples. I would have preferred sleeping on a bamboo bed by the roadside in the villages, but the mosquitos would have devoured us. It was quite the adventure, but Mary and I were both glad to be home.

As the summer of 1946 was winding down, I realized I needed to study Chinese earnestly. I had to learn to communicate and write well to survive in my country. I knew I might need to work hard the rest of my life to master this complex language. That pledge held for a few minutes, then I remembered what it was like before I left for America. Learning Chinese was dreadful. The hardest part was memorizing the thousands of characters, the ancient texts, and other writings. Learning by memorization never worked for me, but that was the traditional Chinese way.

"Jean," Mother said, "I think it's time for us to go back to Kiukiang. I feel so much better. And besides, dear, your school is about to start!"

"You do look much better, Mother." I gave her a big squeeze hug and complimented her sincerely. I thought of how I almost lost the mother I loved so much. I would be completely lost without her. I dreaded the idea of going back to Kiukiang, though, which meant going back to school. How could I study in Chinese? I couldn't even read many of the characters. I hated school in China. I sighed and began to help Mother pack.

Day-Day was so happy to see us coming home, and especially to see how well Mother looked. Everything seemed to be back to normal, and we finally began to settle in. But then Day-Day began to act strangely toward me. My feeling was that he still blamed me for Mother's near death. I was never sure. I also believe Day-Day was beginning to be hard of hearing. He couldn't always hear the conversations between Mother and me at the dinner table. Or worse, in retrospect, perhaps Day-Day felt guilty for uprooting us and bringing us back to China. He did so without anticipating how much things would have changed after the war. Day-Day also ignored the fact that he and Mother were getting older, and that after living for three years in America, our immune systems had become too weak to deal with this harsh environment.

In any case, the first strange accusation came while I was chatting with Chef Tian. Day-Day had never disciplined or criticized me, except the time I peeked through the front gate of the hospital to annoy the Japanese soldiers marching into our city. But on that day, he stormed into the kitchen and said with great agitation, "You told Chef Tian to put ginger in the pumpkin pie. You know your mother doesn't eat ginger!"

Taken aback, I said, "No, Day-Day, I didn't! I don't know anything about cooking, much less what flavors to put in which dishes." Day-Day walked out of the kitchen as abruptly as he'd entered, and I was confused. I stuck my tongue out at Chef Tian, implying I was in trouble.

We all forgot about the incident until three days later, during breakfast. I asked Mother if she wanted the strawberry jam that we both loved, but the jar had very little left.

"No, Honey, you have it." Mother said.

I had no idea Day-Day was watching me like a hawk. I took the jar, spread the last bit of jam on my toast, and ate it all up. After I left for my room, there was a knock on my bedroom door. It was Day-Day, standing behind the screen door staring at me. That was odd, because ever since I had my own room, he would never come in unless Mother was with him. He spoke through the screen door, "I saw you finish the strawberry jam without leaving any for Mother!"

"Oh, Day-Day, I did ask Mother if she wanted any, but she told me to finish it," I explained. Silence ensued. Then Day-Day turned around and walked away without another word. I was never a selfish kid. Living in a home of plenty, there was no need to be selfish. Day-Day's attitude hurt my feelings. "What's going on?" I sniffled softly, and when I recalled the accusation about ginger in the pumpkin pie, I started to cry harder. Then, I remembered my skin rashes. The dysentery made me forget about them, but I was still having them after all these months. Day-Day hardly noticed, and even when Mother said something to him, he didn't do a thing about them.

"He doesn't love me anymore. What's happening? Where is my beloved Day-Day, the beautiful man sitting in the diner in New York telling me the rules of baseball?" With these thoughts,

I sobbed loudly and uncontrollably, which is something I rarely did. But I'd never been accused of wrongdoing, and my heart was broken.

Hearing my sobs, Mother came into my room and asked about it. Day-Day had said nothing to Mother, and she was quite confused. I told Mother between sobs what had happened. She went looking for Day-Day immediately and got the facts straightened out. Day-Day must not have heard what was said between Mother and me.

Day-Day asked me to come to his study. I refused to go. By then, I had cried for three hours. Day-Day was just as stubborn and was still fuming. But being an adult, he finally came with Mother to my room and apologized that he had accused me of wrongfully, including the pumpkin pie incident. He even asked Mother to get some ointment from the hospital the next day for my skin.

It wasn't that easy for me to forget or forgive, especially when I had done nothing wrong. Nothing like that ever happened again, and Day-Day made an effort to show me his love. So, the three of us lived harmoniously together without further incident. I never needed harsh words. A look of disapproval from Mother was enough for me to obey.

In hindsight, I believe Mother's near-death experience took a significant emotional toll on Day-Day, who was no longer a resilient young man. He was already under huge stress trying to get the Water of Life Hospital back up in working order. I believe, too, that he was ridden with guilt and probably wondered, as I often did, "Why did we come back to China?"

23

THE NEWS that we had returned to Kiukiang finally reached Mm-Ma and Mr. Hu, and they visited us not long after Mother and I returned from Ku-Ling.

As was their custom, they went first to the kitchen, where Chef Tian called out my name, "Tren-Hwa, your country parents are here to see you." I ran into the kitchen and gave them a grin of recognition. There was absolutely no hugging and kissing. It is not the Chinese custom, and frankly, as I've said before, I was never a kisser except with Mother, Day-Day, and the aunties.

Mm-Ma now had to look up to me, as she only came up to my shoulders. There was a look of awe and perhaps maternal pride in her eyes. I wasn't that tall, about five feet two, but to her, I must have appeared gigantic. Mr. Hu was, as I remembered, a man of few words, although he nodded his head. He was about my height.

"Tren-Hwa," Mm-Ma began to talk after a long and awkward silence. "Did you see your brother, Kuo-Hsiang (闊祥), in America?"

"No," I replied. I was surprised Mm-Ma would even ask such a question, and to be honest, I could barely remember who Kuo-Hsiang was, let alone that he went to America. "Why do you ask?"

Mm-Ma and Mr. Hu looked startled, as though they'd come to the wrong house and were talking with the wrong person. My Chinese was so faltering and with such a strong foreign accent.

After a pause, Mm-Ma continued, "Not long after you left for America, we received this document."

Mr. Hu showed me the paper. I scanned it and could not read most of it. The document was in old-style Chinese. Mm-Ma kept talking, "It says that your brother Kuo-Hsiang was missing in action while flying on a mission. His military superior returned his coat and some personal things to us, but we don't believe he is dead. We are sure he went to America to look for you. We brought this document today, hoping you could read it to us, so we know whether it's true."

Aside from a photo of him, I had nearly zero recollection of Kuo-Hsiang, the eldest boy in the Hu family. I had heard bits and pieces about Kuo-Hsiang from my American parents but had no idea how much older he was than I. Later I read in Mother's letters to my grandma, that during the terrible flood Kuo-Hsiang had worked at the hospital. He was so bright that Mother and Day-Day sponsored his education. When he took the exams for primary school graduates, he was ranked first in Kiangsi Province. Day-Day arranged for him to enter a Christian High School in Nanchang (南昌), the capital of Kiangsi Province. He and Mother hoped Kuo-Hsiang would pursue medicine, but Kuo-Hsiang entered the Republic of China Air Force Academy instead, and then fought in World War II as a fighter pilot. He was a first-class lieutenant.

"I am so sorry," I said, "but I did not see him in America. America is a huge country. Without an address, it would be impossible to find each other." I handed the document back to Mr. Hu and said. "I cannot read this. I don't understand the old-fashioned characters."

The man of few words, Mr. Hu, spoke only to express disappointment in me. "If Kuo-Hsiang were here right now, he would read and explain it to us. You are no good!" he said. To emphasis his point, he shook his head and added, "How is it you cannot speak Chinese like you used to?" That was the longest sentence he ever spoke to me. With that, Mm-Ma and Mr. Hu left. They were more interested in finding Kuo-Hsiang than in seeing me.

To this day, I wonder whether he became a pilot so he could fly across the Pacific Ocean to America. I often wish he did indeed end up living in San Francisco with a family. With a brilliant mind, he should have had a better life, even though to die in that war for that cause was considered an honor.

Then came another twist of fate. I chose to attend Rulison Girls High instead of the Shanghai American School, which Mother had suggested, and Day-Day almost insisted upon because of the language issue. I had two reasons. First, I didn't want to leave home anymore. And second, I wanted to serve the Lord, my own country, and her people. I believed that was why I was saved from the flood. How could I do this if I didn't master the Chinese language? Mother and Day-Day had to agree with my argument, although it would have been easier for me to study in English. Had I been able to see the future, I might have chosen the Shanghai American School instead. I often wonder what the course of my life would have been if I had. The future is never predictable, and especially in China during that period.

To attend Rulison Girls High in Kiukiang, I would be entering the ninth grade. However, ninth grade in China is the graduating class for junior high, and students have to take an entrance exam first to qualify. The principal of Rulison, Miss Wu, knew there was no way I could pass the entrance exam since I had the Chinese-language level of a third-grader. But since this was the first postwar year and there was room for flexibility, some rules were not strictly followed. So Principal Wu registered me as a transfer student and accepted me as a ninth-grader without having to take the exam.

For once, I wasn't the only Chinese in the room. But it was uphill to learn enough Chinese to keep up with the class. Perhaps Mr. Hu was right that I was "no good." I could speak a bit, but understanding even what I was studying was much harder. I would have had to learn each lesson in English first to comprehend it, but there wasn't enough time for that. So I resorted to memorizing, whether or not I understood. During a midterm exam in Chinese history, there was a question I didn't understand. But instead of leaving it blank, I wrote down a paragraph I'd memorized without knowing whether it had anything to do with the question. I thought at least it would look better than a blank space. Boy, was I wrong! It was a disaster.

While news of my embarrassing history exam was circulating, my essays were even worse. My homeroom teacher, Miss You, asked if I knew the meaning of the Chinese characters I had chosen for the girl's name in my essay. I had found them in a Chinese-English dictionary, so I nodded and replied confidently, "Yes, Miss You. They mean wildflowers, or beautiful flowers."

"No, Jean," she explained in Chinese. "These words suggest a prostitute (妓女)."

"What is a prostitute (妓女)?" I asked.

She repeated herself using the English word "prostitute."

When I still looked puzzled, she shook her head in disbelief and said, "You don't know much about anything, and you lived in America."

"Was I supposed to?" I wondered. "Why would the word *wildflower* (野花) be associated with prostitutes? Wildflowers are beautiful!"

Years later, while walking along a hillside of beautiful wildflowers, I exclaimed, "I love these wildflowers." Those walking with me burst into laughter. Sensing from my puzzled look that I didn't understand, they gave me the same lesson on the Chinese association of *wildflowers*.

I guess I never got it. My Chinese name, Tren-Hwa, means spring flowers (春花), and is considered acceptable as a girl's name, especially for those raised in the countryside. But to me, flowers that bloom in spring could easily include wild ones. There must be a subtle distinction that I'm unable to discern.

Ridiculed as I was and struggling to learn basic Chinese, I still managed to graduate with my ninth grade class in the spring of 1947. I even made a little speech on India. Although I was shaking with stage fright, my face red as a beet, and my voice cracking as though I was on the verge of tears, I managed to finish my speech in the Mandarin dialect, which by then had become the national dialect, although I spoke with an American accent. To my surprise, the whole school burst into applause.

All grown-up at Rulison Girls High, ca. 1947

Miss You stood up and said to the class, "We all remember Tren-Hwa's broken Chinese at the start of this academic year. And now she not only speaks the Kiukiang dialect fluently, she was able to make this speech in Mandarin." Even though it was embarrassing to be in the limelight, I felt great, even knowing she was being charitable.

The next day, Principal Wu announced, "Please all go to the boy's school and wait at their front gate to welcome their teachers and students! They will arrive by boat from Chungking this afternoon." So we all lined up against the wall to welcome them. While waiting for their arrival, I thought of the little boy who had stood next to me in our kindergarten graduation photo taken by Mother in 1937, when he and I were both six. I remembered that his name was Ming-Ming, because during my childhood prayers each night, I would add, "And God bless Ming-Ming." When I was about eleven and went to America, I dropped this little classmate's name from my prayers because he had become too vague in my memory.

I began to wonder what he was like now, after all these years. He certainly had a babyface in that photo. As the group began to trickle in, I asked Miss You, who was standing next to me, "Which boy is Ming-Ming?" She pointed to the one who was running like a crazy horse, complaining, "I am so hot; it's so hot here!"

Miss You laughingly told him, "Silly boy, take off your woolen vest!" He gave Miss You a sheepish grin, and all the girls laughed in good humor, as he took his vest off. I stared at him and smiled to myself because he was still shorter than I was. There were firecrackers, just as when we arrived a year earlier. The new arrivals headed toward their prewar homes on the school compound, and we headed home. Having seen my kindergarten friend, I never gave Ming-Ming another thought, because I wasn't interested in boys.

When I got back home, Mother called out, "I have great news, Darling! The aunties and Chum are on their way back to China!"

"Oh, I can't wait to see Chum's reactions! I wonder if she can still speak Chinese?"

Mother chuckled, with a knowing look that she had been right when she insisted on speaking with me in Chinese in Yonkers.

A few days later, Mollie and I were waiting for the river steamer. The crowd was even more massive than the one that greeted us. So many people had returned to Kiukiang from the western part of China now that the war was over. At last, the boat came into view, and we saw people, although not close enough to make out their faces. Then with a blast of the horn, the ship docked. Firecrackers went off, and when the smoke cleared, I saw Chum standing on the deck straight as a beanstalk with a beautiful figure. She had a perm, and her long curly hair hung around her shoulders. She looked like a movie star, and Aunt Bessie and Aunt Dee also looked stylish, fresh from America!

Chum spotted Mollie and me and began to wave, saying "Oh" and "Ah" in excited tones. Mollie and I had to laugh. That was what I had done when I got off the boat a year earlier. After a year in a Chinese high school, I'd lost a lot of the "Oh" and "Ah" American expressions. Mollie and I looked at each other; we couldn't wait to hear Chum talk.

When the three of them got off the boat, hugs, kisses, and handshakes ensued. I thought it would never end, and sure enough, Chum couldn't speak a word of Chinese. She was in America two years longer than I had been, and she'd lost her native tongue. Finally, we got them home. Everyone was back in their original rooms as though we'd never left. The places where Aunt Katty and Grandma stayed remained empty, waiting for guests who might come. The gateman Grandpa Shui, Chef Tian, and Wang-Sao were all still there too. We had a new, young butler, though. Lo-Ma had

Back together with Chum and our new siblings

become too old to work, but she did visit us. Sadly, Chang-Ma had passed away while I was in America. So began the summer of 1947.

Chum and I had to catch up on five years. It was quickly apparent that the differences between us had widened. Chum was now a real American teenager. Her hobby was to collect car models from magazines and pin them up on the walls. She had an in-depth knowledge about engines and fuels because her Ploeg uncles, the aunties' brothers (four in all), were very knowledgeable about cars. Three of them were mechanics in Grand Rapids, Michigan, and one was a salesman for the Ford Motor Company in Dearborn. I didn't know what she was talking about when she described engines and cylinders. Chum also subscribed to *Miss America Magazine*, which I hadn't even known existed.

Her clothes were up-to-date, and she was fashion-conscious with good taste. It might have been the influence of Aunt Bessie and Aunt Dee's youngest sister, who we called Aunt Louise. She was in her thirties and made sure that Chum dressed in style, but it seemed to me that whatever Chum wore, she looked great.

Most notably, Chum told me about bras. Even though she didn't need a bra yet, she wore one. By that time, all my dresses brought from America no longer fitted me, and I was wearing Chinese gowns, which had very little space around the chest area! Pressing tightly against the Chinese dress, the two bumps on my chest appeared even more substantial, and their presence annoyed and embarrassed me. I even got a strip of cloth to bind myself as tightly as possible.

I didn't know that bras came in different sizes, so I asked Chum to lend me one of hers for Mother to give to a tailor as a sample to make a few for me. When the tailored bras came, none fit me; they were way too small. I used them anyway; they were better than nothing, and way better than my strip of cloth I'd been using. And wearing one helped me psychologically. But I still hunched my shoulders and walked like an old woman to minimize these bumps. I envied Chum's ability to hold herself up straight and look so elegant. Whenever we went out together, boys' heads would turn toward her. I was a homely teenage girl with buck teeth and a hunched back, trying to be invisible.

One day Chum told me I was naive and too obedient. "Why do you listen to everything your Mother says? Don't you ever disagree with her? I always tell my grandmother and aunties when I don't agree with them. I told Aunt Louise I can make my own decisions!"

I thought, "Have I been too much of a baby? Am I too sheltered?" So one time I tried contradicting Mother. The surprised and hurt look on her face was enough to make me feel ashamed. I was so sorry I'd even tried, and I never did it again.

Chum had become much more openly expressive, too. Even though she maintained a solemn demeanor most of the time, she would often hug me. What I always respected about Chum was her determination. She worked diligently to reach whatever goals she set for herself. She could only accept being the best, whereas I was satisfied just doing my best. Here's an example. Chum was upset when she couldn't enter the tenth grade with me. Principal Wu at Rulison Girls High told her and the aunties that regulations had become more stringent by 1947, and there was no way she could pass the exams in Chinese that could validate her standing as a ninth-grader. So Chum began to tackle the Chinese language with a vengeance.

She caught up quickly, and soon she even excelled in Chinese literature. She read the classic novel *Dream in the Red Mansion* (紅樓夢), a book I had thumbed through the first few pages of and given up. My pace of reading Chinese classics remained slow;

there were so many words and phrases I didn't understand. Besides, the Chinese classics often have many characters, and I found it difficult to keep them straight. I enjoyed books I could sail through. Ever since we were kids, I was quick to accept obediently, understand superficially, and learn and then forget easily. I always made more blunders. Chum was the opposite. She did everything with precision and purpose, and at the same time, she remained calm, rarely showing emotion. I wished I could have been more like her—elegant and collected. Despite our striking differences, Chum and I got along really well after her return. We truly missed each other being apart for five years and were now like sisters.

In late summer 1947, Chum and I were invited by Lois and Mary Shubert, childhood friends of ours, to join them on Ku-Ling Mountain. Mother and the aunties consented because they knew the Shuberts well, so Chum and I traveled to Ku-Ling on our own. While there, we were introduced to Lois and Mary's little sister, Jenny, who was three years old. Jenny was a bright kid and a bit spoiled with so many people loving her.

We older kids had a great time, especially at Three Graces, three contiguous long waterfalls—in Chinese: 三疊泉瀑布. They made a natural water slide in the groove of a huge rock. Although we were teenagers, we acted like ten-year-olds. We would slide down the rock into a hole, which would spit us out, and then we'd slide the rest of the way until this natural water slide ended. Nothing could stop the fun, not even the seats of our bathing suits wearing out! We wrapped towels around our butts and kept sliding until Mr. and Mrs. Shubert said, "Time to go home, kids!" Only then would we reluctantly hike home.

We had plenty of fun on this trip and put off studying Chinese. But it was time to go home and get ready to return to school. Chum and I thanked the Shuberts and decided that we'd hike down Ku-Ling. It only took an hour, but when we got to the bottom of the mountain, our legs shook like leaves! We especially bonded on this journey.

In the fall of 1947, I was finally a tenth grader, a year ahead of Chum. The school year went by uneventfully, except that Chum and I made quite the sensation by riding our bikes to school. We also decided to speak English to each other, so we wouldn't forget our English as we had forgotten our Chinese. We whistled to each other when it was time to go home, which amused our classmates. They said we were like foreigners, but some began to follow suit later on. They even rode bikes to school wearing dresses or skirts. We didn't meant to show off. We were just living like the teenagers we knew in America.

The only thing a little exciting was that Chum and I joined the choir, conducted by an American missionary, Miss Maybell Woodruff, who we called Aunt Maybell. Aunt Maybell dressed in long Chinese gowns, which fitted her well because she was tall and thin. I think she preferred the boys in the choir because we girls had fits of giggles at anything even a little funny, such as someone singing off tune, out of synch, or sneezing. The altos, of which I was one, were the most egregious gigglers. Once we started to giggle, there wouldn't be another note from us for the rest of the song.

Aunt Maybell would give me a frustrated look sometimes, as I was usually the one who started the giggles. I think she also liked the sopranos, because Chum didn't giggle the way I did. She was serious about her singing, particularly when she sang solos. She had a beautiful voice. Little did I know that going to choir practice would soon brew a romance for someone.

The summer of 1948 could not have come more quickly. The Nanchang YMCA had organized a Christian Youth Conference

Summer retreat, ca. 1948

in Ku-Ling. Chum, Mollie, and I as well as one of the choir boys attended. Aunt Maybell gave the boy, who she liked very much, an English name, Samuel.

As a small child, I'd pledged that one day I would climb Ku-Ling Mountain on my own. All of us kids climbed up together, and although quite the climb, it was manageable. We had a choice of whether to stay at the Ku-Ling American High School dorm or in our own summer homes. I was supposed to attend this English-speaking school in 1937, but that never happened. Even though Mother had accompanied us up the mountain, Chum and I decided to stay with Mollie at the dorm, thinking it would be fun to be independent. We threw our bedding on the top bunks and then roamed around the school grounds.

The first night was a disaster; there were bed bugs! Mollie sat up the whole night and cried. I finally dozed off but got bitten all over. Since school had been out for a while, the bed bugs were starving, and they feasted on us all night long. We had committed to staying in the dorm, so we were stuck there till the conference was over, not wanting others to think we couldn't cope with a little hardship. When we did finally go home, Mother said, "Girls, leave your bedding on the porch! I'll have Wang-Sao soak them in boiling water!" That night we slept soundly, in peace.

Mollie stayed with us, and we talked about our childhood days, especially during my parent-less months of 1940 when Mother and Day-Day were in Yonkers to get my grandmother. Pointing to the tree near the path, I asked, "Do you remember when I hung a rope over that branch so we could swing on it?"

"Yes," Mollie said, then we laughed. "When the rope broke, I jumped off, but you held onto the rope while it was slipping through your hands and got rope burn."

"Yes," I recalled, "Chunks of skin peeled off my fingers and palms, and it hurt! But I didn't dare say a word to the aunties, as we were dressed up to be guests somewhere."

Then Chum asked, "Do you remember how you took us to the deep end of the swimming pool when the aunties told us to stay at the shallow end?"

"Boy, were they angry!" I remembered.

Mollie began to laugh. "Those were the good old days. It's a miracle none of us drowned!"

"We had lifesaving jackets," I said. "And I was there to protect you, and I did a pretty good job."

The three of us laughed hysterically.

Looking at Chum, I asked, "Do you remember Donald?"

"Oh yes," she answered. "He put ants and caterpillars in his mouth."

Mollie added, "Wasn't he the one who got stung by bees when he tried to steal their honey?"

"That was him, all right," I answered. "His face was so swollen you couldn't see his eyes.

"Those were such happy days," I added. "We were so carefree. And now, we're getting older." What a terrible thought to have at the age of seventeen!

After Mollie went to bed, Chum showed me a letter she'd received from Samuel, Aunt Maybell's favorite choir boy. Samuel had drawn her a beautiful tiger.

I said to Chum, "I want a tiger too. Can you ask him to send me one too?" A few days later, I got a tiger from Samuel, but no letter. I was puzzled. It hadn't occurred to me he might have romantic feelings for Chum.

Weeks before we left Ku-Ling Mountain, the aunties and Day-Day came for medical calls. And then Day-Day was asked to preach at the church. Mother said that the President of China had requested it because Day-Day had received numerous citations of honor from the Government for his work in Kiukiang and contributions to the Chinese people. Lo and behold, Mother, Chum and I sat right behind President Chiang Kai-Shek and his world-renowned wife, Ms. Song Mei-ling (宋美龄). Ms. Song's older sister was the wife of the Father of modern China, Dr. Sun Yat-Sen.

As we were about to be seated, Mother nodded her head and said hello to Ms. Song. Ms. Song stood up and smiled broadly. "Boy, she is beautiful," I thought. "Elegant" was probably the right word.

President Chiang was in non-military attire, and he took off his black hat and gave a respectful gesture to this entire row of ladies sitting behind his pew—including us, two Chinese teenagers. He looked tired, or at least older than I remembered.

I was shocked to see them going to church like ordinary people, like Eleanor Roosevelt riding the Pullman train by herself. Once again, I had a brush with history up close and personal. Unfortunately, Chum and I couldn't control our giggles when we saw Ms. Song's heavy makeup. She even turned around at one point, cringing. We were just seventeen and sixteen, and a little nervous being so close to the country's leader and his wife. We thought she was naturally beautiful and that she didn't have to use all that makeup.

We had no idea this would be last summer we'd spend with our parents on Ku-Ling Mountain. Or that this Sunday service would be the last we all attended at this church. Dark clouds were on the horizon.

24

IN THE FALL of 1948, I was to begin eleventh grade at Rulison Girls High. At home, Mother and Day-Day had been acting strange. It sounded as though they were speaking in code or another language. Then one day as we were having dinner, Mother said to Chum and me, "Girls, you're not children anymore, and perhaps you've heard. The Communists are heading this way."

"What are Communists?" I asked.

"Atheists," Day-Day answered, "people who do not believe in God."

"We've been discussing the situation," continued Mother. "The two of you are at a vulnerable and impressionable age. We don't want anything to happen to either of you, so we've decided to send you to Hong Kong right away."

Chum and I and looked at each other.

"I just got back a year ago!" exclaimed Chum.

"I've been back for two years now, but I'm still in culture shock," I said. "I don't want to be uprooted again." I felt frustrated, but then in a rapid 180-degree turnaround, I said to Chum, "We'll finally get to see Hong Kong."

Chum liked that idea. "Maybe it will be fun, Jean. But if we're constantly yanked out of China, how will we ever serve our country?" She was serious, and I was moved by her patriotism.

Mother was surprised by our reactions. "Jeanie dear, I thought you dreaded coming back to China. Hong Kong will ensure you can get back to America."

I wasn't objecting to going to Hong Kong or even returning to America. I just wanted them to understand how hard it is to keep changing schools, not to mention switching from one language and culture to another. I wished I had spoken my mind before we left Yonkers.

Chum and I didn't know how serious the situation was. Thoughts of moving again and living without Mother and Day-Day terrified me. I wanted only to be at my parents' side and stay with them forever, wherever they might be.

Aunt Dee wasted no time, explaining the urgency of the matter. "This is for your own good, girls. The situation is serious, and we've already made the arrangements. The plane leaves in two weeks. The Danish physician from China Inland Mission [CIM], who is helping us at the hospital, will escort you into Hong Kong. Once you're there, Ms. Wong, our friend from the Bethel Mission, will look after you till we get there. We've also made arrangements for you to attend a boarding school. So, start packing and take what you need."

"Things change," Aunt Bessie added, "and sometimes they change quickly. Perhaps we'll all end up in America again."

Aunt Dee and Mother both said the name of the boarding school, but I couldn't remember it. I thought, "Okay, why not? Why fight about it? It'll probably be great. Maybe Mother is right. If we end up in Yonkers, I can see my friends there again." The conversation ended there, and we continued life as usual during the coming weeks, as we waited for the plane to arrive on the Kiukiang Airfield that would fly us to Hong Kong.

As the days went by, there were more and more rumors about the Communists. Whispers about how frightening that could be became prevalent. We heard they would kill all the rich people, confiscate their land, and take their wives and children. Some rich people in Kiukiang began to leave. Then there was talk about executing all the people connected with the Republic of China's ruling party, the KMT (Kuo-Ming Tang: 国民堂) as war criminals. So officials with KMT affiliations also began to flee with their families. The mass exodus became nationwide, with most heading to Formosa (Taiwan). Many people who lived in coastal cities like Tsingtao and Shanghai went even further; many went to America. The mass exodus by the affluent and influential people created problems for others also attempting to leave the country. Nearly all trains, boats, and planes were booked.

On December 11, 1948, Chum and I stood near the airfield with our luggage for the plane to Hong Kong. But it never came. By spring 1949, with much of China under Communist control, even with assistance from America, President Chiang and his troops could not hold their line of defense along the Yangtze River. The Communist armies captured Nanking, the capital city of the Republic of China down the river and northeast of us. Soon, the Communists took Hankow, a city northwest of us, up the river.

The Communist armies were advancing toward Kiukiang from both directions. It was like when the Japanese occupied our city eleven years earlier, and we again moved to the safety of Water of Life Hospital in case there was a show of force by the Communist soldiers. An unearthly silence hung over our ancient river city. From the time the Republic of China Government deserted its people to save their own lives until Communists took over, the people of Kiukiang, including us, were living in fear. This was called the "Vacuum period," when neither party controlled our little city, and it lasted less than a week. Anything could happen, including looting and banditry. We were terrified, and everyone stayed behind locked doors.

Finally, the dreaded day came. On May 17, 1949, the Communist troops marched into our city without a struggle, as the city and its people had been left defenseless. A day later, we came out from Day-Day's hospital compound, and to everyone's great surprise, these Communist soldiers were friendly and polite. They were young, some not much older than I was. After anticipating ravaging behavior from them, we witnessed an orderly and disciplined army. They formed flawless straight lines and slept by the roadsides or on the streets. They did not enter any homes or private properties, and there was not a single disturbance on the streets of Kiukiang. If we hadn't come out of the hospital, we wouldn't have even known they were there. We learned this was the Chinese People's Liberation Army (中國人民解放軍).

Day-Day and Mother were duly impressed, as these soldiers and their officers did not interfere with any matters related to the hospital, in contrast with the often rude and drunken KMT soldiers we had encountered during the recent Chinese New Year's dragon parade, when we were pushed and shoved while having peanut shells stuffed down our necks.

We soon learned that the Communist leader, Mao Tse-Tung (毛澤東), had strict rules written into an easy-to-remember song. Every soldier and later every civilian had to memorize the words: "All members of the Revolution Army take heed. Bear these three essential rules of conduct in mind, and remember the eight points of Dos and Don'ts and the people's needs—"

The song then stated these rules one by one, such as, "No. 1: Obey orders in all your actions. No. 2: Do not take a single needle or a piece of thread from people. No. 3: Return all things captured."

Then for the eight points: (1) speak politely; (2) pay fairly for what you buy; (3) return what you borrow; (4) pay for your damages; (5) don't harm or swear at people; (6) don't destroy farmers' crops; (7): don't commit adultery; and (8) don't mistreat captives."

SPRING FLOWER: A TALE OF TWO RIVERS

I often wonder if some of Chairman Mao's ideas came from the Ten Commandments. I'm sure Mao had read the Bible, as he was known for being well-read.

As the Communist troops took over the city, Chum and I were sent to board at school until the situation became stable. Given all the rumors, our parents did not want us to be snatched from the streets to become Communists' wives or concubines. But that wasn't happening, so it wasn't long before we were happily back at home.

When the school reopened in the following weeks, things had changed. The school was filled with cadres, or government agents who wore blue-gray pants and long-sleeve jackets, known as Lenin garb. Chum and I found it strange and wondered if female cadres would name their underwear "Stalin bras"?

Soon the Communist government banned traditional Chinese gowns, which were considered aristocratic or bourgeois, and Lenin garb became the fashion nationwide. Dresses and skirts began to disappear on campus, and the whole nation became a sea of gray, black, and blue, with only the Communists' red flag to break the monotony. The clothing did not bother anyone much, but how we addressed one another was awkward. Instead of addressing people with titles, like Miss, Mrs., Mr., teacher (老師), or Sir (先生), as we had, we addressed each other as "Comrade (同志)."

Wives and husbands had to address each other as "愛人 (ai-ren: literally meaning 'lovers')", even mature couples who were accustomed to addressing each other as "我老公 (wo-lao-gong: meaning, my old man)" or "我老婆 (wo-lao-po: meaning my old lady)." And young couples in Day-Day's hospital blushed when being addressed as "lovers" ("qing-ren" or "ai-ren": 情人 or 愛人). After a while, married couples began addressing each other by their names.

JEAN TREN-HWA PERKINS

Some of the changes seemed reasonable; others seemed weird. The intent was to denounce the old ways and establish an entirely new society, with strictly controlled uniformity. The cadres were there to enforce the changes. They recognized that intellectuals and educated people have minds of their own and are less easy to convince than farmers and workers. So, when a cadre was in our classroom, everyone would be hushed. It was clear that the teachers felt uneasy. I avoided the cadres as much as possible.

One day between classes, as I leaned against the balcony staring at the kids on the lawn, I felt a cadre walking toward me. My heart began to pound with fear, and I pretended not to see her, but she felt my anxiety, I think, and asked, "What's your name?"

I couldn't find a way out, so I told her.

"How old are you?" she continued, determined to make me talk.

"Eighteen," I answered.

"I notice you don't say much in class," she said, staring me down. I stood in silence and didn't reply.

"What was there to say?" I thought. "This kid can't be a year older than me. She should be in college — reading and learning — instead of policing a high school campus. Who gives her the right to question me in broad daylight?"

She was about to press on, and I was thinking about where to run. This tense and uncomfortable moment lasted only for a few seconds, but felt like an eternity. Then, she said, "Okay, Tren-Hwa, at ease. It seems you don't want to talk to me," and she walked away. I let out a huge sigh, glad I'd given her my Chinese name instead of Jean.

By the fall of 1949, things seemed more or less normal in Kiukiang. Despite subtle yet noticeable changes in our lives, I was content as long as I could be with Mother and Day-Day. Chum and I still rode our bikes to school but decided it would be better to speak English only at home.

One morning during assembly, one of the cadres announced: "Our beloved, Great Leader Chairman Mao will proclaim to the world on October 1, 1949, that the Chinese Communist Party has 'liberated' all of China from the oppression of the corrupt KMT government; that Chinese people are now finally standing on our feet, free of inside and outside oppression; and that a new China is born. The name will be the People's Republic of China."

The lead cadre then repeated these words, then she pumped her right fist in the air as if to pound the words into our minds, before continuing, "There will be a nationwide celebration that will require everyone, young and old, to learn one of the traditional folk dances. We will dance on the streets during the celebration to show our joy and pay our respect to the Great Leader Mao Tse-Tung. Some students will be selected to learn how to beat a drum, which is tied to the waist, and dance at the same time. Those chosen will need to practice with perseverance."

Even as I was struggling to relearn Chinese, the language was changing. It was now filled with slogans — and not all of them had any actual meaning. Ignoring them was the best way to avoid being grossed out, but often these cacophonous calls for unity were blasted over giant bullhorn speakers and I felt nauseated. All governments inundate their people with propaganda, but this regime seemed especially fond of noisy slogans.

The call for dancing aroused great excitement among the younger students at Rulison, but we twelfth graders could have cared less. After class, the whole school gathered on the lawn to learn the new dance. I stood, watched, and laughed at how funny everyone looked. A cadre came over to me and asked, "Why aren't you practicing?"

I said, "You didn't choose me, and I don't like to dance." I could have also told her that my mother wouldn't allow me to dance. That would have caught her off guard. But at that moment, I was daydreaming about when, in tenth grade, one of my classmates taught me the foxtrot. It was so much fun, but I had to confess to Mother afterward. All she had said was, "I'm glad you know when you do something wrong, but a few dances wouldn't be the worst thing you might do."

Even if Mother had allowed me to dance for the Communists' Independence Day, I preferred not to. It wasn't just because I was shy. This dance looked so kindergarten-ish. I was even laughing at Principal Wu. She was leading the teachers learning to dance like silly kids. It all looked ridiculous.

Then I felt a twinge of guilt for laughing at Principal Wu, who had been good to me since I came back to Kiukiang. She had just returned from a year studying in America, and a year later, she would commit suicide. The two other teachers from William Nast Academy who had gone to America with her were thrown into prison where they eventually died. I'm getting ahead of myself, but their stories could also be a book.

Right then, a male cadre came over and said, "You'd better start dancing—now!"

I reluctantly followed him and joined the crazy crowd. Uniformity was a demand of the new regime. Chum was selected for the drummer dance. She looked much more dignified than the chaotic mess I was forced to participate in. Chum and her drumming mates had to work hard to master their performance.

Well, we still had "free speech" when the cadres weren't around. Darwin's theory on the origin of species became a topic. I would get into heated debates with classmates about how humans originated. I was initially amazed that people who claimed to be Christian were trying to convince me that we came from apes or monkeys. I learned much from these stimulating discussions on Darwinism as well as so-called social Darwinism. I stood firm by my belief that God created the universe and all humankind — and that all men are created equal.

A few months later, I took a course on evolution, "From Apes to Man," during the winter break. Ironically, the class took place in the church where I'd sung in the choir. The church was no longer heated, and it was freezing. I didn't learn much, but I did get chilblains. It was so itchy that the information about Darwinism went in one ear and out the other. The chilblains on my hands and feet were cured by soaking in almost boiling water saturated with dried hot pepper. So much for evolution, but at least I could say I'd taken the course, and perhaps they would now leave me alone.

25

DURING THIS confusing time—politically and socially—the last thing I needed was unwanted attention. Then one day in late 1949, I received a personal letter at school. One of my classmates handed it to me, and then she shouted, "Tren-Hwa has a boyfriend!"

My face turned crimson. "What makes you so sure?" I asked.

"Open it!" The entire class began to clamor in unison.

I stuffed it into my pocket. I was not going to read any letters in front of an audience, especially if they happened to be right. I did not have a boyfriend, nor was I interested in one because I was too shy. Unlike Chum I was a dull-looking kid with not much self-confidence.

After I got home, I quickly opened the envelope and began to read.

> Miss Pei [he wrote in Chinese], I have observed you for a long time. I like your smile. Once during a volleyball game at your school, I watched from the boys' school window. You failed to get the ball over the net and helped your school lose. It was comical. You looked embarrassed. I rooted for you, but of course, you couldn't hear it. Will you be my friend? Please answer.
> Paul

My face again turned red. While I wasn't sure what Paul meant by "friend," I knew I would have to ask Mother, and I wondered what she would say. Screwing up my courage, I read the letter to her.

"Can I be friends with him?" I asked.

"You know boys at this age get excited easily, and then things happen."

"Things?" I asked.

Mother did not answer. Instead, she said, "Remember, your priority is studying. You have to go to college."

"If I study hard, can I be his friend, Mother?" I asked, thinking I might have figured out those "things" that Mother was implying.

"Tell him to come here, if he wants to see you," Mother responded, clear and unexcited.

Paul was no stranger to Mother and Day-Day. He was the fifth child and second oldest son of the headmaster of William Nast Academy, Russell Hsiung (熊祥熙), and his mother, Eve, taught at my school. Still, Mother was cautious, without going into detail. There were no talks of birds and bees. I was left as ignorant as a fawn in the woods, even though I had lived in America. No one except probably Paul would have believed it.

Paul Hsiung, it turned out, was the cute, baby-faced boy I had called Ming-Ming, who stood next to me in our kindergarten photo. He was also the boy who ran around saying, "Oh, it's so hot," while wearing a knitted vest in the heat of the summer. He had become a lean, six-foot-tall teenager. I reached only his shoulder. I finally answered his letter. "My mother said we could be friends, but you will have to see me at our home."

He quickly wrote back,

> Miss Pei, I am scared to go to a foreigner's home. I don't speak good English, and I hate eating with a knife and fork. Paul

I wrote, "My parents won't eat you! And please don't call me

JEAN TREN-HWA PERKINS

Miss Pei! My name is Jean Perkins; call me Jean."

He finally mustered the courage and came to my house on a Saturday afternoon. We stood at the top of the terrace under a sapling while chatting, the first time we talked to each other. Paul seemed more nervous than I was, perhaps because I was at home. Shy as I was, I managed to start a conversation.

"You know what?" I began. "Ever since kindergarten, I prayed, 'God bless Ming-Ming,' after I had prayed for all my family members. I'm not sure why I called you Ming-Ming. Perhaps, I didn't have a better way of remembering your name."

Paul looked surprised and a bit embarrassed, and quickly asked, "Do you still pray for me?"

"Well," I laughed, "I dropped you from my list when I was about eleven and living in America. You've gotten so tall since you came back from Chungking." I continued for the sake of saying something. "You weren't even as tall as I was then."

"I thought you looked very grownup," Paul commented.

"How did you know which one I was?" I asked, curiously.

"You and Chum looked very different from the other girls. You look like foreigners," he said. "And how did you recognize me?"

"Miss You told me you were the little boy running around complaining about the heat. My classmates and I were all laughing at you."

As we were talking, I unconsciously put my hand on the little tree. Paul did too. Then, he slipped his hand down, attempting to touch mine. Remembering Mother's warning about boys, I quickly withdrew my hand, although I still hadn't the faintest idea what would happen if I let Paul touch me. Of course, Paul didn't know what Mother had said, and I wasn't going to tell him. He wasn't even aware that I'd purposely withdrawn my hand. Then he said, with a shy smile, "Now I'm so much taller than you, I have to bend down to talk to you."

We didn't see each other again, as Paul soon left for college in Nanking. We did write to each other a few times.

By early 1950, things appeared to be getting calmer. One evening at dinner Day-Day said, "We seem to be getting along pretty well. The new Communist government is letting us keep the hospital open." He sounded hopeful.

"This has been much better than the first time they came here," Mother said.

"The Communists were here before?" I asked, surprised.

"Yes, in 1927, before you and Chum were born, Honey. The entire Communist movement started here in the Central Yangtze River Valley, very much in our backyard, the Province of Kiangsi (江西)! When they began fighting with President Chiang's KMT armies and local warlords, the wounded from all sides came to our hospital, and Day-Day was pulling bullets out of all of them."

"Then, when it was turning into a civil war, we had to close the hospital and flee to Korea," added Aunt Dee.

"Yes, imagine that! We all spent half a year in Seoul until President Chiang unified the country in 1928," Mother said. "That was quite an experience learning Korean, while Day-Day and aunties worked in a missionary-run hospital."

"Well, I guess we'll survive the new regime after all," I remarked, impressed by Mother's understanding of Chinese history, which was more mine.

Those were famous last words. A few weeks after that dinner conversation, Day-Day was ordered to step aside and nominate a Chinese doctor to be the dean of the Water of Life Hospital. Day-Day was okay with that, because he had confidence in the Chinese physicians, especially the ones he had trained, and he was getting older. Passing the baton to a Chinese physician had been just a matter of time anyway.

JEAN TREN-HWA PERKINS

Day-Day always understood the hospital would eventually belong to the Chinese people. Even President Chiang and his Republic Government had a mandate in 1927-1928 that the presidents and headmasters of colleges and high schools should be Chinese nationals and that foreigners who established these institutions would pass the leadership on to a Chinese national. Such changes had taken place in all the high schools in Kiukiang. Paul's father, Russell Hsiung, had become the first Chinese headmaster of William Nast Academy.

So this turn of events did not dissuade Day-Day and Mother from continuing to live in China and work for the Chinese people they loved. My parents' presence allowed me to focus on school and to graduate. What could be better? I entered the final semester of my senior year at Rulison Girls High in the early spring of 1950. Our homeroom teacher, also our advisor, Miss You, wanted us to think about college. She asked what I wanted to be.

"A journalist," I told her without hesitation. "I want to be a writer."

Miss You laughed. "Jean, you don't read newspapers, and you don't know what's going on currently or what happened in the past. And your Chinese is still unpolished. Are you sure you want to be a journalist?"

"I never thought about that," I admitted. "But ever since I was a child, I've wanted to be a writer. Now neither my Chinese nor my English is good enough. What do you suggest?"

Miss You shared her thoughts. "You have a warm personality and a good nature, although you're quite shy. But I think you'll outgrow your shyness as you mature. Have you thought about being a doctor?"

"Funny," I mused on my way home. "I've lived among medical professionals my whole life, yet it never occurred to me to become a doctor."

SPRING FLOWER: A TALE OF TWO RIVERS

Perhaps I'd been so impressed by Jo in *Little Women* that I fixated on becoming a writer. Or perhaps I knew too much about the dark side of medical work. Day-Day was an excellent and hardworking doctor, but as a father I hardly got to see him. Even while we were in America, he was away most of the time. I sensed I had to face an unfortunate reality. My Chinese was not good enough to be a writer in my native language. So why not a doctor?

When I told my parents, they were thrilled, even though Mother had hoped I'd be an evangelist. I assured her I could do both, just like Day-Day. The aunties chimed in, "Girls, if anything happens so you're not able to finish college, please consider going to the Danforth Women's Hospital for hands-on training to become a nurse. Nurses are always needed." Chum and I agreed to become nurses if necessary. Neither of us had a clue how precious free will can be when making life choices.

A few days later, Miss You announced, "Entrance exams for Gin-Ling Women's University (金陵女子大學) will be tomorrow."

Gin-Ling Women's University in Nanking, later called Gin-Ling College, has a great history. It was established by missionaries in 1913 as a sister school to Smith College in Northampton, Massachusetts, and produced some of the earliest Chinese female college graduates. One of them was Dr. Wu Yi-Fang (吳貽芳), who in 1928 became the first female university president in China. Given that Chinese culture has historically devalued if not abused women, to have women graduating from colleges in the early twentieth century represents a crowning achievement of Christian missions in China.

Since this was a private Christian college, tuition was higher than that of government-run schools, so only a few of us took the exams. Besides, Gin-Ling College was an English-speaking school. Except for the Chinese classics, all classes were in English, which was intimidating to most of my classmates. I thought I did well in all subjects in the exams except Chinese classics and literature. I feared that those scores would drag me down.

When the letter of acceptance arrived, I was jubiliant. Mother and Day-Day could not have been happier and more proud that the little girl they had adopted nineteen years earlier, for better and for worse, was going to attend college. Mother was especially pleased, and she sent my tuition fees in ahead of time. Given how much things were changing, she was afraid the college might change their minds about accepting someone with American parents as well as a religious background. Later, I found out that Mother registered me as Jean Perkins. Most college officials knew who I was, and of course, they knew Mother and Day-Day very well. Mother had contacted the president of the college, Dr. Wu, months earlier and discussed my application.

Perhaps I hadn't done that well on the entrance exams after all, especially on Chinese subjects, and maybe my acceptance was due to my family's influence. But that thought didn't dampen my spirits. I was thrilled to have a chance to attend one of the best women's colleges in China, and that it would be English-speaking only.

Finally, the day came for high school graduation! To my shock and disappointment, Principal Wu advised Mother and Day-Day that they would not be allowed to attend the ceremony. The new Communist government had confined all American missionaries, including American teachers at our school, to their homes. So, it was a bittersweet occasion for my American parents and me. Chum was equally disappointed that her beloved aunties were barred from attending my graduation day, too. Ironically, we had chosen a sorrowful song for this joyful occasion. The words seemed to augur what was to come, although we didn't see it at the time. It went something like this:

"Goodbye, friends, goodbye, friends; the time of separation has come.

"Our golden years have gone; oh, when shall we meet again?"

Tears streamed down my cheeks, and I thought about my kindergarten graduation, then my sixth-grade graduation in Yonkers. I could still see Mother's and Day-Day's proud eyes.

A greater irony was that these missionaries had built these schools. For nearly a century, they had sacrificed their lives and given their collective hearts and minds to the Chinese people. Never did we dream how soon the truth in the song's last stanza would unfold: "Oh, when shall we meet again?"

The sad spring soon gave way to my last summer in Kiukiang, the summer of 1950. Paul came back from college. He had completed his freshmen year at the Private University of Nanking, a boys' college that had also been established by missionaries.[1] Paul came to see me often, and I noticed a change in him. He was no longer nervous or shy. In fact, he seemed confident, even bold bordering on arrogant.

One day as we were walking down on the street, he reached over and held my hand. Despite my struggle to get loose, he wouldn't let go and coyly said, "You should see what they do in college. Couples all walk hand-in-hand, and they even put their arms around each other's waists, like…" He tried to show me, but I pushed him away. Then he continued, "I even saw them kissing in the shadows, behind the trees."

"Well," I said, "We are *not* going to do such things. I don't even want you to touch my hand!" I had in mind what Mother said about boys getting excited.

---

1   This is not the same school as Nanking University. The Private University of Nanking was called Gin-Ling Boy's University (金陵男子大學). In its earlier years, it was called the Nanking Hui-wen University (南京匯文書院: or Hui-wen Shu-yuan, and was founded in 1888 by C. H. Fowler.

Nevertheless, during that summer, the four of us—Paul, Chum, Samuel, and I—would bicycle together. I still loved the powder-blue bicycle that Day-Day gave me. Paul told me that my biking skills left much to be desired, but I didn't care. As long as I could hop on and off and keep my balance, that was enough for me. We even had a picnic at the foot of the Ku-Ling Mountain. We were no longer allowed to go up the mountain. Our homes had been confiscated and transferred to elite Communist officials to use for their summer vacations and conferences. Mother and the aunties didn't object to our outings as long as we stayed out of trouble. We did make a small sensation in this conservative small town, which was not as open-minded as cities like Nanking and Shanghai. Some tongues did wag, but since childhood, Chum and I had always been a little different, a little "foreign" as Paul put it.

Of all the summers, this one felt the shortest, perhaps because I knew I would be packing to leave for college. I didn't want to leave Mother, Day-Day, or the aunties. I would miss Wang-Sao, and Chum too. Chum would be starting twelfth grade at Rulison. And, of course, I'd miss the surroundings I had known for so

Dr. Edith Milner at the left end; Hyla Doc at the right

many years of my life. I'd miss swinging beneath my Japanese maple tree. Thoughts of Jill, Betty, Marie, and Doris C. as well as memories of my other river flickered through my mind too. They felt far, far away.

I knew it wouldn't be easy to head off to college, but I had learned to adapt myself so many times, and Nanking wasn't that far away, just a day's boat ride down the Yangtze River. I knew that I would eventually leave home for good, but as long as I could come back and visit Mother and Day-Day, I'd be fine. Nevertheless, no matter how hard I tried, there was a knot in my stomach that would not go away.

Something uneasy hung in the air. Day-Day hardly spoke to me or anyone; he buried himself in his hospital work. Although he hid it well, I could tell that Day-Day was more and more unhappy. He tried to smile, and he gave me a big kiss on the forehead when I showed him my Rulison High School diploma, telling me how wonderful it would be when I began studying medicine, if I chose that path. His mood had more to do about uncertainty. He was unsure about the future of China, and the future of the hospital under the new leadership. Mother didn't say much at dinners either. Although the Chinese staff who had worked with them at the hospital continued to be respectful and remained focused on those in need, you could sense they, too, were very uncertain about the future.

Of course, my teacher had been right. How could I consider being a journalist? I didn't read newspapers and barely had a clue about world events, although I did know war was already raging on all sides. One war was taking place at China's doorstep on soil thousands of miles from Kiukiang. Like all wars, it would be terrible. One side saw it as "liberation and unification," the other called it "invasion and aggression." In the end, it was one form of idealism struggling against another, for supremacy and legitimacy on a world stage, at the expense of kids of my age, leaving countless civilians as collateral damage.

How else could anyone justify the involvement of so many countries slaughtering one another on a tiny peninsula by the Yellow Sea? None of them lived there or spoke the language. These efforts were all for resolving a civil war between two ruthless dictators, Kim and Rhee, both of whom were executing innocent people. Syngman Rhee had been educated in America but was removed from power decades later by a democratic movement in South Korea. He lived out the rest of his life in shame in America. That was the man the West was trying to save.

Korea had been a colony of defeated Japan at the end of World War II, and dividing Korea into two parts without asking the people what they wanted was a disgrace. The Korean conflict was a civil war between their North and South. How would Lincoln feel if another country had meddled in the America Civil War, assisting in the decision of freedom versus slavery? Let the Korean people resolve their own issues, I thought. The Korean conflict had nothing to do with the powers of East or West, but it became just that.

Having studied history, I knew nothing is ever black and white when it comes to power. But was it worth slaughtering or wounding two million-plus Korean civilians in just three years, in addition to two million soldiers? At the age of nineteen, I didn't grasp the magnitude and ramifications of this war, but I did know that it made no sense, and I felt very afraid. Brave soldiers on both sides were sacrificing themselves following orders, and so many others were "collateral damage." This new war, for me, felt as bad as or worse than the one before, not only because millions more would die senselessly, but because it was actually a conflict between America and China.

I deeply hope these atrocities will stop repeating themselves. But at the time, I was focused on growing up, finishing high school, and going off to college. I barely noticed that Mother and Day-Day were getting older.

"How will they manage when I'm away?" I thought. "Mother has gotten used to having me around. The three of us together wherever we've been—even India.... Now they'll be on their own."

I walked to the garden and sat by my favorite Japanese maple tree, staring at my old swing, tears streaming down my cheeks, as the late summer breeze brushed against my way-too-long hair. "When is Mother going to try to cut my hair?" I mused. "How about now, before I leave for college?"

I so wished the next four years would go quickly and I'd be able to return to Kiukiang to work with Day-Day and Mother at the Water of Life Hospital. I wanted to follow in their footsteps and devote my life to helping Chinese people, making my parents proud.

"Jeanie, dear," Mother shouted, "Day-Day is home early. Let's have dinner together."

"Okay," I shouted back, wiping away my tears, hoping Mother wouldn't notice.

"We'll have dinner on the porch. In just a few days, we'll see you off at the Kiukiang Bund. Our little girl is going to college!" Mother said, with pride and a gleam in her eyes.

I tried to cheer myself up. "Yes," I replied. "That will be wonderful. Let's eat together on the porch. It's been a long while since we have. Okay if I pray tonight, Mother?"

"Your Day-Day will be proud!"

I caught a glimpse of Wang-Sao standing by the kitchen window grinning, yet there was a look of concern on her face. She had been watching me. As I closed the porch door behind me, I took one more look at the beautiful garden where I'd grown up—where I was granted a second chance to live here again. Being able to return and be with Wang-Sao and all these beautiful human beings was the most precious of the many experiences I had had.

26

"WHAT A beautiful campus!" I exclaimed. We six girls from Rulison High entered the big iron gate of Gin-Ling Women's College, the storied sister school of Smith College. It was the autumn of 1950, and I was nineteen years old.

"The lawn looks like a carpet," Phoebe marveled.

"Look at the buildings, half Chinese-style and half Western," said Mollie, now my best friend. Sure enough, the four corners of the sloping roof turned up like Chinese temple eaves, but these buildings were made of concrete, not wood.

"There are more trees here than Rulison," Tsai commented.

"When it gets hot, we can study under their shade," I suggested.

"Better still, you and Paul can sit there while you charm him with your American accent?" Chen teased.

"I'll get you back!" I said, my face blushing bright red. The other kids burst into laughter at my expense.

Tsai added, "I agree with Chen, Jean. Your accent is charming."

Soon, we were all seated in the assembly hall to receive a welcoming message from President Wu (Dr. Wu Yi-Fang). Although I don't recall what she said, she was always an inspiring speaker. Born in the same province I was, Hubei, Dr. Wu had earned a PhD in biology from the University of Michigan in Ann Arbor. Later she found time to teach some of our biology classes. Dr. Wu was one of the extraordinary women in early twentieth-century China. Again, I was witnessing history.

JEAN TREN-HWA PERKINS

After Dr. Wu's talk, the juniors passed out keys for our dorm rooms, and we drew the names of juniors who would become our Big Sisters (大姐). "Big Sister," I thought, "as if we were kindergarteners." My Big Sister was pretty and petite, from Shanghai. Her name was Alice, and she majored in home economics, the most popular subject for women before the Communist "Liberation." Home economics had been introduced to the Gin-Ling campus by Dr. Wu, and students were still allowed to pursue a college degree in "home economics" in the early 1950s.

I hardly understood a word of Alice's Shanghai dialect, but she was an absolute sweetheart to me. That was enough.

And I was thrilled to be assigned a dorm room with two of my high school classmates, Chen and Yen. The room was pretty stark. We had three beds with iron springs, three desks, and three chairs. The cold cement floor was different from the warm wooden floors I had become used to at home. There were no closets and no dresser. So we lived out of our suitcases. I had two, and they had been around the world. I had to drag my old suitcases out from under my dorm room bed every time I needed clothing or cash, and slide them back on the rough cement surface.

I kept a big pile of money that Mother had given me for books, pencils, and daily needs (including snacks)

Freshman year – Gin-Ling Women's College, Nanking, ca. fall 1950

in my suitcase. Although the Communists had been in power for over a year, they had not yet changed the currency of the Nationalist government. But due to the civil war, the old money had become hugely inflated. The smallest unit was now the one-hundred-dollar bill. So instead of trying to figure out where to put this massive stack of cash, I thought spending it would be smarter. It wasn't as if I could open a checking account somewhere. The Chinese banking system was in disarray. Instead of shoring up the dilapidated financial system, our leaders had decided that waging another war was a better use of resources than diplomacy.

My roommates were less fortunate financially than I was. So each time I bought snacks, mostly Nanking's famous roasted peanuts, I would get a bag for each of us. There was a little store just outside our gate, so it was convenient for me to spend money. It was the first time Mother had entrusted me with so much money, and I had no concept of value. Before I knew it, the piles of hundred-dollar bills had vanished. When I wrote home for more, Mother asked me to keep an account book describing how I spent the money. I did as she asked, and was shocked to see how free-spending I was. I decided to manage my money better and change my lifestyle.

I wore a different outfit every day, which my roommates found strange. They wore the same clothes for at least a week. Each night I would change into my pajamas, which seemed to them another odd foreign custom. They just slid into bed in their underclothes, which I thought was weird. I recognized that some of these differences had as much to do with financial resources as with customs and culture.

I also faithfully changed my bedsheets each week and proudly washed them myself until winter set in and the sheets would freeze while still in the cold water, as did my hands. So, I had to give up changing sheets weekly and follow the custom of my roommates, who cleaned their bedding more like once in a blue moon, or never. Without the care of cleanliness, my feet began to itch, and I could hardly concentrate. I told Chen and Yen. They laughed, "You have Hong Kong foot (香港腳), the local name for athlete's foot."

"What's that?" I asked.

"Have you been wearing the wooden clogs in the shower?" Yen asked.

"Yes, why?" I became curious.

"Because that's how you get athlete's foot. You grew up in a doctor's home and you didn't know that?" said Chen.

"No one ever told me," I answered. "What should I do?"

"Get some athlete's foot solution at a drugstore," suggested Yen.

I found the solution, but it didn't help. I wrote to Day-Day, but there was no reply. I did buy a new pair of wooden clogs for myself. Then, weeks later, I remembered Aunt Bessie using gentian violet on a patient who had a skin disease. The solution cured the child's skin problem by drying up the secretion, I suspected. I tried it, and it worked, although it took months and stained all my socks. Since then, I've never worn public clogs or gone barefoot in public showers.

Attending college classes reminded me of Hawthorne Junior High in Yonkers, where we went to different rooms for each course. The most significant contrast was that in Yonkers, I understood what the teachers said, but not here. By the time I got to campus in 1950, most classes were taught in Chinese, no longer in English. To make it even harder, these professors spoke different dialects, coming from different parts of China. Although all the instructors were required to teach in Mandarin, the standardized national dialect, some had not mastered Mandarin and since no one was policing our lecture rooms, many taught in their native dialects. As a result, I had no idea as to what they were saying in many classes. Once again, I was a foreigner in my own country.

My biology instructor, for example, only spoke the Ningbo dialect from south of Shanghai in the Province of Zhejiang. He might as well have been speaking Greek.

The tones of his dialect covered a full octave, and he never looked at us while he lectured. He seemed to find the ceiling more fascinating, and he fixated on one spot up there for the whole fifty minutes. For variety, he would pick a different spot on the ceiling to stare at. I looked up to see if he had pasted his notes up there. I couldn't take notes quickly or accurately enough for any of my classes. So I spent a lot of time copying notes from my classmates or my roommate Chen.

Less than a month into the semester, the instructor of our Chinese Composition class, a core course, said in front of everyone, "I can't believe a prestigious college like ours would accept a student who can't even write a readable Chinese essay!" My face began to burn, thinking he was talking about me. "Listen to this," he said, and he began to read aloud. Yup, it was mine. I slumped into my seat as far as I could, my face beet red. I prayed the floor would open up and swallow me whole. It was so embarrassing, I wanted to dig my way back to America.

Suddenly a voice from the back of the room said, "Professor, you shouldn't criticize before you investigate. Do you know this student's background? She has lived in foreign countries for many years, and she grew up in an English-speaking family." I didn't know her name, but I could tell from her dialect she was from Shanghai. Stopped in his tracks, the teacher gave our next assignment, then left the room before the bell rang. I exited in a hurry too, to avoid the rest of the class. The girl who had stood

JEAN TREN-HWA PERKINS

up for me followed right behind.

"Are you the girl who has an American name?" she asked.

I turned around and smiled awkwardly.

She continued, "I know your registered name is Jean Perkins. I was looking for this new American classmate, but didn't see any Americans. Then it occurred to me that it might be you. You seem a little different—actually, quite different. And you have an accent when you talk. It gives you away." She chuckled.

"Thank you for saving me from further embarrassment," I said.

She introduced herself as Shou and told me she was indeed from Shanghai, and that she was a pre-med freshman. We soon became great friends. From then on, she took it as her responsibility to protect me. Strangely, she reminded me of Jill in Yonkers. Later, I learned Shou was also a Christian.

Being in college gave me a false sense of freedom. For one thing, there didn't seem to be as much homework as we'd had in high school. I was surprised to see my roommates always studying, while I spent a lot of time buying snacks—stress eating—while writing home to Mother and Day-Day, or my friends and classmates in America. I tried to keep in contact with Jill, Betty, Marie, and Doris C., who were also in college.

From the day I arrived in Nanking, Paul kept visiting me. He was a sophomore at the Private University of Nanking (or, Gin-Ling Men's University, 金陵男子大學), which was within shouting distance of our campus. I found his visits disturbing, as I was struggling academically and with the language. Instead of spending time with him, I felt I should be studying more. There was a church near our campus, and so to make his visits worthwhile, I asked him to visit on Sundays and we attended church together. Paul was also raised by a devout Christian family and was no stranger to Sunday services and classical hymns. So this bright idea worked out well for a while, and I figured Mother would approve of meeting him this way.

Once a week, an evangelist would come to our school to preach the Gospel. The meetings were for Christians only. I persuaded Chen and Yen to join the fellowship meetings, and soon, they accepted Christ as their Savior. From then on, the three of us read the Bible every evening before bed and took turns praying. I was proud of myself. "Yes, I could become an evangelist—like Mother and Day-Day," I thought.

Before the semester was over, the ax fell. It happened so quickly I was stunned, unable to comprehend. In October 1950, General MacArthur's army and the UN-backed allies stormed back from South Korea's initial defeats at the hands of North Korea armies. They fought past the 38th Parallel and reached southern banks of the Yalu River, the natural border between Korea and China. So China entered the conflict. Despite condemnation from the UN, they sent the ill-equipped and undertrained Chinese People's Volunteer Army (中國人民志願軍) across the Yalu River into Korea, and China and America were now at war. Slogans like "Resist America and Aid Korea" (抗美援朝) were shouted on the streets of Nanking, and anti-American banners hung everywhere.

The world I had known and understood since childhood was shattered, and I sensed the pieces could not be put back together. These were permanent scars. I walked back to campus, thinking it would be quieter and less insane there, but it was not so for long. There's an old Chinese saying, "The one who speaks means no harm, but the one who hears take it to heart (說者無心, 聽者有意)."

Helen Ferris was one of the last remaining American missionaries in Nanking and one of the last remaining American

JEAN TREN-HWA PERKINS

professors at Gin-Ling College. I had fond memories of her; she had spent her younger years in Kiukiang. In fact, I'd known her as Aunt Helen since I was two years old, and she had given Chum and me piano lessons when we were five and six.

"You were a pain in the neck," she told me one day back when I was at Rulison High. I could only grin. "Each time you and Chum had a piano lesson, you would hide behind the piano and make faces at Chum so she couldn't concentrate. I had to pull you out, but within seconds you were back behind the piano again." We both laughed. "Yes," she added, "you were the mischievous one."

Rulison girls with Professor Helen Ferris

In the past year, Aunt Helen had moved to Gin-Ling to serve as a professor of philosophy. She was so glad to see us Rulison girls that she often invited us to where she and all the other Chinese and American professors lived, on a hill just behind our dorm, known as South Mountain. Although it wasn't really big enough to be a mountain, the name stuck. On that fateful morning, the topic in Aunt Helen's philosophy class somehow evolved into something about Taiwan. In 1949, when the Communists took over the mainland, Taiwan was where the remnants of President Chiang's Republic of China government and the KMT fled. For some reason, many foreigners refer to Taiwan as Formosa, including my American parents. "Formosa" in Portuguese, they told me, means "beautiful island." The Japanese had also called it Formosa, so the Communists disliked the name even more.

In class, Aunt Helen referred to Taiwan as Formosa, which triggered a campus-wide uproar. "打倒 Ferris! (Down with Ferris!). 打倒美國帝國主義! (Down with American Imperial Aggression!)" These chants filled the campus. I'd never seen behavior like this before, and I was frightened and confused. I watched day after day and saw supporters from other colleges and universities in Nanking march onto our campus, shouting more anti-American slogans. Classes stopped, and the Gin-Ling campus became a battleground where Gin-Ling "heroines," as they were called, denounced Americans. I knew anti-American sentiment had been bubbling since my high school graduation day, and by the end of 1950, it was in full swing. I watched it all through my dorm window and thought about what Mother often said, "War is a terrible thing for everyone." Suddenly, it occurred to me, "How are Mother and Day-Day doing? How about the aunties?"

Meanwhile, the university authorities confined Aunt Helen to her home. I obviously did not share in this anti-American enthusiasm. Neither did the other Kiukiang kids. I didn't see why there should be such a fuss over the name of an island. The Portuguese word *Formosa* had nothing to do with the Japanese invasion and occupation.

We would sneak up the hill after dark to see Aunt Helen since no one seemed to be guarding her house at night. She had a strong personality and seemed to be bearing up well. She was more concerned about our safety than hers. We could be expelled or severely punished if the guards caught us. It might be considered treason to be in contact with an American, who was now the enemy. Or they could try us as spies. We were so naive and perhaps too sentimental.

Before the day Aunt Helen was deported, I made one last visit. She gave us all the food she had, mostly canned goods. We didn't want to take it, but she insisted. "Better to have you eat it than strangers, Jean!" she chuckled. She also gave me coats and sweaters and told me to share them with other Rulison alums. Then she said, on the side, "Jean, be frank with me. Do you have enough money?"

"Not much—uh, not enough," I admitted.

I was more than a little embarrassed, but I quickly added, "I've already written to Mother for more."

"As far as I can tell," Aunt Helen said, "I don't think you'll be getting any from them. I think they're having difficulties too. Take this, and I'll see to it that your Mother pays me back in America. All right?"

I nodded my head and said, "Thank you so much, Aunt Helen. Please take care."

The next day, huge posters were everywhere: "We, the Gin-Ling Heroines, had the American Enemy Within—Ferris—Deported."

We, the Kiukiang-Rulison group, celebrated Aunt Helen's freedom going back to America by feasting on all the food she had left for us. A vast upgrade from cafeteria food! It satisfied my craving for American food. "How unpatriotic," I declared, "to be eating American food at this time!" We all laughed and continued to enjoy our feast.

27

WATCHING WHAT was going on around us could not have prepared me for what was to come. The anti-American movement soon entered my personal life. For months, I'd been looking forward to going home in early February 1951 for winter break, which coincided with the Chinese New Year, the Year of the Rabbit. Having been away for nearly a semester, I missed Mother and Day-Day enormously. I thought about Chum and the aunties as well. With America and China at war, I was more and more anxious, and Mother's letters were now fewer and fewer.

Then, in late December 1950, the week between Christmas and New Year's Day, a letter came from Mother. I opened it eagerly looking for the boat ticket she'd promised to send me to return to Kiukiang for the winter break. Instead, it was a brief letter telling me to stay put and focus on classes regardless of what might happen to them. They expressed fear for my safety and warned me not to do anything foolish. They were unsure whether I could leave campus without letting the university authorities know; they imagined severe discipline or expulsion.

Holding Mother's letter, I wept, then started to panic, hyperventilating and seeing horrible images in my mind. Not knowing what to do, whether we would ever meet again, I paced back and forth along the length of my bed. I had no idea what the future had in store, and I was in shock. Then I toughened up and shouted at the ceiling, "Okay, God, you can take my beloved parents away, but you can't take away my faith in you!" My knees shook, and I felt weak and helpless. Then I kneeled and said, "Okay, God, I know I'm not a saint, but I've tried my best to practice what my parents taught and expected of me. So why are you punishing me?"

I stood up, realizing that trying to negotiate with God might not be practical. I believed I should get on a boat or a train at that very moment to see them. "Okay, Jean," I said to myself. "Kiukiang is 300 miles away. How would you get there?" The fight inside me intensified.

Nanking was in complete chaos, and so was everywhere else including both banks of the Great River. The country was at war with its perceived enemy, America. The government was requisitioning most forms of transportation for military use. Then I realized I had no money.

"Oh dear, how can you be broke again? When will you ever learn not to spend money like there's no tomorrow? How is it possible you don't have a cent?" I stamped my feet in frustration, the tears rolling down my cheeks. "What good is crying going to do, Jean?" I said to myself, "I need to be decisive." So, I stopped pacing and sat on the edge of my bed. Moments later, realizing the situation was hopeless, I wrote a letter to Mother asking if they could wait for me to come home before they'd have to leave. I rushed it to the post office, but they never received it.

I would not get a chance to make it to Kiukiang in time. I was not there when my beloved parents of nineteen years departed from China. Just like that, the sight of them waving at me from the Kiukiang piers a few months earlier had become my last image of them. War had separated us.

Years later, I would learn details of their fateful journey back to America and their last trip from Kiukiang. When I read the letters they wrote to friends and relatives, I learned that Mother,

SPRING FLOWER: A TALE OF TWO RIVERS

Day-Day, and the aunties boarded the train at Kiukiang Station and headed to Canton on December 28, 1950. That was when I received Mother's letter, so it would have been futile if I had tried to see them in Kiukiang. When they left China, Day-Day was seventy-five and Mother had just turned sixty-eight.

I think it appropriate to quote from their letters as to what exactly happened and why they had to leave. Disclosure of this letter now will not endanger any of their Chinese colleagues or friends, because like themselves, most if not all of them have passed away.

The letter below was written by Day-Day to one of his relatives, while he and Mother were aboard *SS Anna Maersk* on the journey back to America.

February 15, 1951

Dear Aunt Minnie,

Georgie and I have hardly yet gotten over our surprise at being on our way home. We had decided to stay in China, despite circumstances, as we did at the time of the Japanese invasion when we were in or near the war zone for about five years. Our sources of excitement and hazard were not limited to the day when the Japanese took Kiukiang when we were treated to a naval bombardment, bombing from the sky, and so forth. But we had a great many problems that followed afterward, such as problems of food, fuel issues, issues of getting drugs, financial problems, issues of dealing with the Japanese (plenty of these), and refugee problems. You may remember that we had a thousand Chinese on our hospital compound, for whom we were more or less responsible.

We two thought that we were quite seasoned campaigners, but this time has been very different from anything we've had before. There are such a lot of things we want to tell you that it is hard to know where to begin. You will understand,

I think because we want to write to you very freely if we ask that what we tell you shall not be for publication. The reason is that if echoes of what we say get back to Kiukiang, as they might, they could quickly bring trouble to our Chinese friends and co-workers there, as well as to our adopted Chinese daughter, Jean.

They all have trouble enough already.

The reason for our leaving China and the work was not to escape the dangers of war, nor was it, by any means, entirely concerned with matters that affected us. But Georgie and I decided quite a while ago, that should the time come, when we were more a liability to the Chinese with whom we were associated than an asset, we would consider that an indication to leave. Back in 1927, when the communists first got a foothold in the Yangtze Valley, our best Chinese friends came to us to say that if we remained, we would be a source of great danger and difficulty to them, as they would want to help us and protect us, but would not be able. We evacuated immediately, and that was the time when quite a group of us went over and worked in Korea for about half a year.

The situation in the Yangtze Valley changed very quickly, and we were able to return and take up our work again, at the end of six months.

While not precisely the same, the present situation resembles that. This time it has been the case of the most virulent anti-America propaganda. The Chinese

SPRING FLOWER: A TALE OF TWO RIVERS

people have been told on a daily or more accurately on an hourly basis that the Americans have already begun a war of aggression; the Americans intend to conquer China. They were told that the people of the land must rally to defend their country and their home before Americans would come and subjugate them in total domination and humiliation. Some of that fear, I could understand because of centuries of subjugation at the hands of the imperialistic West. Some of that was just tactics of motivation by fear, and fear works well when one does not have accurate information or is ignorant of knowledge.

Quite a while ago, perhaps three months ago, the news circulated that the American planes were coming to bomb Chinese cities. We had people coming to our hospital compound to seek shelter there from the American bombing planes (the Water of Life Hospital is substantially built and does offer some accommodation). We were told that [in] Hankow, up the Yangtze River from us, the inhabitants were informed that on a particular day, the Americans were going to send planes to destroy their cities. Consequently, a significant part of the inhabitants fled to the country on that day for safety. What chaos and its disastrous consequences! The Americans were likened to tigers in their bloodthirsty attitude toward the inhabitants of China.

What America had done in the past was explained as part of a grand plot. The goal is to despoil the nation and its territory. Money previously given on such occasions as devastating famines or floods was interpreted as a part of the economic invasion. The work of churches and schools was described as culture aggression and subtle form of imperialistic attempts at domination. Indeed, white was just changed to black. The results were that a healthy relationship with our Chinese friends was made impossible. One could not walk with a Chinese friend on the street without casting a shadow of suspicion on him. Any Chinese who is seen to be friendly to us would be regarded as a sympathizer with the plot to conquest.

Towards the close of our stay in Kiukiang, some of our most intimate Chinese friends wanted to show us what their hearts were like, and they gave the little group of Americans a feast. Bowls of excellent food were sent to our home, but the givers did not come. There was no host. Of course, we truly understood what the situation was. The best helper on our hospital staff had been working with us for nearly thirty years. This man was almost like an assistant superintendent, whom I relied very much on his advice, was becoming afraid for his life because of his long association with Americans. They tended to regard such people as traitors to their country.

Two of the most promising of the young Chinese men connected with our mission were given scholarships and went to America for a year's study. On their return, the communists would not allow them to teach in our boys' mission school where they had taught before, and this lasted for a semester. Last September, they were permitted to start instructing again, but late October or November, they were both arrested at midnight on the same night and put in prison where they still are, as far as we know. Nobody is allowed to see them. They have been forever deprived of their license to teach. This all the more pathetic because they each have four or five children, and one of them was being prepared to take over the principalship of that mission boy's high school.

Before we left Kiukiang, a significant part of the Chinese population was in terror, because every night, some persons were arrested and disappeared. When our little party, which was evacuating China, passed through Nanchang, the capital of our Province, the communist newspaper reported seven hundred people in that city had been seized.

In the first part of December, Georgie and I handed in our applications for exit permits. We were told it would be a month or more before the necessary passes would be issued. But after two weeks, we were informed of the day and time to leave Kiukiang.

The time was so short that we had a perfect scramble to get away. Of the few days we had, one was Sunday, and one was Christmas day when there are always programs and exercises to be planned and carried out. We had to break up housekeeping after over thirty years, make an inventory of the hospital belongings, get the hospital ready to be turned over to the Chinese, which involved countless problems; see friends who dared to come to say goodbye, and do our own personal packing. The last night before we left, we didn't go to bed at all.

Quite a lot of foreign property had already been taken over....

Our house would be occupied by the police chief (Communist, of course) as soon as we stepped out of it. We were told that we might have anything we could take with us, but that all the rest of the things were to be left in the house. His wife demanded that we turn the organ over to her, as she wanted to play. I had bought the organ years ago, and I wanted to donate it to a church. Girls' (Jean and Chum) bicycles were to stay too, and I should whisper and tell you that girls' two-wheel vehicles seem to have run away on their own accord! Our large Victrola was a thing specifically mentioned to stay. Well, they did not know we also have a smaller one that Georgie hid.

None of this is in accord with what they "preach" in principle. However, things are "temporal," and we did not go to China for things, anyway.

But what is the most dangerous thing of all is the anti-Christian propaganda and activities.

Part of the communist doctrine is that there is no God. Thus, in every way, difficulties were thrown into the path of religious observance. Meetings that students and teachers had to attend were assigned for church times on Sundays. All spiritual teaching and religious pictures were banished from the mission schools, and students of these schools who were Christians, could not receive any scholarship help. Teachers known to be anti-Christian picketed the church and noted who went in.

May I assume your interest in telling you another event of our last days in Kiukiang. After having preached at Hwa-Sheng-Tang Church, as one of several pastors most of the Sunday evenings, for a good many years, the authority decided that I couldn't preach anymore. I spoke with the authorities that I had been very careful not to approach political subjects in what I said, but just gave a very simple Gospel message. The authorities admitted that I had said nothing bad about the present regime, but they said, "My head was wrong (我的思想不對)" — that I was "too sure I was right." Inasmuch as the Gospel truth is not mine and comes from Authorities higher than any of us here on earth, I was rather pleased than otherwise that they perceived I was sure of the truth of what I said.

With some of the fundamental aims of communists, we should be in sympathy, like their purpose to have everybody get a fair chance to have greater equality in material things; or the thought of a classless society. But these ideas are not put into practice, and during the summer, we witnessed wives and their children of the communists officials, who went luxuriously dressed, and with picnic comforts, to spend the summer up in the mountain resort of Ku-Ling, while the people who had perspired in the rice fields, had most of their crop taken away from them, when autumn came . . . It is perfectly safe to say that people feel very different from the way they did when the new government came in. A Chinese man told me that ninety people out of a hundred had in their heart resentments or discontent.

Left with us from Kiukiang were the Crook family of China Inland Mission (CIM), Miss Annie Pittman, Miss Frances Woodruff, and of course, the Ploeg sisters from Grand Rapids, Michigan. Our last days in Kiukiang were so hectic as to have been more like a bad dream than anything else....

Georgie joins with me in sending love and best

JEAN TREN-HWA PERKINS

wishes to our Aunt Minnie.
Affectionally, your nephew

Day-Day's letter speaks volumes of the great disappointment he felt after serving and helping China and its people for nearly four decades, from 1913 to 1950. Sure, there was an ongoing war. Sure, it might not have been the best time to distinguish friends from foes. That may be true during any war—let alone one that was more about ideological differences and less about righteousness or humanity (or why sacrifice millions of Korean civilians?).

When I think about it from Day-Day and Mother's perspectives, I can feel their devastation, anguish, and the unbearable pain in their hearts. Day-Day's words are not about the bicycles, the organ, the Victrola, the house, Mother's garden, or any "things." They are not about ideals or beliefs. They describe the sad reality around them, two aging Americans who had given their hearts to China. They should have been regarded as New England Mother Teresa's, and instead, they were forced to flee out of concern for the safety of their Chinese colleagues and friends.

In my opinion, the way they dedicated themselves not only to the Christian mission but importantly to people in need everywhere is enough to make them saints. I know this was not what they set out to achieve, but what they and many others, including the aunties from Michigan, accomplished are what churches and religious institutions of any kind should focus on, regardless of denominational or philosophical differences.

After Mother and Day-Day returned to America, the *Hartford Times* interviewed them in October 1951. When asked about China's future, the excerpt below conveyed their sentiment:

"... He expressed optimism for the future

of China—all based on his extremely high opinion of the Chinese as a people. 'There is no question that they are outstanding,' he declared. 'They are physically resistant to diseases, cooperative, willing, intellectually acute and, though not easy to convince spiritually, when they become Christians, they stay Christians...'

"His staff of 70 doctors at his 150-bed hospital was all Chinese. His nurses were natives, except for two Americans (Ms. Deanetta and Elizabeth Ploeg). His patients for 38 years were virtually all Chinese..."

Hartford Times, October 26, 1951

As for me, I felt utterly lost.

28

NEW YEAR'S DAY 1951 came and went. Three weeks after writing to Mother, I had only received one letter from her describing that they had reached Canton and were heading to Hong Kong. Those weeks felt like years. They were gone. Although I wrote to them ferociously, it was to stay distracted from the overwhelming despair I felt.

Mother gave me a Hong Kong address where I could send letters, which would then be forwarded to her and Day-Day. Excerpts from some of our letters are in the Appendices.

If I had not had faith in God and the full support and the understanding of Paul, my parents' leaving China would have been even more unbearable. With help from his friends, Paul got us passes on an old riverboat to Kiukiang. We finally departed on January 29, 1951. Standing on the deck, I dreamed, "How great it would have been to leave with Mother and Day-Day!" I thought of Chum who, like me, was without parents now. Perhaps being with her in Kiukiang might bring us both a little comfort. She had eagerly written for me to come. We missed each other, especially in these difficult times.

I also wanted to see Wang-Sao (王嫂), who was more of a mother to us now. All the others had fled after Mother, Day-Day, and the aunties left. Other Chinese who had been close friends with my parents and aunties looked the other way. Wang-Sao was the only one who dared take Chum under her wing.

An old Chinese saying goes, "True friends appear in times of trial (患難見真交 or 患難之交)." I do not blame those who turned their backs; many had troubles of their own and feared for their lives, having worked for Americans, which was a treasonable offense, punishable by execution.

As the riverboat drew near the so-familiar wharf, I somehow expected to see my smiling mother, aged but healthy except for her elephantiasis leg, waiting anxiously for a glimpse of me.

"Mommy, Mother!" I almost shouted as her image appeared before me. But the cruel reality remained. The pier was bare of people, except for construction workers and those waiting to board. Paul nudged me from my trance.

"Time to get off, Jeanie," he said understandingly. Then he pointed at two figures on the pier, one tall, the other short. They were standing at a distance, scanning for us but showing no emotion. Finally, I could tell it was Chum and dear old Wang-Sao.

There were no joyous demonstrations on the pier as we'd had before the "Liberation," although once in the seclusion of what we called home, we squealed with delight. "Home" was now a room that Paul's wonderful maternal grandparents (Eve Hsiung's parents), Lidiya and retired Pastor Yee, were kindly renting to Chum and Wang-Sao. They were the only other people in Kiukiang who dared show any concern for an American-adopted Chinese child.

I hugged Wang-Sao until she could barely breathe. Not used to Western-style affection, she called me a silly girl (傻姑娘), but I believe she liked it. After the greetings, Paul said goodbye and left to look for his parents and his friend Samuel. His father had asthma.

Chum and I were as close as sisters could be. Being older, I felt responsible for her, although she was actually more mature than I was at that time. Our sisterly love, since I had stepped into her life nineteen years earlier, was a constant. Before I left for college, like any normal teenagers, we did our own things, only confiding in each other when we felt like it. But at this moment, there was too much to talk about. I'd been away for only five months, but it felt like decades.

We chatted and chatted as we walked up the hill from the pier toward "home." Familiar streets that were now unrecognizable. We passed the Water of Life Hospital. I took a peek through the iron gate with no desire to go inside, because I wasn't sure I'd be able to control my emotions. I asked not to stroll on South Ta-Ling Lu or Road (塔玲南路) because I was afraid that sadness and rage would overcome me if we passed our house.

"Your Mother was in a daze the last few hectic days before leaving," Chum told me. "I asked if she wanted you to come home right away. There was a two-week lag time, long enough to rush you a boat ticket. She said you had your final exams to worry about, and they were not going to tell you they'd left until after the fact. Then, your mother said, 'This is her home, and she should stay.'"

"She did?" I asked. "I guess that's Mother, always thinking of others." I felt outraged. I was mad at myself. "I wanted to come home at least to see them off, although Mother told me to stay calm and stay put. They feared for my safety. But the truth is I was indecisive. I wasn't sure if I could leave the campus without university permission. Only later did the school announce they were going to cancel the finals. I'll regret this the rest of my life. Hmmm, why am I blaming this on a stupid exam?"

"It's okay, Jeanie. You wouldn't have been able to catch them leaving anyway. Their leave permits arrived early. Don't be so hard on yourself!" Chum reached out and squeezed my hand. "It's just as well you weren't here. Those of us who saw them off were criticized by the Party for not being able to tell enemies from friends. And I was scoffed at for crying. I could be charged with treason, for saying goodbye to my parents. I'm sure that's why your parents were worried about you coming here and told you to stay put."

"Tren-Hwa, it's all so very depressing. In the end, I hope the world knows these were good people," Wang-Sao added. "Good to Chinese."

"Well, we still have each other. All this is temporary, right? The war could end soon." I was trying to look on the bright side.

"Guess what?" Chum said excitedly.

"What?" I asked.

"Your Day-Day was so brave! When the officials told him that we needed to move out and leave everything in the house, Day-Day sneaked back in and got our bicycles out!"

"They're here, safe in the apartment, Tren-Hwa," Wang-Sao added.

I bit my tongue and held my breath so I could swallow my tears, and finally, I exhaled and said, "Day-Day bought that for me in Shanghai."

"Yes, Aunt Dee bought mine," Chum added.

There was then silence. I was grateful that under the circumstances, they weren't executed or taken as POWs.

"Jeanie, Mother left you two trunks full of things. I don't know what's in them," said Chum.

"I hope there are some sheets and pillowcases and towels," I said.

"If there are, you'll be lucky," Wang-Sao said.

"Why?" I asked.

"One of the pastors at the church we used to attend came to the house with a group of church members, and I suspect they ransacked the house and took your Mother's good linens. I never had a chance to see if your Mother set aside any for you." Wang-

Sao sighed, adding a Chinese saying, "To know someone's face doesn't mean you know what's in their heart (知人知面不知心)."

"I love you, Wang-Sao. You are the most loyal and trustworthy friend!" I said.

"Please look in your trunks," Chum implored, concerned whether Mother had left me enough. She was ready to share whatever I might lack. The aunties had left her with almost everything they didn't take. Chum even gave me some of the money the aunties left for her.

I looked at the two trunks. One was locked and had no keys. So, I opened the other one. There was no money. Mother and Day-Day had no money to give because they had to pay salaries in advance to the hospital staff before they left. They'd had to balance the hospital's books after the Hong Kong bank froze their funds. For all those years, the money to support Chinese and American staff salaries and hospital functions, including building the hospital, came from Day-Day's family inheritance and money my parents raised in America, with a fraction coming from the Methodist Board of Missions. It was challenging to make the final payroll before they left.

Mother had put my precious books — *Little Women*, *Little Men*, *Heidi*, and others — in the trunk, as well as the whole encyclopedia Day-Day had given me for my seventeenth birthday! Mother knew I loved these books. But where was I to put them all? There were no towels or sheets, although I did find Mother's French wedding clock. I wondered why she left that? Did she think I might sell it for money? I decided to keep the clock as a way of remembering Mother, and I would do everything I could to keep it running.

When I was finally able to open the other trunk, it was also full of books as well as some sweaters and skirts. I also found my beloved red reversible coat from Yonkers that I dared not wear during the anti-American era. I had handmade a jacket out of the two skirts. They were gray, so I dared to wear it. Underneath the clothing was a brown envelope with all my official documents, including my adoption papers. I guess that was why this trunk was locked.

"Ah," I screamed with excitement at the next discovery. "Here are my two records." Chum and Wang-Sao came over to see what the fuss was, and I proudly held up the Bing Crosby record from Day-Day with both hands, and then the Frank Sinatra one, a gift from Jill, Betty, and Marie.

Wang-Sao looked startled, then said, "Oh, wait! My goodness, heaven! Your father didn't know." Then she hurried to the corner of the room and moved a stack of boxes and old suitcases. At the bottom of the pile was another big box and she opened it. "I almost forgot, your Day-Day left this here and told me I could sell what's inside the box if I ever needed money. I believe when your family had those picnics on the lawn, sometimes your folks would use it to listen to music, and this box is what those records are for, no?"

"Ah, yes, our gramophone!" I exclaimed.

"All yours! Good thing I was not going to get rid of it, and now, you can use it."

I said, "No, Day-Day left it for you in time of need."

"Tren-Hwa, I don't need money, and even if I did, I would never sell your Day-Day's gift. Anyway, what is an old countrywoman going to with that? I'm not all that smart; in my hands it would be used as firewood."

I chuckled and said, "Thank you, amah. Let's keep it here, and I'll come and use it."

This gramophone was old, even by 1951 standards. It had been brought to China by my Scottish grandmother when she came to stay with us in 1940. She and her attendant, Aunt Katty, loved music. Interestingly, the newer Victrola we had was confiscated. This one still looked in good shape, even though it probably was made before I was born. I wound up the gramophone and put on "White Christmas." Static and all, it sounded great. When the song came on, the mood in the room changed instantly. My mind began to wander to Yonkers, and I wondered where my parents were now, remembering how the three of us used to listen to this beautiful melody.

Since there were few useful things in these trunks, Chum generously shared some of what the aunties had left for her. I in turn gave her the things I'd brought back for her from Nanking, including clothes from Aunt Helen. "Here's the coat and slacks you wanted," I said, handing them to her.

"Oh, great, thank you!" Chum said with delight. "I'm so glad you thought of dyeing the coat black instead of leaving it green. I could never wear it without being criticized. The slacks are okay because they're dark maroon."

"Have you decided which college you want to go?" I asked, trying to change the subject.

"Yes, of course. Same as yours," she replied promptly. "I want to major in music."

"You're certainly talented. And it will be fun to be at the same college," I added enthusiastically. Just then, Samuel and Paul arrived, and we each left with our respective "boyfriends." From then on, Chum and I began to go in our separate ways.

Paul asked me to visit the Water of Life Hospital. He said I had a brother working there named Yan-Feng (延豐: prolonged harvest), who was eight years my senior and six years younger than Kuo-Hsiang, the brother who went missing in World War II. I had almost no memory of either Kuo-Hsiang or Yan-Feng. I'd left them behind when I was a baby, nineteen years earlier.

Yan-Feng had gotten tired of farming life and came to the

hospital after we returned to China in 1946, with Day-Day's consent, to learn the art of cooking. He was now one of the leading chefs. Paul and I found him in the kitchen and surprised him. He was so pleased to see us, proud that he had an educated sister because he understood how problematic it is to be illiterate. He had tried to learn to read and write but gave it up. It was too difficult, and he blamed Kuo-Hsiang for hoarding all the brain cells in the family. I took an instant liking to this brother. He didn't seem to care what people said about my being adopted by Americans. He was just happy to reconnect with his little foreign sister.

Paul said, "It would be good, Jeanie, to have more contacts like Yan-Feng, people who care about you at a time like this."

To avoid unnecessary eyes and ears, we took a walk in Kiukiang, where the hustle and bustle of the streets would make it harder for someone to eavesdrop. But as we approached the riverbank, police swarmed the streets shouting, "Curfew!" It was a word I'd detested ever since the Japanese occupied China. "Why is there a curfew after so-called liberation?" I said out loud, intentionally. "This is no different from the Japanese occupation." My suppressed rage was about to explode.

My brother and Paul were shocked. "Jean/Tren-Hwa, don't shout," they said at the same time. "Someone will hear you."

"I don't care!" I protested. My brother looked around cautiously to see if anyone had heard his stubborn American sister. To his utter surprise, he saw a familiar-looking face, turned to us, and whispered, "Don't look now, but Chairman Mao is twenty steps behind us." Paul and I turned quickly to take a look, and sure enough it was Mao. Crowds began to gather, clapping their hands in recognition and reverence. I pushed myself forward to get a glimpse of him, too.

I was about fifteen yards away and could see two-thirds of his face as he chatted with those around him. The "Great Leader (偉大的領袖)" was an animated man, gesticulating with his hands the way Americans do. Before I could get any closer, two military jeeps swarmed in, and in a swift motion, they whisked the "Great Leader" of China away from the crowd.

"Humph!" I said in disgust. "If he is for the people, why doesn't he stay and talk with these people? In Ku-Ling, President Chiang and his wife, Ms. Soong, went to church like ordinary people. There was no curfew. We saw them in Ku-Ling in 1948. They sat in the pew, right in front of my parents, the aunties, Chum, and me."

"Enough, Jeanie," Paul begged.

But I continued my rant. "We were nervous, sitting so close to Ms. Song and President Chiang, and we were amazed at how thick the makeup on Ms. Song's face was. Chum and I even whispered to each other, 'The paste on her face is as thick as the Great Wall.' She was beautiful and didn't need all that powder and oil. Then, we giggled so hard we shook and had to stuff our handkerchiefs in our mouths. Mother nudged me, but it only made me giggle more. When we finally left the church, Chum and I laughed out loud in relief. Our parents said we'd acted like silly girls."

Paul said nervously, "Will you *please* shut up, Jeanie? Now is not the time or the place to shout these angry, anti-revolution, anti-Communist thoughts!"

I stopped my rant and went into a trance. I was not a fan of Chiang Kai-Shek either. The KMT lost the civil war by their own doing, unable to stop corruption and establish a genuinely democratic government that could champion freedom of speech. They hadn't earned the right to lead the country or receive the respect of the people. And what did they do for the people of Taiwan during their first twenty years on that island? They dragged so many soldiers to Taiwan, separating them from their beloved families while promising a quick return to glory. Those young soldiers suffered even more than I was suffering in my current plight.

In the end, they were no different from gangsters. They only looked after themselves and confiscated all planes, trains, and boats for party officials' evacuations to Taiwan—including the aircraft that was supposed to take Chum and me to Hong Kong. As to who Chairman Mao would turn out to be, it remained to be seen. I, for one, was not interested in politics. All I wanted was to be reunited with my American parents!

29

A WEEK LATER, firecrackers began to explode on the streets of Kiukiang for Chinese New Year 1951, the Year of Rabbit. It was a cold February morning, and I got up early, bundled up, and headed out to the river, where I sat on the wooden pier, looking out to the water. I was in deep thought and completely forgot how cold it was. The river water looked cold too, with mist hovering above. I thought if I stared long enough, Mother and Day-Day would suddenly appear.

"There you are again!"

It was Paul's voice. I looked up, and he said, "Crying again?"

I was not aware of my tears. Paul gave me his coat.

"It's cold, Jeanie. I'm sure your father taught you about pneumonia."

I remained quiet, swimming in my thoughts. Paul nudged my shoulder and asked, "Why so quiet?"

"You told me to shut up, so I did," I grunted.

"That was a week ago." Now Paul seemed as if he was going to cry too, and an awkward silence prevailed.

Then he said, "Yan-Feng had a brilliant idea! Why don't we visit your Mm-Ma and father? I'm sure they would like to see you. Yan-Feng told me he would go today to let them know you're here, and that you and I can go tomorrow."

"Well, okay. All right. I don't even know how to get there," I said.

"Yan-Feng gave me the directions. I'm sure we can find it.

I have a really good sense of direction," he said. I wanted to chuckle at his arrogance, but I held back.

Then I remembered: "The last time Mm-Ma came to see me, she said, 'Get on a boat to cross the river, then ask people where Lan Ni Tao is (爛泥陶: muddy swamp). They will give you directions.' I thought she was joking," I said.

"That's what your brother said too," Paul affirmed.

The next day, Paul and I got on a small boat and went across the cold river. He did have a good sense of direction; I don't. Even though he grew up in a big city, Chungking (重庆), he was also skilled at walking beside rice paddies, while I kept on falling off the ridges and into the water-soaked young rice. My balance was not stable.

"These rice fields must be where I learned to crawl, while my parents and brothers worked the land," I reminisced. "It must be where I peed too. That's what the grownups told me." As we approached some huts, we heard the roar of firecrackers. "What's going on?" I asked Paul. I could never remember the dates of Chinese festivals.

Paul said, "I'll bet it's your family setting off the firecrackers to welcome you home."

"Sure," I murmured, assuming he was teasing me. But Paul turned out to be right. Although it was also because of the Chinese New Year, they were indeed setting off firecrackers to welcome me. Someone must have been on the lookout and gave the signal when we came within view. It was a hearty Chinese welcome, no hugging or kissing, but genuine smiles on everyone's faces. This celebration echoed the one that took place nineteen years ago when I was leaving for Mother and Day-Day's home. Relatives and neighbors began to crowd into my family's mud hut, this time to see the girl who grew up with the Foreign Devils (洋鬼子). They stared at me with a kind of friendly awe. I was their flesh and blood but didn't seem to be one of them. I didn't know any of them and didn't know what to say.

Finally, after a long, awkward silence, Mr. Hu blurted out with mist in his eyes, "Tren-Hwa, you are finally home. You are home at last. This is your home." My eyes welled up, but I couldn't cry. I had nothing to reply, so I gave Mr. Hu a grin and that was it.

Mm-Ma was always more practical. She asked Paul, "Do you think I brought harm to Tren-Hwa by giving her to the foreigners long ago?"

Paul said, "You did what you thought was best for Tren-Hwa at the time. How were you to know there would be so many changes in just twenty years? But you don't need to worry, because no matter what happens, I will always take good care of her. I will do the best I can, Mm-Ma."

I was shocked to hear his words, but Mm-Ma's anxious face broke into smiles, accentuating all the wrinkles on her weather-worn face. She was probably in her late fifties or early sixties, and she looked healthy and well. Mr. Hu, on the other hand, seemed frail, still plagued by asthma and tuberculosis. It was a wonder he was still alive. I went to see him one more time in the summer of 1952. He died two years after that.

The celebration dinner turned out to be more of a goodbye than a hello. The next morning, on New Year's Day, I bid them farewell. Paul, Yan-Feng, and I hopped on a boat and headed back to Kiukiang. Paul and I had to go back to school in a few days, and I was in no mood for Chinese New Year. I also had to study for final exams, which had been postponed because of the Forgotten War (the Korean War) and the anti-American animus.

Just before we left Kiukiang, the *Kiukiang Daily* newspaper announced that Chairman Mao had conducted a historical survey along the Yangtze River Valley. The story confirmed that it had been him we saw while we were strolling down the street;

the curfew had been set up for him.

It was hard to say goodbye to Chum and Wang-Sao. Although my natural parents had welcomed me back so heartily, it was no longer my home. It really never had been. Only Wang-Sao was a symbol of home for Chum and me now. I looked at her as my third mother, and I told myself I would take care of her in her old age.

Paul and I returned to Nanking and went back to our respective campuses. I focused on preparing for finals. I pledged to study seriously, so my mind would stop wandering. But our school was still in chaos. The anti-American movement continued, and schools were about to undergo some physical changes as well. The government had taken over both Gin-Ling College and the Private University of Nanking. Both had been supported by American missionaries, and by the spring of 1951, there was no more financial support from America. So the two colleges merged to become Gin-Ling University. Then in 1952, this short-lived "new" Gin-Ling joined with parts of Nanjing University and became a new college, Nanking Teacher's College, now called Nanjing Normal University (南京師範大學). By the summer of 1951, the famed Gin-Ling Women's College no longer existed, and its campus was occupied by Nanking Teacher's College.

All the merging created bureaucratic chaos. Classes and requirements were shuffled, canceled, and renamed. Confusion reigned supreme in what had been a quiet, respectful, and diligent academic setting. Students majoring in chemistry, physics, math, and biology were allowed to graduate in three years, and were promised teaching positions in colleges and high schools. In retrospect, some of these changes made sense. China was in desperate need of teachers, and so the sooner people graduated, the sooner they could help fill the void.

"I hate chemistry," I thought. "I can't see myself dissecting frogs and earthworms the rest of my life. It gives me the creeps." But there was no time to think about all this. I had to study for finals.

When exams were over, a group of pre-med students from Shanghai, including Shou, demanded that they be transferred to medical schools around the country. Wisely, the new university authorities recognized that physicians were needed as much as teachers, so soon after that, the rest of us pre-med students also demanded we be allowed to continue pre-medical training.

After the government took over our school, Christian Fellowship gatherings were no longer allowed on campus. So when a good evangelist came to town, we met secretly. It was increasingly dangerous to go to church. Christianity was associated with America and Western Imperialism. We were at war with America and its crony allies in Korea. Religion was the idealism the new regime hated. Prayers had become signs of treason. Paul told me that Christian students were beginning to *disappear* from his Boy's College. So for the time being, we felt it'd be better to believe in our hearts.

The anti-America movement never stopped. One morning, shortly after I returned to the university, I saw a Chinese professor being dragged along the walkways by the ravaging heroines, his hands cuffed behind him. They shouted anti-American slogans and called him an American Imperialistic Dog (美國帝國主義走狗) and an American spy.

"Down with the American Imperialistic Dog! Down with the American Spy!" The shouting became louder and louder, as these girls, more or less my age, rushed past me. I was trembling in fear. I closed my eyes, profoundly disheartened. He was being treated that way because his higher education had been in America. After the real Americans were deported, the government began persecuting Chinese who'd had a close relationship with America, including all who were educated in America or had worked with Americans in China.

"I was adopted by Americans!" I thought. "What about me?" Visibly shaken, I ran back to the dorm and slammed the door.

"Mother, Day-Day, come quickly. Get me out of here. I'll be next. I'm dead!"

Chen and Yen, who were always in the room studying, looked up in surprise.

"What are you talking about?" they asked.

Both were brilliant students. No matter what was going on, they remained focused on their studies. I pointed outside as I tried to catch my breath. "Those crazy girls accused that professor of being an American spy. I was adopted by Americans, not to mention by missionaries. And I went to school in America. My clothes are all made in America. Isn't that enough to make me a spy?"

Chen laughed and said, "Calm down. Yes, you were adopted by Americans, and yes, you've been to America; but you are only twenty, just out of high school, how could you be a spy? Besides, the years you were in America, you were only eleven. Who would want a kid to be a spy?" Yen chuckled, too. She did not weigh in on what Chen had just said. Of course, she didn't know.

Finally, I calmed down and hoped Chen was right. "But aren't spies trained young?" I wondered. My fear deepened when I thought about what could happen next. I began to appreciate how those Japanese Americans who were exchanged for me felt during World War II, after Pearl Harbor. I didn't sleep at all that night, so I decided to write Mother for the last time:

April 21, 1951
Dear Mommy,
Just think, about eight more days it will be my

birthday. I don't want any birthday presents, letters, or money anymore. I won't write any more to you either. Instead, I'm going to give you a lovely Bible passage, one that is loved by all. "The Lord is my Shepherd; I shall not want."

Isn't that a beautiful passage? Mommy, please don't write to me anymore, and from here on, I won't write to you and Day-Day either because I can't.

I'll always pray for all of you, and I know you will pray for me too. May God bless His Children! It's getting late, and with the curfew, lights will be out soon, so—I'll stop now. Remember He cares for His own, so there isn't a thing to worry about for He watches over us! Love to Day-Day. Simply loads of love,

Your Jeanie girl

P.S. Things mentioned above include all my friends (Jill, Betty, Marie, and Doris C.). Tell them not to write to me either.

That semester was the most distracting imaginable. Chinese intervention in the Korean War was in full swing. The government urged everyone of age to join the army. Classes were stopped again, while student activists galvanized everyone to join the Chinese People's Volunteer Army (PVA: 中國抗美援朝志願軍). They feverishly recruited students while shouting anti-America slogans with more zeal than ever. One senior student kept urging me to join the army, but not my roommates. She said, "This is a great opportunity for you to show your patriotism, given your background. You probably won't be accepted, so why not make a patriotic gesture and let them know you are willing to bear arms and kill those who adopted you, those who gave you life but are now enemies of China?"

Each time she tried to persuade me, I responded with only a blank stare. I kept thinking what Mother said, "War is a terrible thing for everyone involved." Why can't human beings resolve issues peacefully?

"Patriotic? What do I know about patriotism?" I thought. "When the plane never came to take Chum and me to Hong Kong, we decided to stay. Our parents taught us that we were to serve God and our people. Isn't that patriotism? I think my American parents were more patriotic to China than these raging heroines."

I received an anonymous letter from someone who claimed to have been my primary school classmate, that he or she was delighted I had decided to stay. To this day, I don't know how they knew. But when I decided to stay, I had no idea that my parents would be forced to leave without me, nor could I have foreseen what was to come.

Then I had a bright idea. "Paul," I said one evening when we met. "They're trying to get me to join the volunteer army to fight in Korea. I think I will, not for the reasons they suggest but for American GIs who are getting killed in Korea for nothing. I can speak perfect English. I'll go and persuade them not to fight anymore, to tell the American President to stop, that it's not worth it. I've been on two ships full of GIs, and they were only kids, the same age as we are now, just like the Chinese kids signing up to cross the Ya-Lu River."

Paul looked at me with disbelief and exasperation. He wasn't sure whether to laugh or cry. "Have you gone mad? You are unbelievably naive. No wonder people in Kiukiang said that the Perkinses' daughter was a naive, a *lao-shi-ren* (老实人)."

Lao-shi-ren is a condescending term for those who are naive to the point of idiocy.

"First of all," he added, "you're politically unfit as the daughter of American missionaries. Second, even if you were accepted, you would never be allowed at the front lines—much less talking to American GIs. No one would use a twenty-year-old to be a diplomat despite your perfect English, because you don't understand a thing about politics or negotiation. You will more likely be used as a human shield or a translator for spy work. Of course, if you have your medical degree, maybe you could be a surgeon at the front or on the battlefield."

He shook his head and continued, "Worst of all, I believe they will think you're just trying to cross the river and run away to the America side. So, forget it, Jeanie. Please stop this nonsense!" By then, he was fuming.

I was stunned and, at the same time, moved by his passionate response. My mind was fixated on his last point. Maybe becoming a doctor would be a reason to join the army. Perhaps I could join the military as a medic, go to the front, and then run away.

"Why are they recruiting you? You're an easy target, and if you were to join the army, it would be a public relations coup for the whole recruiting process—All-American kid rises up to shoot those who gave her life!"

"What?" I wanted him to repeat what he'd just said, but my mind was too confused.

"Listen!" Paul shouted impatiently. But I had drifted away. "If I can't stop the war, maybe I can run away."

Seeing I wasn't listening, Paul repeated himself, speaking louder each time. "Jeanie, I don't always have answers. You think I know everything; I don't. But I do know it would be crazy for you to go to Korea and try to run away. Besides, I came to tell you something." His mouth was quivering.

"What?" I asked.

"My parents are in trouble. After my father was asked to step down, he was accused of embezzlement. It's patently untrue, but no one believes him, and they're demanding he pay up in full. I might not be able to finish college. My father's punishment is to kneel under the hot sun on a cinder block every day for hours. With his asthma, he can hardly bear the pain. My mother has pleaded to take his place in kneeling. My oldest brother has given up his postgraduate studies so he can work to support the family."

Immersed in my own turmoil, I had forgotten to ask Paul about his family. My focus shifted, and I began to wonder how they were surviving during this chaotic period. Both of his parents received their master's degrees in education from Northwestern University. They returned to China in 1926 to teach and to help. It was an extraordinary accomplishment for both of them, but especially for a Chinese woman, to get a master's degree in America in the 1920s.

Paul continued, "My youngest brother is ten. He's now with our grandmother and is bewildered by all that's going on around him. My little brother is smart and has the good sense not to say anything. He answers, 'I don't know' to anyone who questions him about our parents."

I listened attentively. Besides the war and the anti-American fever, a massive communist movement of Three-Antis and Five-Antis (三反五反: San-fan Wu-fan) had been going on internally. These movements were for stabilizing the newly unified country and its young regime, and they did so at the expense of perceived enemies within. The process involved identifying, purging, persecuting, and executing those regarded as anti-revolutionary, which meant those who had been middle- and upper-middle-class in the Republic Nationalist era—landowners, the affluent, and the influential who had not left the country. To flee persecution, people were volunteering to fight in Korea, and once there, some surrendered to the American side just to be taken to POW camps. I wasn't the first to have had this thought.

How was it that I, Paul, or his parents hadn't already been executed? The fact that we were still alive—so far—was astonishing. There was nothing I could do to help Paul or his family. I just wondered what would happen next.

30

CHAOS AND TURMOIL continued on and around the campus well into the spring semester of my freshman year. In late spring of 1951, my roommate Yen received a letter that her aunt, Ms. Wu, who had been the Principal of Rulison Girls High, couldn't bear the wrongful accusations and persecutions, and committed suicide by drinking formaldehyde. This was the first time I learned that my principal at the Rulison, Ms. Wu, was Yen's aunt.

Ms. Wu had been so kind to me. She had taught us biology in high school, much like the President of Gin-Ling College, Dr. Wu Yi-Fang (no relation). It was a huge shock and loss for a country that claimed to be desperate for teachers.

And my other roommate, Chen, told me that her father had been imprisoned. He had been a high official in the Ministry of Education during the Republic Era. He had fled to Hong Kong before the Communists swept through the South, but he got homesick and came back to meet his daughter secretly. The police caught him. I began to contemplate running away.

Many students joined the army. I didn't; Paul was right. How could I shoot Americans? They could be Jill, Betty, or Marie's brothers or even be my nephews, Evvie's sons. My mind began unraveling as I watched these young women marching from the campus into oblivion.

The campus became quieter with fewer people there, and attending classes became routine again. I had to settle down and study. Oddly, the return to normalcy made me even more homesick for my parents. I kept writing to them. My letters went to Hong Kong first. I had a "big sister," Hannah Wu, who had been under the care of my parents before I was born. Hannah had worked at the Water of Life Hospital as a nurse before she and her family relocated to Hong Kong. She was able to forward my letters despite it being risky for her, even from Hong Kong.

I wondered how many letters actually reached her in Hong Kong and went on to my parents. I did get a few letters from Mother while I was still at Gin-Ling College saying that she and Day-Day were in excellent health. I learned they were staying with Uncle Henry in Hartford until they decided to go to a place in Tennessee to help Americans who were in need. Mother's few precious words were the water of my life. I continued to think about how I might run away, to get out of here and see them. I began to focus on an escape plan. Perhaps I could still get to Hong Kong.

Paul came more frequently now, on weekdays too, not just on Sundays. While he genuinely cared about how I was doing, his visits started to bother me. They were interrupting my studies and taking time away from writing to my parents and planning how to reach Hong Kong. I wanted him out of my life.

My roommates also began to annoy me, too. They would say, "You never have time for us anymore. Paul takes so much of your time, we'll soon be strangers." When he would call up to me from outside the window, they'd say, "Here comes your needy boyfriend." For months, I couldn't decide whether to stay with or leave Paul. I liked him as a friend, but I didn't love him. I loved my parents more than anyone else. So, one evening, when Paul tried to kiss me for the first time, I nearly slapped him and blurted out, "How revolting! If this is what it's going to be like, we might as well forget it."

SPRING FLOWER: A TALE OF TWO RIVERS

Always bearing in mind Mother's warning that boys could get excited and then things would happen, though I still had no idea what that meant, I wasn't going to take any chances." That night I wrote a letter to Paul.

> Paul,
> Please don't come and see me anymore. I prefer to be a bird free to fly at will. I don't want to be bound to anyone. I want to do what I want—what I need to do. Why do I have to be with you every single weekend? I want to be with my girlfriends sometimes too. You have been coming far too often lately, and it affects my studying. I don't mean I will never marry someone in the future, but not now. Now, I want to be free—free—free!
> Jean
> P.S. Oh, by the way, I don't like to be kissed either.

Paul came immediately, but I refused to see him. My roommates tried to get me to talk to him, but I was stubborn. My mind was made up, and I would stick to what I wrote. Paul was utterly unprepared for my actions. Not able to see me, he finally wrote.

> Miss Perkins,
> I understand your feelings, but please let me still see you on weekends. I won't come on weekdays anymore, and I promise no more kissing. I will give you all the time in the world to study.
> Paul

I didn't answer his letter. Nor did I consent to see him, even on the weekends. To me, it was over. Paul's second-oldest sister, who was at Gin-Ling College at the time, said, "Jean is a weirdo who has not grown up mentally or physically."

Almost everyone on campus knew I had rejected Paul, and it seemed unbelievable to them. To me, it was puzzling; this was none of their business. During the treacherous times we were living in, how did they have the time to worry about these picayune issues of someone else's life? Perhaps I hadn't grown up yet, but none of them knew what was on my mind.

"Would I have fallen in love with some man by now if I were in America?" I asked myself.

Shou tried to talk me into seeing Paul again. She seemed to know so much. She told me, "You're stupid to turn down such a young, handsome, all-around college boy. When the two of you go out together, you're the envy of every girl here. Even many seniors don't have boyfriends yet, and you're just a freshman."

I was surprised by what she said. I had no idea. Nor did I have any intentions to make anyone jealous of me. I knew Paul was handsome, tall, and athletic, being on the college basketball and soccer teams, and he boxed too. And he was brilliant. Most of all, Paul was always kind to me, even during this most difficult time. He might have reminded me of my very own Day-Day, but none of these qualities mattered to me at the time.

Maybe I was weird or a loner, and perhaps destined to be an old maid, but I didn't know what I wanted and my mind was entirely occupied with my parents and how I could reach them. I needed the freedom to think, to choose, and to speak my mind. I did not want anyone to dominate my life—not the government and not Paul. My mind was made up, and no one could change it.

"How can I reach them? How can I get to Hong Kong?" These were the questions I pondered, over and over. Then one afternoon when Chen and I were alone in our dorm room, I asked her, given that her father had escaped to Hong Kong in 1949. She looked shocked, but didn't ask me why, except to say in a matter-of-fact tone, "You need to get to Canton [Guangzhou] first." Chen's answer reminded me that Mother's first letter was from Canton.

"Where is Canton?" I asked.

She smiled quizzically and said, "You're really a foreigner." Then she stood up from her desk and pointed to the map on the wall. I followed her fingers, then took a breath.

"Oh, my," I said. "Canton is a million miles from Nanking, and Hong Kong is nowhere near Canton."

"You're thinking about touring Hong Kong?" she asked with a gleam in her eyes. "Yes, my dear American roommate, Nanking to Canton first! It's maybe 1,500 kilometers. After you get to Canton, you'll have to find a way to get to one of those small towns south of Canton along the Pearl River (珠江). It may take another half a day by train or buses."

I nodded my head, and Chen continued, again pointing to the map. "There should be several small towns along Pearl River that are near Hong Kong. The Pearl River runs a long way before reaching the South China Sea. Some people even swim to Hong Kong across the Deep Water Bay."

"Really? I'm a good swimmer," I murmured, staring at the map while recalling that Mother had written that they had been sailing out of the Pearl River to Hong Kong. Chen walked away without asking a single question. She was smart and probably knew what I was thinking.

The following week, all I could think about was how this might work. I used a ruler to measure the distance I might need to swim. I traced the map of the Canton area on another piece of paper, including the shape and the flow of Pearl River. I wrote down the names of some small towns south of Canton. I'd sit in the middle of campus away from everyone else, thinking and memorizing what I would do. People probably thought I was sad about breaking up with Paul.

Another week went by, and I figured that the water in the deep South should be warm enough by now not to suffer from hypothermia. So, on a cloudy Sunday afternoon in May 1951, when my roommates were away for lunch, I took out a small bag I'd already packed and hidden in my suitcase. I counted whatever money I had left and checked the quality of dry food I'd gathered the past week. The less stuff I carried, the better, I thought. So I took only some dry food and a refillable tin of water, and headed out the campus gate, where I hopped on a bus to Zhong-Hua-Men Railway Station (中華門火車站).

"That was simple!" I thought.

Upon arriving at the old station, I was immediately overwhelmed by the sea of people and the utter chaos. Nervously, I inched forward in a long line in front of a ticketing booth. "Are there any more trains to Canton?" I asked.

The man behind the tiny ticket window said, without looking up, "The last train will leave in four hours."

"How much is a one-way ticket? And how long does it take?" I asked.

"Two-plus days—if there are no problems or delays along the way!"

"Two days? Are there beds available?" I gulped, thinking of the Pullman train or the ones I rode crossing the plains in India.

"No, standing room only." The agent finally looked up at me through his old wire-rim spectacles and cringed. I became flustered, and people began pushing from behind.

"Uh, what?" I asked.

"Do you speak Chinese, Miss? I said two days at least if you are lucky and do not have to change trains somewhere en route!"

The man began to look impatient and stuck two fingers in my face, representing two days.

"Why—wait, what? Change trains? Where do I have to change trains?"

"I don't know, Miss, maybe Ning-Tong (宁铜) or Wu-Hu (芜湖), I don't know. You change trains if they tell you so and buy additional fares when asked." He started to look angry.

"Oh, where am I going on the first train? How far is Wu-Hu (蕪湖)? Where is Ning-Tong?" By then, I was trying to get whoever was behind me off my back.

"Are you going to buy a ticket or just ask stupid questions?" An older woman finally jammed her bag into my kidney and started shouting right in my ear. "Oh, okay, okay, one way," I said, and out of panic I threw a bunch of wrinkled bills from my sweaty palm toward the man. He threw me a ticket, and I grabbed it.

I was in shell shock, but determined nevertheless to make the journey. "Standing for two days? Okay, I can sit on the floor, I guess, or wherever I find. That's not a hardship. Where there's a will, there's a way," I thought.

I found a quiet corner and sat on the floor, clutching my bag, and looking to see how much money I had left. "Do I have enough for more food and water, and for a good meal before the swim? Will I be able to swim across? I've been exercising every day for two weeks. How cold is the water? Canton is in the Deep South, so the water must be warm enough by May."

I was shaking as I took out the piece of paper with my chicken-scratched notes on it, along with the traced map mimicking the one on the wall. I wished I had drawn the whole route or taken the one on the wall. "So if I can get on a boat heading south toward one of the coastal towns by the Deep Bay, then find a close spot and jump, it's only a mile, I think." People had done that. With war in the north and limited resources, the southern coasts were not well patrolled. "It's almost summer. Why is the station so cold?" I wondered as my shaking increased.

"Maybe there are other ways of getting across. You can't think that far, Jean. You don't even know how far south this train will take you! Or where to get off the first train and get on another one? Focus on getting to Canton first, and hope for the best." I spoke to myself, and I was breathing quickly. To calm myself, I began to pray. "God, I pray you will be with me, and I pray Mother and Day-Day are with me. Please, are you listening?" I asked.

Suddenly, I heard a familiar voice. "Jeanie, there you are! What are you doing? I've looked for you everywhere!" It was Paul.

I stood up and asked, "How did you find me? I told you I don't want to see you."

"I went looking for you, and no one had seen you all afternoon. Chen joked to me that you were thinking about going to Canton and then Hong Kong. Knowing your stubbornness and some of our conversations, I thought it might be true. And it is, here you are! Have you gone mad?" He pulled me toward a quieter place with fewer people. "Do you have the faintest idea how difficult a journey to Canton will be?"

"I know, but that's okay. I am determined, and God will be with me. And so will Mother and Day-Day, in spirit," I replied.

"No, you don't know. You won't even make it halfway to Kiukiang, let alone Canton, and you'll be dead. It's not about your determination. Just listen to your American accent! The way you behave and speak will immediately give you away! You are a foreigner in your own country!" Paul didn't know whether to laugh or cry.

"But I'm sure there will be good people along the way who

will help." I bit my lip.

"Before or after they shoot you? I know you miss them terribly, but please listen. This is not the way to do it. It's way too risky. You'll be lucky if you're shot and killed. If they catch you, like Chen's father, it will be all over. It's treason."

I stayed silent. It was less than an hour till boarding.

Seeing that I wasn't moving, Paul continued, "Things will get better. There will be other and better ways—and this is not one of them. The war will be over, maybe soon. Why not be patient? As long as you stay alive, there will be a path, and you'll get to see your parents again. It's not worth it if you go south now and get yourself killed."

I didn't want to hear any more, fearing I would lose my courage. I started to walk toward the platform as another roar of the engine came from afar.

Finally, Paul became desperate. "Okay, Jeanie, look. Come back with me, please. I won't bother you or see you again after you go back. But please come back with me. You must, before people start to realize what's going on."

My running away had nothing to do with him, yet after I prayed, strangely, he showed up. I had planned all week how to run away, and here I was facing a journey that would likely lead to a dead end, as I had no real clue what to do after Canton, or if I'd even get that far. At the same time, I could no longer endure the madness. I just wanted to be with Mother and Day-Day again. I wanted to go home!

Paul grabbed my hand, then quickly released it, fearing I'd get mad at him for touching me. Then he said calmly, "Please, Jeanie, what are you still pondering? Come back to campus with me. We'll find other ways."

"What ways, Paul? What other ways are there?" I shouted. "I need to go! Just let me go!"

JEAN TREN-HWA PERKINS

A colossal roar of the engine resounded accompanied by a sharp whistling and blinding steam. The train rushed into the station at what seemed like full speed. I wasn't sure where it came from, probably from the north, or whether it would stop. We could see through the windows that it was filled with people, and others were camped out on the top of this old green-and-yellow workhorse.

"No, Jeanie, I can't let you go. I can't let you get on that train!"

"Why?" I found his passion strange, if not amusing.

"What am I going to tell your parents when they come back looking for you, and you're dead?" Paul shouted above all the noise.

"What?" The cacophony was so loud I could only guess what he'd said, and I shouted back at him. "It's my life, my fate, not yours! It's none of your business!" I was angry and sad.

"What do you mean, Miss Jean Perkins? Back home in Kiukiang, who doesn't know Dr. and Mrs. Perkins' daughter? You were their princess; you and Chum were the princesses of that small town. If and when the war is over and your parents come to look for you, only to find out that you're dead, they'll find out that I was the last person with you and that I let you get on the train. They'll never forgive me!" Paul was staring straight into my eyes.

The chaos around us kept increasing, as people began to jostle for positions to board the train. Hearing those words, suddenly I felt he might be right. What if the war is over next week, next month, or next year? And what if Mother and Day-Day do come back next year? Maybe I should be more patient. I have no money left. Looking at the ticket clutched in my hand, I said, "I already spent half of my semester allowance on this ticket. I might as well go."

"I know you spent a lot of money on this ticket. I will loan you however much you need." Paul seemed to be panicking. He tried to grab my hand, but quickly withdrew his again, and instead, he threw his hands in the air. "Don't board that train, Jeanie, please!" He was on the verge of tears, and he reached out and firmly grabbed my hand. A swarm of sadness rushed into my heart like the hot steam surrounding us. Then, a mixed feeling seeped in—an immense disappointment in myself for my lack of courage and determination, and the realization that perhaps patience would be a virtue. How foolish it would be to get killed halfway.

I slowly began to walk away from the platform, while others—many others—rushed toward the train. Silently I sat on the bus looking onto the streets of Nanking. Paul was next to me, still holding my hand. He, too, had few words except when he shook his head and murmured, "This is unbelievable. I never thought you were serious about this." I didn't move my head. I was exhausted.

I didn't know if Paul had just saved my life, or if he had merely delayed the inevitable.

*****

I opened this memoir with the question, "Where shall I begin a story that spans more than half a century?" Now I must ask, "and where shall I end it?" I think I'll end the first of two volumes here. I apologize if it feels abrupt. In Book Two, the final volume (anticipated publication in early 2022), I will finish the story.

As China became isolated from the world, I remembered my parents encouraging me to serve China and its people. And so I determined to shed my accent and learn more about my country's culture and history. I found support from a loving husband and some success as an ophthalmologist specializing in glaucoma. I

JEAN TREN-HWA PERKINS

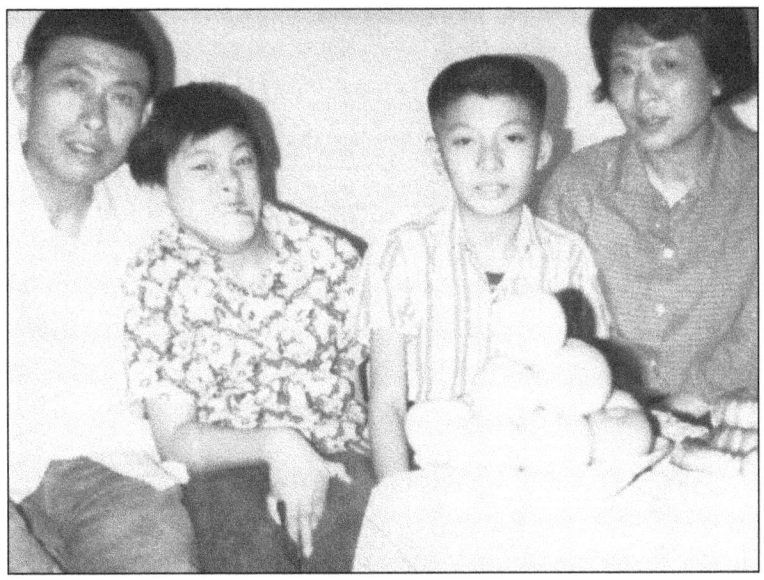

A rare family portrait, ca. 1978

raised a daughter with a disability while living in a Westerner-built district in Shanghai, which was an oasis for me.

After that, I moved to Hangchow (杭州), and Mao's Great Proletariat Cultural Revolution began to raise hell for many of us. Yet, despite my American and religious background and the Red Guards imprisoning my husband and destroying so much around us, I was always blessed to encounter helpful souls who intervened on my behalf, as though divinely orchestrated. In the late 1970s, while serving as a translator for Communist Party Chairman and Premier Hua Guo-Feng (华国锋主席) at the time China was reopening to the West, an American doctor found me and began the process of helping me return to America. Book Two reflects the pain of a nation, and the heaven and hell I experienced as brave men and women banded together to survive these years of terror.

APPENDICES

1. A Tribute to My Beloved Parents
2. A Brief History of Modern China, Including a Tribute to Missionaries
3 & 4. Letters with My Parents: December 1950 – March 1951

Appendix One
A Tribute to My Beloved Parents:
Dr. and Mrs. Edward Carter Perkins

MY FATHER, Dr. Edward Carter Perkins, was the son of Mary Evelyn Dwight Perkins and Edward Henry Perkins, and the younger brother of Henry Augustus Perkins. He was born in Hartford, Connecticut, on July 11, 1875. Records have it that my father and his elder brother, who later became an accomplished professor of physics and engineering and twice served as acting president of Trinity College in Hartford, were descendants of the wealthy Connecticut Perkins clan. Their great-grandfather Enoch Perkins, husband of Anna Pitkin, was cofounder of both Hartford National Bank and one of the oldest and continuously running law firms in the US, currently known as Howard, Kohn, Sprague & FitzGerald. Their grandfather, also named Henry Augustus Perkins, served as president of Hartford National Bank from 1853 to 1874.

For generations, the Perkinses were a powerful family through marriages. Their great-grandmother Anna Pitkin was a sister of US Representative Timothy Pitkin (1766–1847). Their great-aunt, Emily Pitkin Perkins Baldwin, was wife of Roger William Baldwin (1793–1863), the thirty-second Governor of Connecticut and a United States Senator, and became the mother of the sixty-fifth Governor of Connecticut, Simeon Eben Baldwin (1840–1927). I could go on and on with other influential family connections.

In the literary world, they were both grandnephews of Edward Everett Hale (1822–1909), author, historian, anti-slavery advocate, and minister, who was a descendant of the American Revolutionary War hero Nathan Hale (1755–1776). For decades, the Perkins family were close friends, neighbors, and confidants to Samuel L. Clemens, whose pen name was Mark Twain (1835–1910). In short, my father, Dr. Edward C. Perkins, was a direct descendant of an elite, blue-blood New England family!

So, how did he obtain the Chinese name 裴敬思, "Pei Jingsi" in pinyin?

My father was said to have led a playboy life during his youth, squandering his time and his fortune. He was handsome, charming, smart, and athletic, captain of the Yale University track team around 1893–1898, winning numerous meets in high and low hurdles. A member of the class of 1898, he was Phi Beta Kappa with a Philosophical Oration rank in political science, law, and history, and went on to obtain a law degree from Columbia University in 1899. He was also dismissed from the First Church of Christ in Hartford (which is still at 60 Gold Street), where he'd been a member from the age of fifteen. We can only imagine that it might have been related to his hard-drinking, womanizing lifestyle.

Then it all changed. My father fell off a horse during an outing in the countryside and somehow this led to finding his "higher" calling. He attended Hartford Theological Seminary in 1902, spent a year at the Baltimore Medical School, then enrolled at the College of Physicians and Surgeons of Columbia University and obtained his MD in 1910. During that time, he also attended Yale Divinity School. I don't know if he was formally ordained, but later he was referred to as the Rev. Dr. Edward Perkins.

My father, Dr. Edward C. Perkins (裴敬思医生)

JEAN TREN-HWA PERKINS

In 1910 post-medical school, without knowing a word of Chinese, my father traveled to China by sea, visiting Korea and Japan en route, a life-changing excursion. During this maiden voyage to China, he managed to find his way to Kiukiang in Kiangsi Province in Central China. He spent some time at the Elizabeth Skelton Danforth Memorial Hospital (但福德醫院) in town, where he met Dr. Mary Stone (玛丽・斯通 or 石美玉: "Shie Mei-Yii" in pinyin), superintendent of the hospital. Their interactions became the basis of his book, *A Glimpse of the Heart China* (一窥中国之心) (New York: Fleming H. Revell Company, 1911), documenting the life and work of Dr. Stone in China.

Soon after returning to America, my father completed his three-year residency as a surgeon at St. Luke's Hospital in New York. In early 1913, accompanied by his mother, he sailed to London, where he trained for three months in tropical diseases. He and his mother then visited Paris and Lausanne, before heading to Berlin, where they went their separate ways. My father traveled to Moscow and embarked on an adventurous train ride on the Trans-Siberian and Trans-Manchurian Railroads. Along the way,

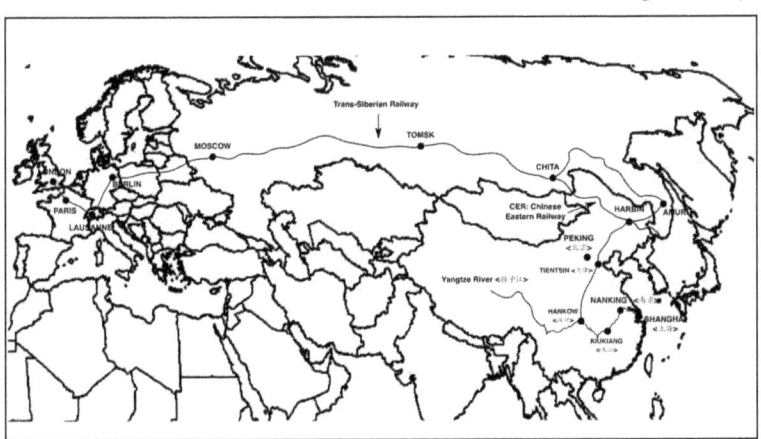

My father's odyssey to the Far East via Siberia in 1913
Blank map downloaded from http://geography.about.com/library/blank/blxeurasia.htm

My Mother, Mrs. Georgina Perkins (裴家紀 – 裴师母)

he managed to learn Russian.

He got off the train in Harbin, the northernmost metropolis in China. From there, the Trans-Manchurian Railroad took him to Tientsin (天津), the gateway city to the capital Peking (北京), where he knew many missionary compatriots. While in Tientsin, he learned that the City of Nanking (南京), where he would attend language school, had been nearly destroyed from the fighting among local warlords, so he detoured to the city of Hankow (汉口), and from there boarded a steamer downstream onto the Great Yangtze River.

On July 17, 1913, after a monthlong journey from London, my father returned to the ancient city of Kiukiang (九江), where he became involved with the local Chapter of the Methodist Episcopal Church (江西美以美), predecessor of the United Methodist Church (联合卫理公会). He spent a year as a staff surgeon at the Elizabeth Skelton Danforth Memorial Hospital (但福德醫院), the only hospital in Kiukiang and devoted solely to women's health, duly noting that there was no hospital or clinic for men in the city.

The newlyweds spending their own quiet time on a Yangtze River steamer

JEAN TREN-HWA PERKINS

My father would not have left China were it not for someone special waiting for him stateside. That was my mother, Georgina MacDonald Phillip, the daughter of William and Jean Sword Phillip. My mother was born in 1883 in Edinburgh, Scotland. When she was five, her family moved to Toronto, and stayed there for about two years before emigrating to the United States. Her father went to work for an architectural firm in New York. My mother then grew up along the Hudson River Valley, moving from Hastings-on-Hudson to Irvington before finally settling in Yonkers.

My mother, who also has a Chinese name 裴家紀 ("Pei Jia-Ji" in pinyin), had a far less exciting youth than my father. She lived with her parents in Yonkers until she was well into her thirties. For women of her time, that was rather old not to be married, and she had accepted that she would live out her days with her parents, a quiet and non-adventurous life. They were all devout Christians, and while life was uneventful, they were happy, just the three of them and their dogs.

In 1916, that all changed. That was the year Mother married Father. A few years earlier, my father spotted her riding on a

Shanghai Bund in the early 1920s

SPRING FLOWER: A TALE OF TWO RIVERS

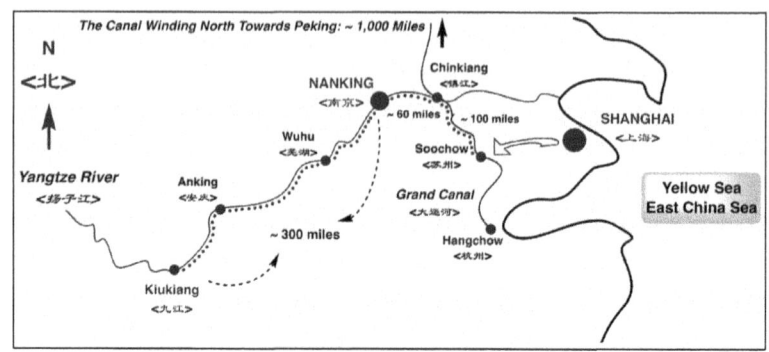

Mother's journey toward Kiukiang

Traversing the Grand Canal near Soochow (大运河: 苏州)

Edward handing out Bibles to those standing on the banks

trolley in New York City. As the trolley made a turn, Mother glanced through the windowpane, and when their eyes met, my father was in love. He chased the trolley, hopped onto it, and proposed.

They were married in 1916, and shortly after the wedding, Mother left Yonkers for the first time in her adult life and became a missionary, traveling halfway around the world. Much praise should go to her parents, my grandparents, who were willing to part ways with their only daughter and sacrifice their happiness.

Together they boarded a Trans-Pacific steam liner at the San

SPRING FLOWER: A TALE OF TWO RIVERS

Kiukiang Pagoda on the banks of the Yangtze River

Francisco Ferry Terminal and bade farewell to America, where Georgina had lived since she was seven. After months at sea, with brief stops in Honolulu and Yokohama, they landed at the famed Shanghai Bund (上海外灘). Mother was already an avid photographer, and she began to document her lifelong journey into China through her lens. In the early twentieth century, carrying around a camera was most unusual.

From Shanghai, my parents went west to Soochow (蘇州), the Chinese Venice, and took a boat ride on the Grand Canal (大運

My parents at work in the hospital office: Part of a motion picture taken by the Methodist Photographic Bureau

JEAN TREN-HWA PERKINS

河), a manmade waterway completed in the sixth century that runs from Hangchow (杭州) to Peking, 1,100 miles in length. Not to overlook the brutality of slavery during the Sui Dynasty (隋朝: 581–618 CE), the Grand Canal represents an engineering feat on par with the Great Wall, testimonies of Chinese ingenuity. This human wonder modernized north-south travels and transport of goods, alleviated flood damage, and transformed the Chinese economy.

After nearly 100 miles of riding on an equivalent of a gondola, they reached the town of Zhenjiang (镇江), where the Grand Canal cuts across the Great Yangtze River. From there, they headed west, upstream on the Yangtze for about sixty miles toward Nanking, which my father had failed to reach three years earlier. They stayed in Nanking for almost two years and began a long and intensive language training. During that time, my father worked as a surgeon for the University Hospital of Nanking, and my parents began planning a new hospital for men in Kiukiang.

In 1918, Edward and Georgina set sail again on the Yangtze River, continuing upstream another 300 miles toward Kiukiang. It was Mother's very first time seeing this ancient city in the rural central regions of China, and my father's third. From that year on, they devoted all their time and energy to the well-being of Chinese people, both medically and spiritually, for nearly half a century.

My parents' earlier years in Kiukiang

SPRING FLOWER: A TALE OF TWO RIVERS

A Brief Reflection on My Mother

I often think about what Mother's expression must have been when she arrived in old Shanghai and when she meandered by gondola through the narrow and congested Grand Canal before sailing up the Yangtze River for the first time. I imagine her being completely captivated when the Kiukiang Pagoda

My mother with her Sunday School students

JEAN TREN-HWA PERKINS

(锁江楼塔) slowly and majestically unveiled itself. At the same time, she must have been awestruck by an alien world. I wonder what she was thinking when she finally landed in the town of Kiukiang, after spending most of her life along the Hudson River in Yonkers, New York. I can only imagine the magnitude of her culture shock, particularly during her first years. She did speak of her shock when she learned that the centuries-old practice of "bound-feet" was still prevalent. Chinese women had their feet tightly wrapped with strips of cloth at a very young age so they could grow up with small feet, which was attractive (and marketable) to men. Despite creating a lifetime of pain and deformity, this antiquated practice was adopted by nearly all social classes, because having tiny feet was considered a thing of beauty. It would be impossible to find a woman with feet longer than three inches. To my mother, this was a desecration of women's bodies, which was consistent with historical disregard for women, including their health and education.

My beloved parents in the 1950s

SPRING FLOWER: A TALE OF TWO RIVERS

My mother was not new to Chinese faces, as her family had generously hosted numerous Chinese medical students and physician-interns in New York. Had she stayed in Shanghai, it would have been less shocking, since Shanghai was already an international city in 1916. But Mother migrated from the US to a rural town in the Central Regions at a time when war and famine were ravaging China.

One might think she was merely following her husband, fulfilling the traditional duties of a loving wife supporting her man's dream. But this was much more than that. What must have sustained her? I believe she had a mission, a calling of her own, which was a life of compassion, an ideal in which women everywhere have an equal right to life, education, and medicine. She was following her hope that Chinese people could see the heart and feel the warmth of Western civilization. Georgina Phillip Perkins was doing what she could to make a difference in this world.

Here is what my father wrote about her: *"It would be quite impossible to describe how great of a blessing the Lord conferred upon me in my life. He has given me someone who has always been ready with sympathy, with comfort, with patient understanding, with wise counsel, and all kinds of practical help, under extreme conditions and harrowing experiences throughout our active and ever-changing life. In short, she has been patient in trouble and fearless in danger."*

Appendix Two
A Brief History of Modern China

If I can sum up the history of China from the mid-nineteenth to the early twentieth century, it would be war, famine, and plague. By the mid-nineteenth century, China was beginning to descend from 2,000 years of invincibility. The ruling of an increasingly corrupt, divided, and weak imperial court of the Qing Dynasty (清朝: 1644–1912) was eroding that invincibility. Their ineffectual governing weakened China's diplomatic ability to deal with the imperialistic West. The insatiable demand for Chinese products led to an imbalance of trade and mounting debt from the West.

Consequently, the British East India Company began bootlegging opium, the most active ingredient of which is morphine, and that effectively paralyzed an entire nation. In an attempt to eradicate the widespread addiction and control the trafficking, China engaged the West in the Anglo-Chinese Opium Wars. With its vastly superior, modernized naval force, Britain won the first war (1839–1842), and a rare Franco-British alliance demoralized China in the second one (1857–1860). These defeats led to one-sided treaties and cessions of land, including Hong Kong Island to Britain at the end of the first war (Treaty of Nanking, 1842).

Contrary to what I've read, I do not believe this was all the fault of the embattled Empress Dowager Ci-Xi (慈禧太后: 1835–1908). Much of the criticism stems from the fact that she was a woman in power (from 1861 to 1908). I believe the greedy, incompetent men around her should have been held guilty of treason for weakening and selling out the country. These men were too busy lining their pockets, suppressing whoever they could still oppress, and persecuting their political rivals.

Ironically, the Opium Wars have come to represent the beginning of modern Chinese history. China was unable to strike a balance of honorably preserving cultural strength and identity of 3,000 years, while selectively engaging the values of Western civilizations. China was confused, I believe, whether "to fight or flight," or "to resist or sell." One can only be envious of what took place so effectively three decades earlier in Japan, the Meiji Restoration (めいじいしん; 明治維新), which transformed feudal Japan in the wake of Western colonialism. China, on the other hand, failed to modernize through the "Hundred Day Reform (百日維新)" led by the ambitious Guang-Xu Emperor (光緒帝: 1871–1908), the eleventh emperor of the Qing Dynasty. Where would China be if there had been an equivalent peaceful transformation?

Instead, China was ushered into the modern era with blinding force and profound humiliation. On the one side, there were many rebellions, including the Taiping Rebellion (太平起义) from 1850 to 1864, and the Boxer Rebellion (义和团运动) in 1899-1901, valiant attempts to resist Western domination and restore dignity. These rebellions also targeted missionaries and churches, which were regarded as instruments of Western colonialism. Most of those rising up were desolate farmers suffering from famines, droughts, and plagues, who had no hope in sight. Without any sustainable support from the imperial Qing Court, the rebellions all ended in devastating failure. The Boxer Rebellion lit the fuse for the ultimate counterattack from the West, after rebels killed Clement von Kettler, a German diplomat who had executed a Chinese boy in broad daylight on the street in Peking. In 1900, the infamous Eight-Nation Alliance (八国联军) was organized, consisting of Japan, Russia, Great Britain, France, the US,

JEAN TREN-HWA PERKINS

Germany, Austria-Hungary, and Italy. Under the pretense of humanitarian intervention, the allies quickly captured the Port of Tientsin (天津), a gateway to China, and shortly after, in August 1900, besieged the capital Peking (or Beijing, 北京).

The once-proud and invincible "Middle Kingdom" (中国: "Zhong-Guo") was brought to its knees by the "foreign devils" (洋鬼子: "Yang-Gui-Zi"), which is how Chinese referred to Westerners. Horrific atrocities followed—burning temples, pillaging homes, and beheading those associated with the rebellion, while allied troops stood by and watched. China was beaten into submission by the West.

The chaos that followed became accentuated when the West began preparation for its own Great War. It had neither the time nor the resources to deal with the mess it had created. In 1912, Dr. Sun Yat-Sen (孫中山: Sun is the last name) toppled the Last Emperor of the imperial Qing Court and established a Provisional Government of the Republic of China ruled by the Chinese Nationalist Party (国民党: "Kuo-Ming-tang" in pinyin or "KMT").

China quickly fell into anarchy, and for more than a decade, the country was trampled by warlords and bandits and devastated by endless coups and factional wars. Dr. Sun and his young, ambitious successor, Chiang Kai-Shek (蒋介石: Jiǎng-Jièshí), tried to unify the fragmented country through military campaigns (Northern Expeditions: 1911 through 1927), which only led to further bloodshed. A brief unification of China took place in 1928.

As if all these wars were not enough, famines, pandemic diseases, and natural disasters brought China to the abyss. By the early 1920s, the concept of communism, already spreading around the world, was emerging in China, not as an ideal, but a real revolutionary force. Further internal conflicts would follow, spilling into World War II. For the first half of the twentieth century, China struggled mightily for freedom, independence, and legitimacy, both within and on the international stage.

Medical Missions in Kiukiang

The spread of Christianity began in China as early as 630 CE, during the Tang Dynasty (唐朝), when China was at the height of its civilization. By the mid-nineteenth century, it had grown from isolated efforts into a widescale religious crusade. The China Inland Mission (now Overseas Missionary Fellowship or OMF International), established by Rev. J. Hudson Taylor from Great Britain, and the Presbyterian and Methodist Churches of America were leading the charge. Although a stark contrast to Western brutality and colonialism, Christian missions were not always well received in China.

In 1867, two men came to Kiukiang by way of Foochow, Fukien (福州, 福建: "Fu-zhou, Fu-Jian"), and set up the first missionary station in China for the Methodist Episcopal Church (江西美以美會). The Rev. Dr. Virgil C. Hart and the Rev. Dr. Elbert S. Todd were the earliest missionaries to venture into the Central Yangtze River Valley. Their arrival would make Kiukiang the first mission station for the Methodist Episcopal Church, or indeed any Protestant missions from North America, in Central China.

The Rev. Dr. Hart (an honorary doctoral degree was conferred on him later) became a key figure in Christian missions for Central and Western China—spanning almost the entire length of the Yangtze River. His most influential work and that of his wife, Addie, was done in Chengdu in Sichuan Province (成都, 四川), at the head of the river. Mrs. Hart was Canadian and Dr. Hart was from Watertown, New York. They established schools with a modern curriculum, advocating educations for girls and women, and called medical missionaries to bring forth Western medicines and build modern hospitals. Sichuan University in Chengdu currently has a building named after the Rev. Dr. Hart, whose pioneering work preceded my parents by a generation or more.[1]

Much less is known about Rev. Dr. Elbert S. Todd, from Adrian, Michigan. He attended Adrian College and later enrolled in the Union Theological Seminary in New York. There is a beautiful portrait of him, and a chapter describing his journey to China with his family and ultimately to Kiukiang in 1867, in a book by his niece, Eva Todd Burch. Neither of these men spent much time in Kiukiang. There are no records of them or any other missionaries or physicians opening medical clinics in Kiukiang before 1900. There is a record of Dr. William E. Tarbell opening a dispensary in 1875, but it was discontinued the following year.

Schools, however, were built by the Kiangsi Chapter of the Methodist Episcopal Church. In 1881, the William Nast Academy (九江同文中学) was founded by Thomas C. Carter (Chinese

William Nast Academy Chapel (九江同文中学)

---

1   E. I. Hart, D.D. *Virgil C. Hart: Missionary Statesman. Founder of the American and Canadian Missions in Central and West China* (New York: George Doran Company, 1917).

name: 托马斯·卡特), and Dr. Carl Frederick Kupfer (Chinese name: 库思非), a German missionary, became its first headmaster. The Rulison-Fish Memorial High School (儒励女子中学) was founded earlier in 1873 and an American, Ms. Gertrude Howe (Chinese name: 昊格矩) from Lansing, Michigan, became its first headmistress. Education for women was a key focal point for these missionaries at the turn of the century—how forward-thinking! My mother taught at Rulison, and at one point in the 1920s, my father served as the acting headmaster for Rulison Girls High and also taught at William Nast Academy. Both high schools remain in existence today.

A series of elementary and day schools opened in succession. In 1906, Knowles Bible Training School for Women was established, and Ms. Jenny V. Hughes (Chinese name: 胡遵理) became its first principal. Both my father and mother taught at this Bible School. Later, the Gracey Center was built for rehabilitating and teaching disabled children, another human triumph ahead of its time.

In 1901, missionary Dr. Isaac N. Danforth from Chicago established the first hospital in Kiukiang, named the Elizabeth Skelton Danforth Memorial Hospital (但福德醫院) in honor of his late wife, focused solely on women's health care. Today, it is called Kiukiang Women and Children's Hospital (九江市妇幼保健医院).

Besides Dr. Mary Stone (石美玉), there was another extraordinary Chinese woman in that era: Dr. Ida Kahn (康成: "Kang Cheng"). She was the adopted daughter of Gertrude Howe, the first headmistress of Rulison Girls High. Both Dr. Kahn and Dr. Stone attended the School of Medicine at the University of Michigan and in 1896 became the first Chinese female physicians trained in America. Upon returning to China, they served as the first superintendents of the Danforth Memorial Hospital. They were among the most influential Chinese women at the turn of

Rulison-Fish Memorial High School (儒励女子中学)

the twentieth century.

In 1913, when my father worked as a staff surgeon at Danforth Memorial and realized there were no clinics or hospitals for men in Kiukiang, the seed was sown. Between 1916 and 1918, while he and my mother were studying Chinese in Nanking, they were also laying the groundwork for a hospital for men there.

Elizabeth Skelton Danforth Memorial Hospital (但福德醫院)

In 1918, the first clinic for men in Kiukiang officially opened, the Kiukiang Water of Life Hospital (九江生命活水醫院)("WLH"). Shortly after its opening, Deanetta and Elizabeth Ploeg (浦乐姐妹), American nursing graduates of Calvin College in Grand Rapids, Michigan, arrived and became the cornerstones of my parents' endeavor.

The phrase *Water of Life* comes from a Biblical passage my father loved during the days of his spiritual reckoning: "…And the Spirit and the bride say, Come. And let him that heareth say, Come. And let him that is athirst come. And whosoever will, let him take the water of life freely..." (Revelation 22:17, King James Version). To stumble upon this rather obscure phrase in The Book requires a personal story.

The Water of Life Hospital (WLH) rented a facility from 1918 to 1927. When it opened, my father was the only surgeon,

Kiukiang Water of Life Hospital (九江生命活水醫院) opened, ca. 1918

Kiukiang Water of Life Hospital (九江生命活水醫院), ca. 1918

operating on as many as 140 Chinese patients a month. As time went on, he received help from visiting physicians, in particular a young woman from Tupper Lake, New York, named Dr. Hyla Watters. She was a missionary working at Wuhu General Hospital (芜湖总医院), downstream along the Yangtze River. In addition, with the help of the Ploeg sisters, my father was able to train hundreds of young Chinese physicians and nurses.

In the early twentieth century, diseases such as Asiatic cholera, malignant malaria, leprosy, diphtheria, smallpox, tuberculosis, and typhoid fever were pervasive in China, particularly in the Central and rural regions, including Kiukiang. The line between isolated events and a disastrous pandemic was thin. My father's training in tropical medicine became beneficial for the Chinese people.

In 1924, there was an Asiatic cholera outbreak in Kiukiang, and my father himself nearly died from the infection. It was not uncommon for missionaries to die of infectious diseases. Nora Evelyn Kellogg, an American nurse from Wheaton, Illinois, died of typhoid fever while working at the Danforth Memorial

The arrival of the Ploeg sisters

SPRING FLOWER: A TALE OF TWO RIVERS

Lining up for the morning clinic

Hospital, when she was just thirty-nine.

My father did not remain in Kiukiang all the time. With my mother serving as an effective general manager and financial officer of the WLH enterprise, Father helped out in other regions of China. In 1921, the northern part of China suffered from great famines after three consecutive years without a harvest due to droughts and wars. Although this pales in comparison with great famines in earlier decades (circa 1876 and circa 1907, killing 10 and 25 million people, respectively), the 1920–1921 disaster still killed half a million people. My father, along with famine relief personnel from the American Red Cross, went to Tehchow (德州: "De-Zhou") in the Shandong Province (山东) and helped the staff at Williams Porter Hospital. My father wrote a short memoir documenting this period, excerpted below:

> *The whole experience of the months of famine work in North China brought out, to my mind, one of the outstanding characteristics of the Chinese, namely, their long-suffering patience. Although [the] famine was dreadful beyond words, I neither saw nor heard of anything [that] savored of mob*

JEAN TREN-HWA PERKINS

violence [even] in their distress and starvation. The people did not do what one might have expected, namely, get a mob together and loot the stores, but they died at home or out in search [for] food. Any time, all day long, one could look out across the great level expanse of the Shantung plains and see groups of people in varying numbers, walking single file on the narrow paths, and trekking in every direction in search of food...

Amidst starvation and cold, a pneumonic plague broke out in the Tehchow (德州, 山东) region. In his diaries, my father described his efforts working with Dr. Sam Cochrane, a physician at Williams-Porter Hospital, to stop the spread of the deadly plague. He documented their efforts to convince the Chinese Railroad Commission to prohibit trains from Tientsin stopping at stations within the region, preventing the spread of the disease.

In 1926, my father was called to Nanchang (南昌), a city not too far south of Kiukiang, on numerous occasions, to help the staff

Nearly completed new Water of Life Hospital, ca. 1931

SPRING FLOWER: A TALE OF TWO RIVERS

Water of Life Hospital, 2016 (九江市第一人民醫院总院-生命活水醫院)

Water of Life Hospital physicians, nurses, pharmacists, aides, and staff (ca. 1949–1950) Georgina took the photo, so she is not in it

at Nanchang General Hospital treat a flood of wounded Chinese soldiers. Some days, stray bullets flew by while they operated. There were casualties both from Chiang Kai-Shek's (蒋介石) Northern Expedition to unify the country and from the escalating conflict between Communists and Chiang Kai-Shek's KMT Nationalists. As the wounded from all sides arrived at the hospital, my father saw only faces with pain and suffering, not their beliefs or ideologies. By 1927, conditions in the country had so deteriorated that my parents and

Deanetta and Elizabeth Ploeg at WLH, ca. 1920

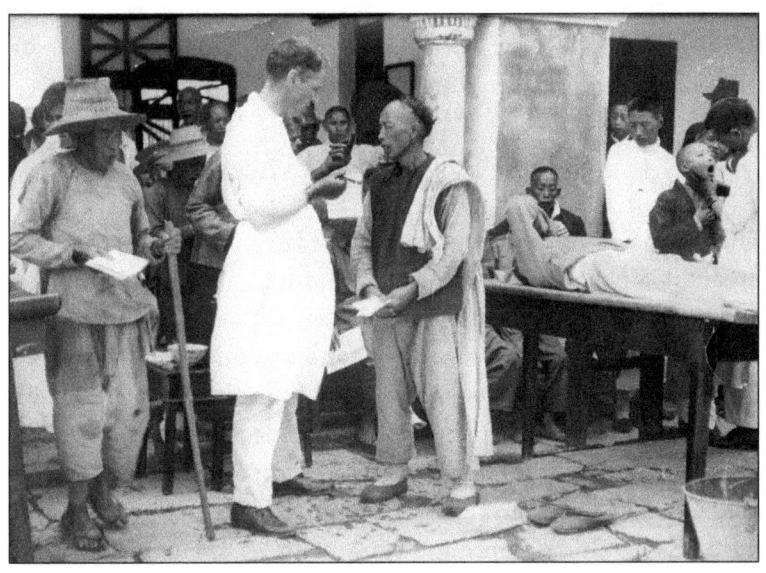

Morning clinic at the Water of Life Hospital

the other foreign missionaries from Kiukiang were ordered to evacuate, and they relocated to Seoul for six months.

In late 1927, my parents returned to Kiukiang. They purchased a piece of land near the facility they had been renting for WLH, to build a state-of-the-art facility. Construction began in early 1928 and was not completed until 1931. By 1932, the new facility was fully operational. The construction of Kiukiang Water of Life Hospital was funded mostly by my father's share of his family inheritance as well as whatever other resources he had.

Along with many others, my father treated tens and thousands of poor and desolate people at the hospital. They never discriminated which side of conflicts the casualties came from, whether Chinese, Japanese, or allies, whether communists, Republic nationalists, or Americans. They trained generation after generation of Chinese physicians and nurses. The Water of Life Hospital (九江生命活水醫院), founded in 1918, is still in existence (九江市第一人民醫院总院-生命活水醫院) and fully operational, with the lineage of the "Perkins School" of physicians still practicing in China.

My Last Thoughts and Tributes

That was a different time in China. Despite her beauty and ingenuity, her ancient history and myth, and her strength and perseverance through 3,000 years, China was ravaged by internal strife, natural disasters, famines, and pandemics, all the while enduring transgression and humiliation at the hands of the West. During these same trying decades, the collective efforts of Christian missionaries' endeavors must be recognized and cherished, because they brought modern education and hospitals to China, offering a stark contrast to colonialism and revealing a redemptive glimpse at the heart and humanity of

Western civilization. These are the people who sacrificed their brief but invaluable moments on this earth to help the Chinese people.

Most of all, I appreciate how they related to my people and took the time to learn Chinese so they could communicate. When it comes to the pride and symbol of any culture, language is at the top. Thus, in any given era serving any purpose including religious, the willingness of foreigners to learn Chinese represents the most positive indication that they are here to respect and help, not to oppress or rule.

I believe China should honor these missionaries because their sacrifices were for her people and her cause. I realize, however, that it may be too much to ask a country to take this responsibility, especially one that was struggling against oppression and trying to attain independence and freedom. To me, the church—the Methodist church, in particular—can do a much better job of honoring and recognizing these missionaries—doctors, nurses, and teachers—because they represent an essential part of church history. They devoted their resources, energy, skills, and intellect while living a selfless life, all for the cause of the church and its God. We know so little about the experiences of Methodist missionaries in China and their accomplishments for their church during the first half of the twentieth century. I can only mention a few of their names in the context of my parents.

It would be a shame if the church forgets them. Although I have not thoroughly researched the literature and so I will stand corrected if this is not the case, from the research I've done, the records about them are spotty. I believe when someone does something, let alone sacrificing their lives for a *belief*, the institutions representing that *belief system* should honor them to the fullest extent and not let them become mere footnotes to history or obliterated.

SPRING FLOWER: A TALE OF TWO RIVERS

Nanking University Language School, ca. 1916

To do what these Kiukiang Methodist missionaries did need not be set on an altar with a bronze bust. My parents would tell me exactly that; they might even scold me for thinking this way! But I do believe they are saints for what they and others accomplished. If they were Catholic missionaries, they would be canonized for their sacrifices. All of them lived extraordinary lives.

Appendix Three
My Letters to Mother
December 1950 – January 1951

After Mother and Day-Day left China, I wrote to them furiously. My letters, excerpted here in appendix three, are from Mother's preserved collection. Selections from the letters she and Day-Day wrote to me, in appendix four, are based on carbon copies she kept.

December 23, 1950

Dearest of Mommies,

I know this won't get to you on your birthday, as it is your birthday right now, but I thought I would write on this pretty stationery anyway, just to let you know I thought especially of you! May God add His blessings to you, Mommy.

I doubt I will get good marks in English as I did at Ruli [Rulison Girls High School in Kiukiang]. Speaking of marks, I just saw two of mine for the first half of this semester. One was biology, in which I got 80 — I don't know how but I did. The other was chemistry, and I received 75. I don't know what's the matter with me — I don't seem to dig it with chemistry.

Another girl and I visited Miss French at her home yesterday. She showed me letters you wrote to her and Miss Schulman. We got coats there too! I told her you said I could get money from her, but I didn't know how much. Just now I have borrowed from my roommate Chen and probably will again until I know just how much I should have. Mommy, I wish I wouldn't buy so much eats. But I do! Oh my, wish you were here to scold me!

The weather has been okay. It looks like we're not going to

have a white Christmas. Well, a nice sparkling sunshine day is just as lovely or perhaps more.

This evening we have our own Christmas program. I'm in a play called "Other Wise Men." I play a passerby. I only have to speak one sentence.

We hear there are going to be three days of vacation for New Years. Boy, won't that be fun? As if I haven't had enough already. Ha-Ha.

Well, Mommy, I should settle down to my Chinese essay now but thought I'd drop you a few lines on your Birthday.

Happy Birthday, Mommy!

Lots of love,

Jean

January 5, 1951

Dear Mommy,

Was so glad to receive all the news from you folks today from Canton! The last two weeks had been like years. I see—what a dashy sort of time you folks have had. Bet you are all tired out. I hope your voyage will be more restful. Are you going by way of England?

I am glad there were friends to see you off. It shows how well the Kiukiang people liked you. I am so sorry I could not, and I was not.

Is this the first time you were in Canton? I wonder if by now you have sailed for the U.S.? I wonder what kind of letters I should write hereafter. Airmail perhaps would be quicker but more expensive. I cannot bear the fact that you will not hear from me for months at a time.

No, God has not forsaken His own Children yet. I forgot to tell you Miss French gave me a coat, which was given to her from Aunt Helen to give to someone. It is a very lovely one, but more importantly, it is a warm one. Grace H. the other day gave me a pair of knitted socks. They were too big for her, and she heard that mine had many holes. You see, I will be warm this winter — people around me have been kind.

Oh Mommy, I can't stop buying eats. I spend on nothing else frivolous, but I seem to be eating and eating and eating out of anxiety.

Chum has not written to me in a long while, neither have I. I should, as I am the only person she could confide in. I don't know how she is making out by herself still in high school. She must miss the aunties terribly.

I still have Miss French and Miss Schulman. Auntie Helen has been asked to leave soon. In any event, seeing them is like seeing you. I feel I still have a home. Well, she has one that is greater than us all. I hope she will be comforted by Him.

However it works out, we shall be contented with God's will.

Dear Mommy, you will never go out of my mind or thoughts or prayers. None of you will! All four of you are part of me, even though we are not the same nationality. Still, we are one with God.

Lots of love to you all!

Jean

P.S., Please give my love to Aunt Mabel and Aunt Annie. I will try to write to the aunties, and right now, I am wearing Mommy's pajamas. They are nice and warm. I can even feel your warmth. I find comfort in them.

January 7, 1951

Dear Mommy,

Your letter written in Canton on the 2nd came yesterday! My but am I happy to hear from you all again. But I know there will come a time when mail will be far and wide apart. Perhaps we can begin writing our letters like our diary.

I have just taken my English final exam that came earlier than expected. Miss Spicer, our teacher, left for England last night. Perhaps you were on the same boat, wouldn't that be something. She is a brilliant person with a fantastic English accent.

I said I would write to Day-Day, but here I am again writing to you.

I went to SS [Sunday School] this morning. I am thankful that two of my roommates came. They had promised to attend some time ago, but today, at last, they came. I am delighted that they are seeking God's salvation, and I certainly will be glad if you can pray for them. Maybe for me too. Last night when I prayed, I didn't feel God's presence at all. Perhaps Satan has been busy at work. Or maybe it was just me.

Church attendance is still good. Even though it was wet and damp, people came. Wonder how many more English services I will be able to attend. Pretty soon all these people will be gone, and then there won't be any more.

I am thinking of you always!

Lots of love

Jean

P.S. How awful of me not thanking you for the money that came with the letter. I still have what Miss French lent me. I had offered to return it to her, so this is great. Thank you.

January 11, 1951

Dear Mommy,

No letters from you the last four days.

Days are going by so swiftly. Here it is the eleventh already. Wonder if you are now sailing on the ocean. Will you probably stop off in India somewhere too? My, it will be a familiar sight to you, won't it? I'd have loved to be on the trip—I so wanted to be, even though I knew that was not possible given all the circumstances. And I guess like you and Day-Day have said to me, this is where I should stay and that I should help my own people. My calling is here. But if I were with you, I would surely appreciate much better what I'd see now, more than ever. Instead of seeing it myself, though, I will hear it all from you. So will you drink it all up and then describe everything to me, won't you, Mommy?

It snowed here today, and it's so cold. I just had a gym class, and that is why I can write to you, as my hands are sufficiently warmed. They were like blocks of ice.

There have been no letters from you since the 2nd, and I know I am not forgotten. You probably have not received any from me either. Aunt Helen is still here, but she has been giving away many things. So, you know what I mean. Anyway, she gave me so many eats (Ha-ha, you know your daughter). The half jar of peanut butter which all six of us from Rulison enjoyed.

In two weeks, finals will be done, and I will head back to Kiukiang for the first time without my mommy and Day-Day...

The bell has gone off, and so I must go now.

Lots of love

Jean

January 13, 1951

Dear Mommy,

Since I wrote to you last, I've received two letters from you, both from Hong Kong! They are surely welcome! My, how I love to hear all the news. It'll be a long time now before I'll hear from you again, I guess, especially when you set sail.

Mommy, I'm glad you folks can all go together, and that you're having a nice visit with Ms. Wu in Hong Kong. Is she as beautiful as ever, and her children Marie and Helen too? Please send my love to her.

Many events have occurred since I last wrote to you two days ago. We are not going to have our final exams next week after all. How I wish I had known that, and I could have sailed down to Kiukiang to see you and Day-Day one last time. We may not even have those winter vacation days off, and so it looks as though I will not even be able to go in a few weeks to see Chum. I know she had been looking forward to it. We will have to pray for it.

We have also learned that our school will become a public one, owned by the government. All the chaos, well, we'll see.

I am wondering how many letters you have received from me. I will try getting this one in the mail tomorrow before you set sail on the 19th.

Mommy, please write to me all you can. I don't believe there will be any danger in it. At least, I am hoping the letter could be okay. I mean I don't think it matters—we write very carefully in case they read them. Why don't we get Miss Pool to be the middle person transferring our mail, or I can send mine to Mr. McCoy and then he can forward them to you. Maybe you can send me a bit more money for stamps, and I can try airmail, and perhaps we try just one letter and see what happens, I mean I will send it directly to where you are going. Okay? Oh, what am I talking about, I'm just rambling here, but you understand me, don't you, Mommy?

I cannot bear the thought of not hearing from you. You are all I got left.

So, you will be stopping by Japan instead of England? Which is the quickest way? Wonder if there has been considerable change there since the war ended. Mommy, how strange life is—the last time we set sail, we went away from that direction; but this time, you will go right to the coast of Japan. I am envious of where you and Day-Day are now, you know how I love to be on the ocean.

JEAN TREN-HWA PERKINS

Please don't mind me, I'm okay here, I'm just expressing myself. I mean it would have been fun to set sail again with you.

Nope, I have not taken serious measures to get rid of this nagging cough. I don't like to go out to get my medicine. Interacting with these pharmacists in Chinese is still a challenge. I'll see how I fare after this winter. I am reminded of when I was little, all I had to do was to tell you, and you would tell Day-Day, and then he'd prescribe, and you'd bring it to me. Ha-ha, I guess I have to grow up at some point.

We went downtown and got a farewell present for Aunt Helen, and she gave us even more useful things that she said she'll no longer need. She is leaving tomorrow night, and so she threw a party instead, wanting us to finish all the food in her pantry—ham, eggs, cookies, more meats, and fruits. Boy, were we filled! We sat by her fireplace, it kept us warm, she kept us warm, but this would be the last time.

I will write to the aunties. Let's keep writing—this is the only way. Oh, Mommy, I love you in heaps.

My love for Day-Day—Jean

January 14, 1951

Dear Mommy,

The day was made happy by two letters from you! One came in the morning and one in the afternoon. I just sent one by special mail or registered mail—and hope it reaches you before your voyage—it will be a long while before we could hear from each other again.

By the way, mail came in about a week from Hong Kong. Not bad, I could live with this. When you get to America, maybe you can send to Mr. McCoy, and Mr. McCoy can send to me by airmail, and it would be even faster.

Yes, the stationery that I am writing on belongs to Aunt

Helen. None of us dared to see her off. Instead, we celebrated her freedom in our dorm room by having a party eating all the things she gave us.

I got a few letters from Kiukiang. I was told that the principal of the nursing school burned her bible and hymnbook. More people are now turning away. It's sad, she always gave inspiring talks to students.

I guess you folks aren't so cold — it's freezing here now. Did I tell you Miss French gave me an overcoat?

Each Sunday, there are fewer and fewer people attending the English service. Soon, there won't be any. I will miss it.

The light in the dorm room will go out soon.

Love, Jean

January 15, 1951

Dear Mommy,

Here I am again! There were no lessons today, again, and there won't be any for the next few weeks. I'm not sure if exams will ever come. It is somewhat chaotic here. We were told to listen to announcements from bullhorns hung high above the trees and telephone pole.

I will visit Miss French and Miss Schulman. Soon they too will be gone. Don't know what's on tomorrow. We are living from day-to-day.

Lots of love,

Jean

January 16, 1951

Dear Mommy,

Another day is nearly done. We just listened to some announcements. Well, they are not real announcements, but speeches given by students, teachers, and workers on the topic of you know what.

This afternoon, we were led to the University of Nanking campus. We were there to see all the history of the school. Of course, it would be the kind of history that we are to denounce. I need not go into details; it would be too much. In short, I saw a photo of Day-Day standing in an old hospital among the flood refugees. He was helping them.

I don't know how it got there. They even made it into a slide, and so it was on a big screen. I just stood in the back and did not dare to make a sound. Nor did I want to hear their heresy. I was tough, Mommy, I didn't cry, although the photo made me very sad. I miss you so much.

No mail from you today—I am complaining. Anyway, it's okay for me to tell you events of my day anyway, Mommy. You will be leaving in three days.

Hope all goes well with your voyage!

Lots of love to you and Day-Day,

Love, Jean.

January 17, 1951

Dear Mommy,

Another letter from you! It was written on January 10. Letters take precisely seven days to get here. I sure hope you are receiving my Sunday weekly letters. I've written quite a few since you have left.

No school today either, we are really having an easy time of it. Miss French gave me another coat to give to Chum. I sure hope I will see her soon.

It's getting late—Mommie's girl is going to bed now!

Lots of love to you both!

Jean

SPRING FLOWER: A TALE OF TWO RIVERS

January 19, 1951

Dear Mommy,

I received another letter from you yesterday. Boy, do I like to receive them!

Yes, we do need faith. We usually lack it too. So many times, we don't trust ourselves to God. We must always pray for more faith. God will guide us safely through this life and lead us into eternity.

Wonder if you are now on the ocean. Hope you are having a pleasant voyage—how I wish I am with you, well, I am in spirit.

We just found out we will have an exam next week. So, we may be able to go back to Kiukiang for a few days after all. Paul Hsiung, you know Wm. Nast Academy's Principal Russell Hsiung's son, told me that he would try to find ferry tickets, which are hard to come by because—well you know, and that was also why I couldn't go and see you. Paul wants to go and see his parents too. He is worried about them.

We have to listen to some announcement over at the University of Nanking, and so I have to go. It's raining now, but I'm not going to take a raincoat. Hmm, I can see Mommie's look, ha-ha. I sure wish my letters could go by airmail.

My own mommy, I love you loads! Love to Day-Day,

Lots of love,

Jean

January 20, 1951

Dear Mommy,

Another letter from my mommy! It was written on January 14. Sure, I've been receiving letters from you since you were in Hong Kong. I wonder why you have only received two from me. I know you are looking forward to them, and I have been writing. I sure hope they are not lost or something. But don't believe for a second that I've forgotten you, Mommy. I couldn't possibly do that!!!

Bet my "mudder" and Day-Day are on the ocean just now. I wish this could reach you right away. Wonder when this letter will find its way to you. Oh Mommy, how I'd like to give you a big hug just now. Well, you can pretend you are being hugged just now! Okay? Dear Momma.

Oh, Mommy, your dear Jeanie is terrible at budgeting money. Oh, Mommy, I am simply awful, that's all. Oh dear! I've put aside enough for the next semester which I will not touch if I can help it at all. I will spend just a bit to go back to Kiukiang — boat tickets and all.

Enclosed are two photos of our fellowship group. See how many you recognize.

My turn to turn off the lights, and so, goodnight my dear Mudder, you know I love you lots. Hope you do receive my letters.

Love to Day-Day,
Lots of love, Jean

January 22, 1951
Dear Mommy,
So sorry that I did not get to write to you yesterday. I felt bad about that. But Mommy, you were in my thoughts all day. At the English service today, I got to thinking and longing for you that I nearly cried; but I know I shouldn't. What would I say if they ask me what my tears are for? I have Jesus Christ as my comforter and protector, and so I should be fine. I so want to be spiritual — I so want to love Him more than anything, as the Bible teaches us, and as you have always taught me; but I love you so much — and I miss you so much.

Oh, Mommy, just a hug just a kiss from you one more time,

is that too much to ask? But don't let me make you sad. I know sometimes I should not let you know my real feelings because I know that would make you feel bad; but sometimes, I just cannot help it. Oh Mommy, please pray for me that I will have the strength and that I will be brave with everything in front of me.

I am so glad you have finally received a letter from me. My, it took a long time and much longer than yours coming my way. Does it look like someone has already opened it? Anyway, I got yours of 11th, 14th, 15th, and 16th. Thank you for the postcards, they give me a sense of your surroundings.

I will be heading to Kiukiang on the 28th, exactly a month after you left Kiukiang. How strange that will be to not see you at the dock waving at me. Paul got us 5th Class tickets, so we will be outside bundled up—cold—but that's okay. I still want to see everything of which I am so familiar.

How is your wrangled finger doing? And you are typing to me, oh Mommy. I hope you are okay. On a brighter note, guess what, I got to play the piano last Sunday when the pianist was sick and their backup was not able to attend. It had been a while, maybe even dating back to Yonkers. I think I did okay with the hymns. I wish I had paid more attention to learning piano, as Chum did; but anyway, I did it.

I'd better get this one off to you now—the sooner, the better—uh?

Simply oodles of love to you both,

Lots of love, Jean

P.S. Enclosed is a photo taken last week. I have Miss French's coat on. Still recognize your very own Jeanie?

JEAN TREN-HWA PERKINS

January 24, 1951

Dear Mommy,

How glad I was to receive your more letters from you. My, am I glad to know that you have been receiving mine. I really had begun to worry—it just seems to be taking much longer in getting to you.

Well, I guess my mommy is sailing on the deep blue sea, or rather the Ocean. I can imagine how excited you will be to see all your familiar places! Many things will have changed since the war. It's been a long while. Will you and Day-day get to see Dr. Takata?

Mommy, in three days, we will be making our journey on the river homeward bound. I hope all things go well—please pray for us. I'm not sure what Kiukiang will be like now. Anyway, I bought slacks Chum had wanted, and I will give her the coat from Miss French. It will surely be good to see her again...

I'm not even packed yet. I suppose I should start before the boat goes tooting off to Kiukiang. Can't you imagine me? Ha! Ha!

I am sticking to my plan of leaving the money set aside for next semester. I'm learning, although I still seem to eat a lot. Maybe when I get home—I mean to Kiukiang—I will eat everyone out of house and home. Ha! Ha!

Miss French and Miss Schulman are still here. I don't know when they are leaving, as they have not gotten their exit permit to leave the country. Guess it won't be too long. Miss Schulman invited us this week to her house before my journey to Kiukiang. I guess you will see her in New York when she returns.

I should be packing—my very own "marmar"—I so love her.
Love to Day-Day,
Love, Jean.
P.S. Consider yourself kissed and hugged.

SPRING FLOWER: A TALE OF TWO RIVERS

January 26, 1951

Dear Mommy,

Boy, was I glad to receive your letter of the eighteenth written on the boat but sent before you at last set sail for Japan! Oh Mommy, I am so glad you are actually on your way to safety. May God bless you all along the way! My own dear Mommy, I really am terribly happy in the Lord. I am unsure how to describe my feelings. If it weren't for Him, I know I couldn't possibly bear one bit of this departing! But I know you are in His care.

We can't get off until the 29th again. When it happens, it will happen, and even if just for a day, I would love to see Kiukiang again and cheer up Chum in any way I can.

I guess you have not received many of my letters. I hope you will someday soon. Anyway, I said goodbye to Miss French yesterday. Miss Schulman asked me to drop by, but I have not had time. I fear that she too will leave soon. Then I will have very few to remind me of you and Day-Day.

Please do remember me — please ask all my friends in the U.S. to remember me.

Please don't forget me.

I would have loved to see them all again, but they are in my thoughts as always.

Mommy, you know how much I love you. I would love to give you a big squeeze just about now. Probably Mommy would go — ooof! — 'cause I'd nearly squeeze the breath out of you. Ha-ha!

Do tell Day-Day that I love him so.

Simply heaps of love to my sweet — and only parents.

Jean

Appendix Four
Mother and Day-Day's Letters to Me
January – March 1951

Aboard the *S.S. Anna Maersk*, in the harbor of Kobe (神户), Japan
January 25, 1951
My dear precious Jeanie,

Kobe is a place of memories of other days, and so a familiar place. We went yesterday afternoon ashore and walked the long distance from the place where the ship landed, into the town, and we viewed various places that have memories of other days. Truly a remarkable nation that is working so hard to pay off the war debts and is rising from its ashes, although it is pathetic to be still seeing visible effects of the war on buildings and the land.

For two days, we ate lunches at the same places. Today, I bought postage stamps, envelopes, note paper, carbon paper (I never saw anything like it before—it is carbon paper on each side), photos, and gospels in Japanese. Day-Day bought two volumes of self-taught German.

Everyone is extremely polite and pleasant, there is this stillness and calming presence, which is perhaps what we all desperately need.

Mommy needs to soak her feet, I'm quite tired from all this walking. More later, my precious.

January 26, 1951
Back again! We are in the same harbor and are due to sail at two o'clock this afternoon. We haven't seen the aunties' ship

yet, which I call the *Tungus*. Not sure if they will catch up with us, as they left a day later than we did. It would be nice to see them once more at least in the Far East before we meet them in America.

Mother has been praying for her Jeanie. Yes, I gave you our address in the USA before, but here it is again: c/o Board of Missions and Church Extension

150 Fifth Avenue

New York, N. Y. U.S. America

Still more loads of love from your marmar

S.S. Anna Maersk, in the harbor of Nagoya (名古屋), Japan
January 27, 1951

My own dear Jeanie,

We sailed again yesterday about 3:30, and as we came out from the harbor of Kobe, we passed the *Tungus*; Mother waved her red sweater, and Day-Day waved a white towel, and two people on the top deck of Tungus waved at us. We are just going to assume it was Aunt Dee and Auntie Bessie who were waving!

Early this morning, we came up to the dock at Nagoya. We see the *S.S. Emily Maersk* up against the pier opposite us. Emily and Anna must be glad to see one another again! Wonder how often that happens.

We went ashore and took the tram to the city. We walked around and did window shopping and then a little real shopping. Do you remember Mother's brass-colored little tea kettle, which we used all the time? Of course, that was left behind in Kiukiang along with almost everything else. So, Day-Day bought one like it as a souvenir of Nagoya, and I am glad to have it to remind me of our Kiukiang home!

The shops are just incredible at Nagoya, most attractive and tempting window displays — like those of New York City. You will be interested to know there were small piles of snow and ice on the streets, now well sprinkled with dust, which showed that there must have been a snowstorm not too long ago.

Mother could not help but notice the girls of my Jeanie's age. Half of them wear trousers and jackets, and the others skirts instead of trousers. I was pleased to hear that in the summer, the female population still wears kimonos.

I think of you often — you must be in Kiukiang now — I will be so glad to hear everything, but I guess I will have to wait till we reach America. The ship is due to spend the night here and sail in the morning for Shimizu.

S.S. Anna Maersk, leaving for Shimizu (清水) in Shizuoka Prefecture (静岡县)

January 28, 1951

Precious darling Jean of mine —

Mother has just been reading her lamb's letters, written December 23, 25, 26, 27, 28, 31, and Jan 1. These are her last letters, and oh, how she looks forward to receiving a letter when we reach New York!

Anna sailed this morning from Nagoya and is expected to reach Shimizu sometime tonight, but passengers will get no permits to go ashore, even though we will not be very far away from Mt. Fuji. The ship will take on more freight in Shimizu, although we have been loading much of the time in Nagoya. The expectation is that *Anna* will start tomorrow morning for Yokohama. We are hoping to see the aunties at Yokohama!

Day-Day and I had our "church" together this morning. After dinner tonight, we took a walk on the deck, and we saw an ocean liner passing us by.

With the beaming sunshine and the white-crested waves, our thoughts are with our precious dearie.

SPRING FLOWER: A TALE OF TWO RIVERS

Anna Maersk
January 29, 1951
We have been anchored in the harbor at Yokohama for a few hours waiting for the pilot to come and guide us in. I see now that we have started, so we'll soon get ashore and have a look-and-see. We'll probably have about two days here before we set sail for Vancouver, I mean San Francisco. The spaces between letters will then be longer, but I plan to send this one off from here.
Loads of love,
Mother

S.S. Anna Maersk, in the harbor at Yokohama, Japan
January 31, 1951
My precious darling Jeanie,
I can't get it through my wooden head that this is our last night in the Far East. As you know, we are due to sail tomorrow at 3 in the afternoon for San Francisco. So, Mother will be writing "a line a day" and hang onto the letter until we reach San Francisco.

Just think what a pleasant afternoon and evening we've been having with Auntie Dee and Auntie Bessie in their stateroom on the *Tungus*. Aunt Mollie came from Tokyo to spend a day with us. What a reunion it was, and we even had our prayer meeting and all. Day-Day then treated us all with a sukiyaki dinner at a restaurant in the town near the harbor of Yokohama.

Aunt Mollie then took us to Tokyo to see the Children's Center where she has been working. There are 900 children in all at the center. Aunt Mollie seems to be very happy with her new work. We also managed to track down Dr. Takata's residence in a suburb of this great city. You remember them when they worked at Danforth? Unfortunately, they were away in another town!

I hope my dearie is doing well and isn't coughing. Take care of yourself, as well as your ducats [money], and be faithful to your studying. The better you study, the more prepared you'll be for your life work. I will be beginning the next letter to you tomorrow, but it will take longer to reach you than this one. Imagine I'm squeezing and hugging my dearie.

Dad-Day sends his love. Loads and loads of love from Mommy.

Your very own—very loving,
Mother

S.S. Anna Maersk, Yokohama Harbor
February 1, 1951
My own dear Jeanie,

Mother now begins her line-a-day letter! She hopes that her Jeanie is having a happy day. The sign was posted this morning that our ship was going to sail at 10 a.m. Then we heard it would sail at noon, maybe!! So, Day-Day and I sallied forth in a pedicab to the shopping street and got a necktie for Uncle Henry, and a slip-slip with embroidery on it for Aunt Olga. It's now 9:25 p.m., and we are still here at the harbor of Yokohama. You would have loved the beautiful twinkling blue lights by the harbor. Tonight will be the last night Mother and her precious are on the same side the earth.

We had more visits with the aunties—including Auntie Mabel Woodruff, your old choir teacher, and Auntie Anne Pittman. Their *Tungus* is set to sail tomorrow....

S.S. Anna Maersk, at Sea
February 1, 1951
Jeanie dear,

When looking out my window this morning, I realize we have left Japan. At last, we are no longer at the same half of the earth.

The sun was ever so bright, and the ocean looked beautiful. There were no whitecaps, and the motion of *S.S. Anna* was gentle. No one knows just when we sailed! Some say midnight, some say one o'clock, and others say that it was between twelve and one! I should think Day-Day and I would have heard the commotion involved in starting, but we didn't.

On this ship there are two parlors or social halls, the smaller one is marked "for non-smokers." It's a lovely room; the furniture has gay-colored chintz covering it. I do my morning work, Bible reading, and prayer there, and always have the place to myself. Then I take a walk on the deck, back-and-forth, for exercise.

Wondering if you are now in Kiukiang, and how Chum is doing.

Love from
Mother

S.S. Anna Maersk (from Day-Day)
February 7, 1951
Dear Jean,

Chum's birthday has just gone by, and in realizing that Chum turned nineteen, I woke up with a start to the fact my little daughter Jean would soon be twenty years old. We shall be thinking of you and remembering you in prayer on that day. I hope that the year between twenty and twenty-one will be the best yet so far as the important matters of life are concerned.

Word came that because of various interruptions, Gin-Ling would not be having its mid-year holiday and we are ever so sorry to hear it, being apprehensive that the happy time that you and Chum had planned in being together in Kiukiang would have to be postponed. Perhaps you will have a little get-together after all. Kiukiang and Nanking are not very far apart — much closer than where we will be.

We are having a happy voyage so far. I'm doing some writing on Mother's typewriter, Bible studying, reading, reflecting, and a bit of exercise. We are delighted to have this opportunity to prepare for the next chapter in life.

Some sea birds are following the ship. We are many hundreds of miles away from land and they certainly cannot go home at night. Perhaps they are hoping something nice will be thrown overboard as their meals. If the Lord looks after them, as He does, surely, He is going to care for us in times of great needs. He does not forget us for a minute — believe that, my dear daughter.

Did Mummie tell you that we brought along a full lunch basket so we would be sure to have enough to eat. This boat is a freighter, and we didn't know what the meals would be like. Having that basket is more or less a joke now, for the ship's food is delicious and we are far more in danger of overeating than in not having enough.

Mummie and I send loads of love and special birthday love for April 29. With frequent prayers, I am thinking of you, as always.

Your affectionate,
Day-Day

S.S. Anna Maersk
February 8, 1951
My dear Jean,

Last evening, Day-Day and I had our prayer meeting, as it was Wednesday. You and Chum were surely remembered. Later in the evening, we had our word game together, and Day-Day's record was 63, and Mother's, 80. Praise expected for winning!

There have been no white caps on the sea today, and we are rolling along nicely. Mother has been helping Day-Day write letters, and as usual, wrote one herself to her precious.

This forenoon, Day-Day and I went to the deck and threw some of the bread we brought from Japan to the birds that have been following the ship.

Lovingly,
Mommie

S.S. Anna Maersk (from my father)
February 9, 1951
My dear Jeanie,

Mother is trying to recite John 3:1-21 correctly in Chinese. I have known verses 1-16 for quite some time, and now I am adding five more bible verses in Chinese.

I hope your study at Gin-Ling College is going well with fewer interruptions. How is Chum — do you hear from her often? How is dear old Wang-Sao? Hope you got to see her as well during your trip back in Kiukiang.

Mother threw another bun today into the water for the birds. Many of them ceased to follow the ship, but over time, they have all returned!

S.S. Anna Maersk
February 10, 1951
Jeanie dear,

Mother helped Day-Day type more letters this morning. Then, I did some tramps on the deck. There wasn't a single white cap on the ocean today, and the swell was slower and longer. Of course, my precious was on my mind. I thought of our last trip all together on the sea to America. I also wondered what sort of weather the aunties are having with their ship *Tungus*, which has gone the northern route, while our *Anna* is taking the southern course.

Today is Saturday, and the Captain informed us we would

reach San Francisco on Tuesday.

I keep hoping that my darling has an opportunity to study peacefully at Gin-Ling. I keep wondering so much how things are everywhere.

Loads and loads of love from your mommy.

S.S. Anna Maersk
February 11 and 12, 1951
My own dearie,

Yesterday was Sunday. Day-Day and I had two services together. I am so glad we have a Methodist hymnal book between us, and that we can still carry a tune without an organ or a piano. If my Jeanie dear or Chum were here, you would be playing for us. That would be so wonderful.

All was very quiet when we sat on the deck reading. I hope you, too, had a peaceful day.

Today, Monday, I am helping Day-Day type more letters, and have written a letter myself, like right now. This evening will be a Captain's dinner, as half of us passengers (12 of us altogether) will be getting off in San Francisco. I presume the dinner is to honor those who will be leaving.

Much love

S.S. Anna Maersk
February 13, 1951
Mother's Precious Jeanie,

It is now half-past ten Tuesday morning, and the ship is due to arrive in San Francisco at about twelve, and Mother and Day-Day plan to go ashore and "wobble around" and mail our letters. This part of the journey letter will start back to my Dollie from San Francisco, and then a new one will be begun after that.

I hope you are well. Tomorrow will be Valentine's Day! I will see what I am able to find for my Valentine, though I fear it will not reach her on time!!!

Loads of love from Mudder. Day-Day sends his love.

Mother

S.S. Anna Maersk, in port in San Francisco
Tuesday, February 13, 1951
Dear, dear Jeanie,

We are now Tuesday evening, and Day-Day and I had a walk on the streets of San Francisco this afternoon! Imagine, we are back on American soil.

After our dinner, Day-Day went to get a haircut. Mail was brought to the ship for us from Uncle Henry. He reports that Aunt Olga is home from the hospital and there is a slight improvement. Do pray for him at this difficult time, for he is not strong either.

The Board of Mission Office here in San Francisco says we have letters from Aunt Adelaide, Miss Coral Houston, Miss Edith Fredericks, Miss Frances Woodruff (Aunt Mabel's sister), and also Mr. and Mrs. Wilber Wilson.

There was a letter from Philip Watters, Aunt Hyla's brother, welcoming us back to America, and that we could stay with them when we arrive in New York. Come to think of it, Mother has been saying to herself that this was her first time to live in the USA when she had no home to go to. Home had been Kiukiang for all these years.

Loads of love from
Mother

S.S. Anna Maersk, in port in San Francisco
Wednesday, February 14, 1951
My own dear Jeanie,

Day-Day and Mother started out for the Methodist office to

collect our mail. You remember Miss Ellen Smith who works in the office? She and her coworkers and we had a nice lunch together. She asked about you.

Then we made some modest purchases, including a Valentine for my Jeanie.

San Francisco streets are fascinating. Some are on high hills, and indeed, I'd be terrified to ride up and down these hill streets in an automobile, as the folks here do. They go fast, too!!

I certainly hope to see Mr. and Mrs. Wilson, who live in Arcadia, California. We've known them since we first arrived in China and attended Language School in Nanking.

We will be passing the aunties' ship again, as they are due here tomorrow morning at eight, as we sail out to the port of Pasadena before heading toward the Panama Canal.

Mother keeps hoping her darling keeps well, especially in the winter. God bless you…

S.S. Anna Maersk
February 15, 1951
My own dear Jeanie,

There is a chance to mail another letter to my darling tomorrow, as we'll be making a stop in Los Angeles. The ship left San Francisco this morning at about five o'clock, and ever since, we have been sailing along the California coast.

Before I was entirely dressed, I realized that the aunties' ship, the *Tungus,* was passing, so I put on a coat and shoved my bare feet into my shoes, grabbed the red sweater, and dashed up to the deck, only to find that the *Tungus* had passed us. I could see it well, but we weren't near enough to wave the red sweater!! The captain told me that someone on board the *Tungus* waved at this ship! That would be one of the aunties. I hope they have a good time in San Francisco.

SPRING FLOWER: A TALE OF TWO RIVERS

Yesterday, we received more letters from Aunt Adelaide, Aunt Maybell, and Miss Edith Fredericks. One from Uncle Henry too. He hasn't been well. Aunt Olga is confined to her home with two trained nurses looking after her, one during the day and one at night.

Aunt Maybell told us that Mrs. Ploeg — the aunties' mother — is thrilled to know Auntie Dee and Auntie Bessie are on the ocean and will be home in Grand Rapids soon.

God bless you and keep you, my darling
Lovingly yours very own,
Mother

S.S. *Anna Maersk*, in the harbor at San Pedro (the port for Los Angeles)
February 16, 1951
My dear Jeanie,
Today has been a great day!
As *Anna* was gradually siding up to the dock, we saw Mrs. Holland and son, Bruce, a tall and handsome young man, standing on the pier. Bruce drove us to the Moral Rearmament Building to show us where they have been working. Later, Mr. Holland came to greet us and took us to a Chinese Restaurant, where we met many of our old friends from China. What a wonderful reunion it was.

The officer on the *Anna Maersk* told us to return at three in the afternoon; so Julia Wilson drove us to our ship, accompanied by her mother and father. It is now six o'clock, and we haven't started yet! Someone told me that the *Tungus* is arriving this evening, so I am going to watch this evening and see if I can sight the *Tungus* again.

Loads of love from your
Mother

JEAN TREN-HWA PERKINS

S.S. Anna Maersk
February 17, 1951
Jeanie dear,

Today is another beautiful sunshiny day, with the blue sky, deep blue sea, and the white seagulls sitting around here and there on the water. I have the stateroom window open to enjoy the outside air. Day-Day is in the upper room, finishing his devotional work. Mother has finished hers and is now having her first chat with the dearie.

I am always hoping that you are keeping well. You understand how much we are thinking of Kiukiang and everyone there, and how we are wondering about everything. Of course, we have no news.

S.S. Anna Maersk
February 18, 1951
My dear Jeanie,

Today has been one of great beauty, with bright sunshine, blue skies, and very blue water. We have sailed past islands and pretty beaches. We are passing Mexico now. We've sat on the deck in the sunshine, enjoying the views and the open air.

We hope to get tanned before we reach New York.

Loads and loads of love from your loving,
Mother

S.S. Anna Maersk
February 19, 1951
My dear Jeanie,

How are you today? I hope that all goes nicely and that you are feeling satisfaction from the daily progress you are making. Today has been another day of bright sunshine and blue skies and a blue Pacific without whitecaps. A flock of birds has been skimming along the top of the water alongside the ship. They don't seem like anything we have seen before.

I helped Day-Day with his correspondence, which Day-Day read out loud to Mother. The captain informed us it will be very warm soon. Today Mother removed her union suit and got into summer underwear and wore a cotton dress. The warm spell will probably last all the way to the Panama Canal and beyond. Of course—as you know—New York won't be warm when we get there at the beginning of March!

Loads of love from
Mother

S.S. Anna Maersk
February 20, 1951
Dear Jeanie,

With another beautiful day. Mother darned socks, and Day-Day read out loud from the February issue of a magazine called *Coronet*. There were many interesting articles in it. A fellow with a nice Scotch name—Macintosh—handed the magazine to me.

Believe it or not, Mother is now in summer attire: no corsets, stockings, or socks, and no warm underwear. I'm wearing a summer dress in February!

The captain told us that we will be going through the Panama Canal soon and then starting up the Atlantic Ocean, toward New York. It will be colder!!

Lovingly,
Mommy

S.S. Anna Maersk
February 21, 1951
Jeanie dear,

Today's program has been the usual one: Blue skies, blue

water, sunshine, Mother helping Day-Day write letters, darning more socks, and Day-Day reading out loud.

I wonder now, which is your favorite subject in college? I hope you enjoy everything.

I'm loving you always in the same old way, my precious one.
Lovingly
Mommy

S.S. Anna Maersk
February 22, 1951
My own precious Jeanie:
We have just come down from the upper deck after another day of the same old program—darning socks and reading out loud, except the water is very green today.

You must be wondering if we are losing our mind to be at sea for so long.

You are always in my prayers and thoughts, precious one.
Lovingly,
Mommy

S.S. Anna Maersk
February 23, 1951
My Jeanie dear,
Our ship is now sailing along the shores of the Republic of Panama. We can see islands as well as the mainland, which is mountainous. Some of the hilly bits remind us of the Palisades opposite Yonkers.

The captain expects to anchor at this end of the Panama Canal about two o'clock this morning. Then he plans to pull up the anchor around six in the morning and begin to sail through the Panama Canal to the other side. This process will take about eight hours. Of course, each ship has to wait its turn before starting to go through the canal. Passengers are permitted to get off the boat at the other end of the canal and get a little exercise walking around before reboarding for the last lap of the journey to New York. (Incidentally, the ship lands at the Brooklyn side, so after arrival, we'll have to get across to New York City!)

I just cannot get it through my thick scalp that we are so near the end of a very long journey that started from our home in Kiukiang...

I expect to mail this letter tomorrow when we get off the ship, and then the next one will be mailed from New York!

Other than that, today's program was the same, mending, darning, and reading out loud.

I hope you had an exciting day, and that all has gone happily for my dear, dear one. I pray God is guiding and directing you day by day.

Loads and loads of love from,
Mother

S.S. Anna Maersk
February 24, 1951
Jeanie dear,
How often I think of you during this voyage, and how you would be enjoying it, and racing around and up and down the decks, and telling me all the beautiful things you see. I think too, how everyone would love my Jeanie, and how kind and helpful Jeanie would be to everyone else.

We will soon be entering the Panama Canal, and then once more on the Atlantic Ocean. I am hoping I can get more postage stamps when we are ashore!!

Day-Day sends love to Jeanie, and so does
Your loving Mother

JEAN TREN-HWA PERKINS

S.S. Anna Maersk, in port at Cristóbal Canal Zone
February 25, 1951
My own dear Jeanie,

By now you will have enjoyed another Sunday. Day-Day and I went ashore and attended the morning service at Cristóbal Union Church. You would be interested in the choir of young people. They wore white robes and sang very well. I thought you and Chum, how talented you both are in playing pianos—the ways you have helped the Lord's work with your music.

The *Tungus* has also entered the Panama Canal. *Anna* is supposed to reach New York on Saturday. It's hard to believe that we'll be attending church service next Sunday in New York City!

Lovingly

S.S. Anna Maersk
February 26, 1951
Jeanie dearie,

As I write, our ship is pitching and rocking more than it has during the voyage thus far. We have left Cristóbal and now are speeding thro' the Caribbean Sea. When ashore this morning, Day-Day and I bought a few small presents for Philip and Grace Watters, and also for our niece Evelyn's daughters Olivia and Joan (little pins made of china, only to find that they were made in England). *Well!*

Word is that *Tungus* is still waiting for its turn to go through the Canal. So now we hope to meet with the aunties at the New York pier.

I hope the Lord make his face shine upon you and keep you safe and give you peace.

Lovingly,
Mummie

SPRING FLOWER: A TALE OF TWO RIVERS

S.S. Anna Maersk
February 27, 1951
My dear Jean:
All day long this ship has rolled and rolled from one side to the other; one has to be careful when walking, lest one fall! Day-Day finally got seasick, and he blames himself for eating too many different things at lunchtime.

We have a letter from Aunt Hyla, who is now working in Liberia, Africa.

I should tell you that our Danish captain is a very nice man. He too is hoping to reach New York City quickly. After this long journey, he can skip across the Atlantic Ocean to Denmark and rest for three months before his next voyage. He received a telegram that his wife has been ill. Naturally, he is very concerned.

Seafaring men have a hard time, don't they? They always seem to be away from home and family for months or years at a time.

Lovingly,
Mummie

S.S. Anna Maersk
February 28, 1951
Dear Jeanie,
A few minutes ago, we passed the island of Cuba. It's almost 5 in the afternoon, and until this time, we have had a calm sea. Everyone but Day-Day was at the tea, which has not happened before.

We might be arriving on Saturday or Sunday. I certainly hope it won't be Sunday since Rev. and Mrs. Philip Watters won't be able to meet us on Sunday.

How I look forward to receiving letters from my Dollie when we reach New York. I hope they are there.

Lovingly,

JEAN TREN-HWA PERKINS

S.S. Anna Maersk
March 1, 1951
My own dear Jeanie,

"March has come in like a lamb here," and I hope it has done the same in Nanking!

Patsy has just gotten us to write our name in her book. She will be 19 in July—just a year younger than my Dollie. She is Portuguese with long and flowing black hair. She is a very dear, loving, outgoing lassie, who was traveling with her mother.

She wants to train to be a nurse in New York. She just gave us a photo, and on the back, she wrote, "You are both the sweetest folks I have ever known. I hope you won't forget me because I will never forget you. Love, Patsy."

Today, Day-Day and Mother finished packing and then with much labor, we filled out our U.S. Customs Declaration, which is always a job.

I am so looking forward to seeing my darling's handwriting(!) when I reach N.Y. We know nothing about our beloved China since we left.

For some reason this morning, I began to figure some years, a mathematical problem, and Day-Day was studying Organic Chemistry when we both sat under the sun in the steamer chair on the deck. That is a mathematical problem!! Mother is 68. Time spent in Edinburgh, Scotland, Toronto, Canada, Hastings-on-Hudson, and Irvington-on-Hudson, 17 years; time spent in Yonkers, 17 years; time spent in China 34 years.

I hope this day can be a very happy one for my darling.
Lovingly,
Mother

SPRING FLOWER: A TALE OF TWO RIVERS

S.S. Anna Maersk
March 2, 1951
Mother's own girlie,

The good ship has been speeding along at a great rate today. We have seen no land nor any vessels, but seagulls that followed us.

We are due in Brooklyn in the afternoon. Day-Day received a telegram from his 1898 Graduating Class from Yale, welcoming him back to America!

What is going on in Gin-Ling today? Mother thinks of you always.

Loads of love from your mudder

S.S. Anna Maersk
March 3, 1951
Mother's precious,

Today has been dull and cloudy and misty, but our brave *Anna* has rushed along through the rough and thrashing Atlantic.

This evening, we anchored near the Statue of Liberty, and then tomorrow morning we'll be allowed to get ashore. We have a few more things to pack, and so I'll run along. Mother's next letter will be written onshore!

Day-Day and I just prayed in thanks for a lovely voyage. I don't need to tell you that you are in our prayers, dear heart.

Day-day sends his love, and loads and loads from your very own,

Mummie

New York City, N.Y.
March 5, 1951
My own dear Jeanie,

Think of Mother's joy over receiving *eight* letters from you yesterday and the one dated from February 12 through the 18th.

Thank you, my precious one for giving Mother the news. Your idea of a line a day is undoubtedly excellent.

Thank you again for letting us know something about the place where we worked, the place we have come to call home.

I am glad you are learning that it is wise to be careful with money. Always be vigilant—money is never easy to get. You may need it for essential things, then if you have none, what's to happen, just because you did not use "Scotch Thrift." I had a letter from your institution and learned about the fees that we have to pay. We will do our best, dear.

Yes, dear, you know before one takes a medical course, it is always well to get good general knowledge first. Day-Day had his four years at Yale, then his medical course at Columbia, and then post-graduate experiences in a hospital in N.Y. and at the London School of Tropical Diseases. There are really no shortcuts with a medical education.

Oh my, I am so happy that you think of medical missionary work, as the life work—just like Day-Day. He is so proud to hear that. He nodded his head, as I read your letters aloud to him.

Washington Square Methodist Church
March 7, 1951

Again, let me say, my darling, it was a joy to receive your letters. We were glad to know what you said about the institution where we worked. Any items you may glean from time to time will be gratefully received.

I am terribly sorry that my letter was interrupted at numerous junctures but am now set to take up the thread of our conversation!

I think you know now that we got off our *Anna* on the 4th, which was a Sunday. We had just enough time to attend the

Sunday morning service at Rev. Philip Watters' Church (Aunt Hyla's brother). Frances Woodruff met us at the Church. It was a happy reunion.

On Monday morning the 5th, we were due at eight on Pier 82 in Brooklyn to shepherd our trunks through customs. First, we went to another Pier to meet the four aunties on the *Tungus*, which had just arrived. Aunt Frances was there, and so were Auntie Annie's sister Ellen, and her brother Horace and his wife.

Guess what, we met Aunt Dee's real twin sister Henrietta, or rather Mrs. Veenstra. I know my dear always gets confused— Aunt Dee and Aunt Bessie are not twins. Anyway, there were two nephews (who are likely Mrs. Veenstra's sons) there too, very tall and handsome.

You could imagine how happy the two aunties are—please do tell Chum all of this.

Then all of us went back to our Pier 82 to see our trunks taken off, and no duty to pay—another thing for which to be thankful.

We also had to have our physical examination, and so we went to the Board of Mission on 150 5th Avenue, where my darling has been sending her letters. It took a long time, but thankfully, Day-Day and I passed all right. Last night, all of us had a great reunion at Mrs. Watters' place, and we had strawberry shortcake—yum! Yum! Yum!

Uncle Henry called, and we will be heading up there soon, and Aunt Adelaide asked us to spend a day with them at their home in Brooklyn.

Back in dear old New York, where do you suppose Mother went yesterday afternoon? To Hearn's Store on 14th Street and purchased a new navy-blue dress for herself, and a navy-blue long coat, and a navy-blue hat.

Now, she feels a little less like a country cousin! Ha!

Day-Day has just come in, and he had been trying to get in

touch with the aunties—so we could have our regular Kiukiang prayer meeting at five, and then we will have a Chinese meal at a restaurant across the street—yum—oh how I miss Kiukiang food.

I am glad your lung examination came out alright. Please remember to fix your cough—because it can lead to something else. Mother even takes it here in the USA, and in China, flu, TB, pneumonia remain a significant problem.

How I long for my precious Dollie. I love you more than tongue can tell. I am thankful to God for the privilege, which has been mine, to live with my dearest Jeanie for all those happy— happiest years.

You are much in our thoughts, my dear heart.

New York City
March 9, 1951
My precious one,

How constantly I have been thinking of you and remembering you in prayer. How much I love you, my own precious daughter.

How kind the New York people seem, and cordial, as one passes them on the street, or sits beside them on the 5th Avenue bus, and everywhere else. We thank God for friends as always— especially these days—from anywhere.

Dearie gave mother such great joy with letters of February 19 and 21. Day-Day was ever so happy today to receive your letters. Mr. McCoy has been forwarding them via airmail. This morning, I typed some of your letters for Day-Day. I typed everything capital letters so that he could read it easily. Yes, he intends to use them and read some of them for a sermon he shall deliver at the Washington Square Methodist Church next Sunday!

I am so happy you could spend some time with Aunties Helen (Ferris), Laura (French), and Clara (Schulman), and that you could feel at home with them—until they too have to leave. In your letters, you spoke of how much you would be interested in sailing with us. Darling, let me say that over and over again, I thought of, "O, if my Jeanie were here with us, oh—how much she would enjoy this, and how much fun we would have had together...."

When you become a mother—someday, you will know exactly how I feel.

Yesterday, Day-Day and I went to the hotel where all the aunties are staying in N.Y. Most opportunely, when we reached there at 5 p.m., they were just leaving the hotel and their taxi was waiting for them, so we all piled into the cab and went to the dear old New York Central R. R. Station (you would remember). Mother stood in the middle of this beautifully ornamented and marvelously spacious waiting room and guarded the suitcases amid the bustling of so many people, while the aunties checked in their baggage. Auntie Francis was there with us and watched it all in so that she can do it today when she and Auntie Maybell leave for their home in Upstate New York.

So, at last, the two aunties were on their way to Grand Rapids, Michigan.

After the aunties left, we went back inside Grand Central Station, and there we sat in a lovely restaurant, and at the appointed time, Mrs. Mildred Drescher met us for dinner. Do you remember her, darling, we lived with her in Bombay?! She asked much about you. It was most wonderful to see her. Day-Day was going to arrange her as our guest for dinner, but she saw to it that *we* were *her* guests. We are thankful for that happy evening with another friend.

Yes, you mention seeing that slide of Day-Day at N. U. [Nanking University] Hospital. That photo was taken when Day-Day was at the old W.L.H [Water of Life Hospital] ground.

During that time, he worked for Nanking University Hospital three different years. They begged him not to go to Kiukiang, but to remain there. Wasn't that heartbreaking to hear what they have to say about Day-Day now, and about Lord's work, and the burning of Bible and hymn book. We also received a letter from my "older" daughter, graduated from Rulison years before your time. Anyway, things are not good—and she is having an *awful* time. She too mentioned how newspapers are accusing Day-Day of being a hypocritical man.

Please do tell us more about what you can, and what you hear from the place we lived and worked and loved very much.

Tomorrow we start for Hartford at 9:30 a.m., from Penn Station, which you also know. Uncle Henry will meet us at the station in Hartford. He called. Aunt Olga is in poor health, and I think there are three trained nurses at their house, among other medical folks. She has arthritis and hardening of the arteries. Never comfortable being old, and as I have often said, how grateful we should be for the troubles we don't have and managed to make it through this long journey.

Both Uncle Henry and Aunt Olga inquired *most* kindly about you. They felt terrible you were left behind and that you will have to brave the elements on your own. They told me to give you their love when I wrote. We will probably spend the weekend with them. We're not sure if we will get to see our niece Evelyn. She and I had a telephone call. From Uncle Henry, we did hear that Evelyn is becoming quite an accomplished author and that her four children are doing very well. The oldest, Oakes, is in college, and so will not be drafted for the war. It would seem that Edward, who is brilliant like his Uncle Edward, may be drafted next month. He could be bound for the navy and be shipped to your part of the world. Isn't that an irony, Jeanie? You cousin is at a close distance offshore from you, on the opposite side.

SPRING FLOWER: A TALE OF TWO RIVERS

The two girls, Olivia and Joan, are doing well in school. These are your family, my precious, I so wish and pray that you can meet them someday.

My goodness, your friend Phyllis Hall has a letter here addressed to Ta-Ling Nan Road, but someone had returned it to 22 Hennessy Road [in Hong Kong]. My goodness, darling, they thought you were there and had come back here in New York with us. Oh dear, sometimes, how I wish that were true.

Day-Day just came in, and he had his suit cleaned. He looks terrific, and with my new navy-blue coat, I think we will look alright for Hartford!

Please keep well, my darling, and keep close to the Lord and our savior, and there will be a way. There will always be hope.

Till our next conversation, loads of love from your very own,
Mother

Glossary of Names

My American Parents and I
Mother: Georgina MacDonald Phillip Perkins (裴家纪: Pei Jia-Ji)
Father: Dr. Edward Carter Perkins (裴敬思: Pei Jin-Si)
Me: Jean Tren-Hwa Perkins (胡春花: Hu Tren-Hwa)
Hannah Wu (吴): One of the girls whom Mother and Day-Day supported before I was born. She was a nurse at Water of Life Hospital (WLH) before moving to Hong Kong and became my sole contact to the outside world.

My Extended American Family
Maternal Grandma: Jean Sword Phillip
Maternal Grandpa: William Phillip
Uncle Henry Perkins, my father's older brother: Professor of Physics at Trinity College
His wife: Aunt Olga
Two children: Henry Jr. (Harry) and Evelyn
Four Children of Evelyn and Amyas Ames: (Evvie) Oakes, Edward, Olivia, and Joan.

Aunt: Ms. Deanetta "Dee" Ploeg (浦大: Po-Da): Nurse at WLH
Aunt: Ms. Elizabeth "Bessie" Ploeg (浦二: Po-Er): Nurse at WLH
Their Daughter: Chum: my *de facto* sister

SPRING FLOWER: A TALE OF TWO RIVERS

My Biological Parents: The Hu Family and Known Siblings
Mother: Mm-Ma
Father: Mr. Hu (胡)
Brother-1: Kuo-Hsiang (阔祥): The MIA pilot, fourteen years my senior
Brother-2: Yan-Feng (延丰): A cook at WLH eight years my senior

Chinese Staff at Our House
Amahs: Wang-Ma (王妈, and later as Wang-Sao 王嫂) for Chum
Chang-Ma (常妈) for me
Lo-Ma (罗妈) for my grandmother
Cook: Chef Tian (田) and his daughter "Sarah"
Doorman–Gardener: Grandpa Shui (水爷爷)
Butler–Laundry Man: Uncle Paddle (大板叔叔)

Yonkers, New York, 1942–1945
Yonkers Public School No. 16
Teachers: Mrs. Hughes and Ms. Ryan
Friends-Classmates: Jill, Betty, and Marie

Nathaniel Hawthorne Junior High in South Yonkers
Teacher: Mrs. Eaton
Friend-Classmate: Doris C.
Lake George–Silver Bay: Ju-Ju

India, 1945–1946
Woodstock School:
Friends-Classmates: Phyllis and Joe
In Nadiad:
Friends: Nancy and Patrick

JEAN TREN-HWA PERKINS

Kiukiang, 1946–1950
Rulison Girls High School:
Teacher/Principal: Ms. Wu (Grace Wu – 吴懋诚)
Home Room Teacher/Advisor: Miss You (尤)
Friend-Classmate: Mollie

The Hsiung (熊) Family
Father: Russell, Headmaster of William Nast Academy
Mother: Eve, Teacher at Rulison Girls High
Six Children:
Bart, Ruth, Grace, Mary, Paul (振民), and Simon

Freshman Year at Gin-Ling College, Nanking, 1950-1951
The six girls from Rulison Girls High to attend Gin-Ling in 1950:
Mollie, Tsai, Yen, Chen, Phoebe, and I
My Roommates at Gin-Ling:
Yen (尹): From Rulison High
Chen (陈): From Rulison High - Died young

Friends:
Shou (寿): From Shanghai
Teacher: President and Biology Professor, Dr. Wu Yi-Fang (吴贻芳校长)

Acknowledgments

First and foremost, I thank my cousins Olivia, Joanie, and Ned for their unwavering support throughout this entire process of compiling and editing my mother's memoir, including the initial efforts to set up a website honoring my grandparents, Dr. and Mrs. Edward Carter Perkins (https://www.yangtzeriverbythehudsonbay.site/home-page.html).

I am also indebted to Olivia for introducing me to Arnie Kotler, who generously agreed to work with me on this book and became my editor, consultant, and literary agent. I am grateful for his skillful and knowledgeable editing, as well as his timely encouragement and invaluable advice. I've learned so much from him about writing and expressing things in a plain, simple, easy-to-understand manner. Aside from his in-depth linguistic insights, I am awestruck by his incredible knowledge of history and geography.

In terms of editing, Doti Browning, mother of my good friends at Calvin College, Daral and Kip Smalligan, edited the early chapters of this book. My academic mentor at Milton Academy in Milton, Massachusetts, Barclay Feather, had helped my mother with her writing. My mother submitted some chapters as writing assignments for courses she was taking at the Institute of Children's Literature (ICL, today's Institute for Writers in Madison, Connecticut). The names of the ICL instructors I was able to gather with whom she corresponded are Tom Bethancourt, Mimi Bourne, and Pat Murray. My apologies to anyone I've missed.

Although these collective editing efforts took place more than thirty years ago, I remain appreciative, as I am confident my mother would be if she were still in our lives.

I would like to extend my heartfelt appreciation to Mark Woodworth for his meticulous proofreading. And last but certainly not least, through perhaps angelic intervention, Arnie and I met Graham Earnshaw, founder and publisher of Earnshaw Books. I am eternally grateful for his in-depth experience in publishing as well as his command of the Chinese language, culture, and history. I am also grateful to Jason Wong for patiently designing the book—the cover and the interior layout, including the photos and figures.

I gratefully acknowledge Helen Zia, the author of *Last Boat out of Shanghai*, and Margaret Sun, the author of *Betwixt and Between*, for their generous endorsements. These two women's stories and journeys are in the same spirit and equally inspiring and amazing as my mother's.

I would say only one thing about my spouse. Thank you, Professor and Dr. Jun Dai, for a singularly greatest gift anyone could have in life: *Freedom*.

I could not have completed this book without Dr. Margaret McCray of Westminster Counseling Center at the Presbyterian Church in Minneapolis, Minnesota. "Putting one foot ahead of another and staying in the moment" became my mantra, getting up every morning during this long and arduous journey, which is not yet complete. There were times it was the only way I could survive the bitter winters of Madison, Wisconsin.

There are numerous people whose encouragement has been paramount for me to persevere. Unfortunately, I need to withhold their names for the time being. If you happen to be reading this book, you know who you are! I hope you will understand; I am incredibly grateful from the bottom of my heart.

Given the historical elements in this book, I've tried my best to be accurate, relying on these valuable sources: Wikipedia, the Chinese version of Wikipedia (维基百科), New World Encyclopedia, and Britannica. I also found an excellent website called *A Blog out of the Wall* (http://www.cnblogs.com/wildabc/p/3798219.html), which has an insightful summary of the History of Methodist Missions in Kiukiang (九江), and its author has in-depth knowledge of the Water of Life Hospital. Some documentation is from the Yale University Archives, while other information was drawn from letters preserved by the Perkins family. I read and abstracted information from voice transcripts recorded by Deanetta and Elizabeth Ploeg in 1978. These valuable transcripts were kindly given to me by their nieces and nephews. I also consulted on many occasions with my cousin Ned and his wife, Jane Sokolow, who coauthored *Chronology of Dr. Edward C. Perkins*.

Two other books have been useful as resources. The first is *Hyla Doc: Surgeon in China Through War and Revolution 1924–1949*, edited by Elsie H. Landstrom (Fort Bragg, California: QED Press, 1991). Dr. Hyla Watters was a close friend of my grandparents. My maternal grandmother, Georgina, was Dr. Watters' Sunday School teacher. My maternal grandfather, Dr. Edward Perkins, became a missionary because of the direct influence of Dr. Watters' father, the Rev. Philip M. Watters. The phrase "Water of Life" came out of their fellowship. Dr. Watters herself was a surgeon in Wuhu General Hospital (芜湖总医院) in the city of Wuhu (芜湖), downstream from Kiukiang. She and my grandfather helped each other in times of need.

The editor of the above memoir, Ms. Landstrom, also wrote a manuscript describing the history of Wuhu General Hospital. My grandfather as well as numerous other physicians and nurses who were also missionaries are prominently featured in these writings.

JEAN TREN-HWA PERKINS

The second book is *My China Years* by Helen Foster Snow (New York: William Morrow and Company, 1984). Helen Foster was married to the American journalist Edgar P. Snow.

My grandmother Georgina took most of the photos presented here; others are from the Perkins family collection. Or else I took them.

Lastly, although I have been careful in arranging my time and allocating my space to work on this book project, I would like to thank my colleagues from the School of Pharmacy at the University of Wisconsin–Madison for their support and encouragement. I would also like to acknowledge the Kremers Family Foundation and Vilas Foundation of University of Wisconsin–Madison. When readers follow with this story in its entirety, they will surely agree that this writing project is very much within the spirit of these academic foundations and the distinctions thereof.

Richard P. Hsung, PhD
editor of *Spring Flower*, my mother's memoir
Madison, Wisconsin
December 2020

About the Editor

After coming to America, Richard attended Milton Academy, Milton, Massachusetts, as many of the Perkins children had. He then went to live with his adoptive mother, Kate Louise Ploeg, the youngest sister of Deanetta and Elizabeth Ploeg, and earned his BS in Chemistry and Mathematics from Calvin College in Grand Rapids, Michigan. He studied organic chemistry and obtained his PhD at the University of Chicago. After working as a research associate at the University of Chicago and Columbia University, he became a faculty member at the University of Minnesota–Twin Cities before moving to the University of Wisconsin–Madison. Richard received a National Science Foundation Career Award and was a Camille Dreyfus Teacher-Scholar. He is currently the Laura and Edward Kremers Professor of Natural Products Chemistry and the University of Wisconsin–Madison Vilas Distinguished Achievement Professor.